BOLIVIA

BOLIVIA

Land of Struggle

Waltraud Queiser Morales

Westview Press

BOULDER • SAN FRANCISCO • OXFORD

Westview Profiles/Nations of Contemporary Latin America

"Quechua Fifth Hymn," from Grady Hillman with Guillermo Delgado P., *The Return of the Inca* (Austin: Place of Herons Press, 1986), is reprinted here with permission.

Published in 1992 in the United States of America by Westview Press, Inc., 5500 Central Avenue, Boulder, Colorado 80301-2847, and in the United Kingdom by Westview Press, 36 Lonsdale Road, Summertown, Oxford OX2 7EW

Library of Congress Cataloging-in-Publication Data
Morales, Waltraud Q.
  Bolivia : land of struggle / Waltraud Queiser Morales.
    p.   cm. — (Westview profiles. Nations of contemporary Latin
America)
  Includes bibliographical references (p.   ) and index.
  ISBN 0-8133-0197-1
  1. Bolivia—History.   2. Bolivia—Social conditions.   3. Bolivia—
Economic conditions.   I. Title.   II. Series.
F3321.M75   1992
984—dc20   91-35091
                                                                                   CIP

Printed and bound in the United States of America

10   9   8   7   6   5   4   3   2   1

This book about the struggles of the Bolivian people
is lovingly dedicated to the memory of my son John Peter,
who never came to know his Bolivian heritage
but nonetheless struggled fiercely throughout the four years
of his brief, painful life.
And to my wonderful son Carl
for having bestowed on me the love and trouble of two.

The weak do not struggle.
The strong struggle perhaps an hour.
The stronger yet struggle many years.
But the strongest struggle their entire lives.
They are indispensable.

—Bertolt Brecht
Gedichte, Vol. 4

Kausachiy, qawachiy
Ama muchanaypaq
Hinata muyuspa
Wiñanpaq

Let the people live.
Prevent our suffering
and let us return
forever.

—Grady Hillman, with Guillermo Delgado P.
"Quechua Fifth Hymn"
The Return of the Inca

Contents

List of Tables and Illustrations	ix
Foreword	xi
Acknowledgments	xv
List of Acronyms	xix

Introduction   1

1   *Diversity of Land, People, and Culture*   4

Geopolitical Forces, 4
The Land and Its Regions, 6
The People: An Ethnic Mosaic, 14
Culture and National Identity, 19
Challenges Ahead, 29
Notes, 29

2   *Early History: The Pre-Columbian, Colonial, and Republican Eras*   31

The Pre-Columbian Era to Independence
(600–1825), 31
The Postindependence Era (1825–1880), 40
Republican Government (1880–1930), 47
Notes, 53

3   *Contemporary History: The Chaco War to the Revolution (1930–1952)*   55

The Chaco War: A Precursor of Revolution, 55
The Postwar Reformers (1936–1939), 57
Formation of Radical Political Parties, 61

Resurgence and Fall of the Oligarchy (1939–1952), 65
Notes, 74

4   *The Bolivian National Revolution and
    the Political System*   77

Revolution and the MNR in Power, 77
Restoring the Revolution? Return to Military Rule, 86
The Move Toward Democracy, 94
Civilians in Power, 99
Notes, 107

5   *Postrevolutionary Society*   110

The Struggle to Consolidate Old and New
    Social Groups, 110
The Social Problem of Narcotics Trafficking, 125
Notes, 138

6   *Postrevolutionary Economy*   141

The State and Dependent Development, 141
The Dependent External Sector, 148
"Restructuring" State and Economy: The Debt Crisis, 155
The State and Cocaine, 160
Notes, 169

7   *Bolivia's Foreign Policy*   173

Determinants of Foreign Policy, 173
Objectives of Foreign Policy, 177
Foreign Policy and the Future, 196
Notes, 197

Conclusions   200

Notes, 204

Selected Bibliography   205
About the Book and Author   213
Index   215

Tables and Illustrations

Tables

4.1   Voting results for general elections, July 14, 1985   103

4.2   Voting results for general elections, May 7, 1989   106

5.1   South American graduates of SOUTHCOM in relation
      to total armed forces and population   124

6.1   U.S. aid to Bolivia   154

7.1   U.S. narcotics-related assistance to Bolivia: Fiscal Year
      1991 allocations and Fiscal Year 1992 requests   189

7.2   U.S. narcotics-related assistance to the Andean region
      and estimated coca leaf production by major producers   190

Maps

Bolivia   xxii

Photographs

The craggy lunar landscape of La Paz   8

Indian shepherds minding their flock on the Altiplano   9

The main plaza of Santa Cruz de la Sierra   12

A Camba woman and her child by their home   13

Chola women wearing the distinctive mestizo dress of Bolivia   18

Chola women at a traditional religious festival in the
town of Jesús de Machaca   20

A celebration in the name of the Niño in the town
of Jesús de Machaca   22

Morenada dancers at a folkloric festival on the Altiplano   24

An amateur folkloric group demonstrates their skill
on drums and vertical flutes   25

La Paz, Bolivia's administrative capital and center
of political life   73

Ex-president and general Luis García Meza   98

The lowland city of Montero   112

Low-income migrant housing in the city of Santa Cruz   117

The Club de La Paz   127

The Plaza San Francisco   129

Kolla men in migrant barrio in the city of Santa Cruz   133

Little Cochabambinas take a bath   135

The May 1990 Festival of the Chica in Socaba   163

A Yapacaní colonist and her child standing outside
their homestead   167

Foreword

Few Latin American countries are as little known or poorly understood in the United States and Europe as is Bolivia. The Western Hemisphere's only completely landlocked country, Bolivia has had a melancholic history repeatedly tinged with tragedy. Even the famous Venezuelan "liberator" from whom it got its name never considered Bolivia anything more than the appendage of Peru it had been throughout the colonial era. Stripped of its rich lodes of silver by the Spanish *conquistadores*, Bolivia—upon achieving independence—lost its coastline to the Chileans (along with valuable mineral deposits) through two wars, one in the 1830s and the other at the end of the 1870s. Between 1932 and 1935 it fought a third disastrous war, this time with Paraguay, over land falsely presumed to have rich oil deposits. Although Bolivia was long a major source of the world's tin, the wealth from this irreplaceable resource went into the hands of a few absentee oligarchic families who lived mostly in Paris and New York. Even now, at a time when the country is of great importance to the United States (at least in the negative sense of being a leading producer of the raw material of cocaine), it generally remains in the shadow of much larger Colombia and Peru with respect to this pressing problem.

Textbooks consistently describe Bolivia as an extreme case of political instability. They frequently refer also to the halfway successful revolution in the 1950s that subsequently lost its way. And college students know this unique and fascinating country as the place where Ernesto "Ché" Guevara—the Argentine physician turned Cuban revolutionary—met his death. But few know that Bolivia was also the first country he had observed upon leaving Argentina in the early 1950s. Indeed, most Latin Americans have as partial, distorted, and superficial a view of Bolivia as does the rest of the world. Tourists are a rarity in this quite inaccessible country, and few Bolivians emigrate to the industrialized nations of the Northern Hemisphere. Although the major cities of other Andean lands are at reasonable altitudes, La Paz is perched so high in the mountains as to make acclimation a somewhat formidable task.

Professor Waltraud Queiser Morales has been deeply interested in and involved with Bolivia for most of her professional life. She brings a highly sympathetic, yet far from uncritical, approach to what is perhaps physically the Tibet of Latin America (given Bolivia's mountainous terrain and isolated location, wedged as it is between much larger countries more active on the world scene). But her portrait demonstrates that Bolivia might more aptly be termed the Guatemala of South America in the sense that it is essentially Indian country that experienced at least a partial sociopolitical revolution in the post–World War II years. Appreciative of the aspirations of the Bolivian people, Professor Morales does not hesitate to champion them without unduly becoming an advocate. Given the very heavy Indian elements in Bolivia's heritage and present-day makeup, she appropriately places substantial stress upon the pre-conquest indigenous culture and society of the Quechua and Aymara peoples.

The author then shows the patterns in the at-first-view chaotic profusion of "presidents of the year," tracing out their weighty influence on contemporary Bolivia by way of its colonial experience. Yet given that her portrait does not necessarily reflect a comic opera kind of "Banana Republic," it behooves us to remember that the French Third and Fourth Republics (from the 1870s to 1958) averaged well under a year per premier and cabinet. Dr. Morales's analysis of the Chaco War and its profound impact upon Bolivia provides a fascinating counterpart to the Paraguayan side of the same story as told in *Paraguay: The Personalist Legacy*, a recent volume in the Nations of Contemporary Latin America series.

The circuitous and obstacle-ridden road from this military defeat to the 1952 Revolution is clearly shown, and the complexities of that never-quite-finished social and political movement are aptly portrayed in a manner that contributes significantly to the difficult quest for understanding certain phenomena that recur in different Latin American countries. For Latin America in the period since World War I has repeatedly seen voters put back into office individuals who had already served much earlier and been written off as discredited. Professor Morales adds significantly to our comparative understanding of this perplexing problem that I call "Return, Resurrection, and Recycling" through her perceptive treatment of Presidents Víctor Paz Estenssoro (1952–1956, 1960–1964, and 1985–1989), Hernán Siles Zuazo (1956–1960 and 1982–1985), and General Hugo Banzer Suárez (1971–1977), a leading candidate in 1985 and holder of a major share of power following the inconclusive 1989 elections.

Strongly committed to the priority of social needs over economic orthodoxy, the author provides an explanation of the policies that halted Bolivia's runaway hyperinflation in 1987–1988. She also emphasizes the immense social costs involved in following such stringent orthodox austerity policies—now advocated in many of the larger South American countries on the basis of their "success" in Bolivia. But, above all, Professor Morales ably carries out a task unfortunately crucial to the comparative analysis of contemporary Latin America: She deals with the coca/cocaine problem frankly, fully, and objectively—avoiding both skittishness and sensationalism. This problem is extremely important at the present juncture because it is the war on drugs that has U.S. military as well as civilian "advisers" deeply (and soon, perhaps, controversially) involved in Bolivia. This excellent book casts a great deal of light on a subject that promises to become a very heated one not far down the road.

Ronald Schneider

Acknowledgments

My work on Bolivia has encompassed over a decade of growth in my professional and personal life, and many individuals have been directly or indirectly instrumental in those important changes. I sincerely thank everyone who has extended to me friendship and assistance in this project, and I am especially indebted to numerous Bolivians and Bolivianists whose excellent research and writing have made this task both easier and more challenging. If along the way I have failed to always be professional and caring to my colleagues, friends, and family, I hope I am forgiven. The pressures and competitiveness of academia have not always brought out the best in me. But working on this book has taught me many things, above all that people come first. In short, the book itself has been a lesson in life and the meaning of struggle.

I would like to thank, first of all, Mom and Dad and my son Carl, as well as Jorge Morales, Maria Luisa, and many Bolivian relatives, especially Anselma de Morales and Abuelita Pancha. Señora Anselma taught me one essential phrase that every Bolivian woman of her generation seems to have internalized, "Ay, paciencia, paciencia!" (Oh, patience, patience!). And Abuelita Pancha showed me with relish and gusto, "como gozar" (how to enjoy life) and afterwards "como curar el cuerpo" (how to put the body to rights afterwards).

In 1982 various Bolivians took the time to extend interviews to me for which I am extremely grateful: Former Archbishop of La Paz, Monsignor Jorge Manrique; the Rev. José Gramunt de Moragas, S.J., of Agencia de Noticias Fides (ANF) and Radio FIDES; General Juan Ayoroa Ayoroa; Hugo González Rioja of the newsletter Actualidad Boliviana Confidencial (ABC); Eduardo Navo Morales, political science professor at the Universidad Mayor de San Andrés (UMSA); the staff of the UMSA library, especially its successive directors, Dr. Jorge Siles Salinas and Dr. Alberto Crespo Rodas; the staff of the Bolivian Permanent Assembly on Human Rights; Dr. Carlos Serrate Reich, director of *Hoy;* and former

Bolivian ambassador to the United States and editor of *Ultima Hora*, Dr. Mariano Baptista Gumucio.

Also in 1982 the U.S. Embassy in La Paz allowed me to consult their extensive clippings library and interview individuals on the embassy staff: U.S. Ambassador Edwin G. Corr; Rudolph P. Peña of the U.S. Embassy Narcotics Control Program; Air Force Col. John Hargrove; Steve Valdéz, Economics Officer; David Wagner, Labor Attaché; Mary Jeanne Reid Martz, Political Officer; and Stanley S. Shepherd, Information Officer. Special thanks to Peter McFarren, Bolivian resident and occasional *New York Times* correspondent in La Paz, and to John Enders, then Associated Press (AP) correspondent in La Paz, who was kind enough to provide the photograph of ex-general García Meza.

At the University of Central Florida (UCF), the Office of Sponsored Research, the UCF Foundation, the College of Arts and Sciences, and the Department of Political Science assisted with travel and research funding in 1982 and 1990. The University of Florida and Florida International University Travel Consortium also contributed to my travel support in 1982. I am most grateful to the United States Information Agency, the Council for International Exchange of Scholars, and the Fulbright-Hays Program for a 1990 Fulbright Teaching Grant to the Universidad Mayor de San Simón (UMSS) in Cochabamba. Various individuals of the U.S. Embassy staff in La Paz facilitated this experience: Thomas Mesa and Christopher Midura, Cultural Affairs Officers, and Carmen Pardo, Educational Assistant.

Colleagues of the UMSS Faculty of Law and the Instituto de Estudios Internacionales (IDEI) were an inspiration and a delight: especially Dr. Oscar Alba Salazar, IDEI's outstanding director; Dr. Alfonso Camacho Peña; Dr. Ramiro Arze; Lic. Alvaro Guzmán; Lic. Marcela Iriarte; and Dr. Juan Mejía. I offer kind personal regards to Dra. Isabel Maldonado Pinto, colleague at UMSS-IDEI and director of the Centro de Estudios y Consultoría Jurídico Económica (CECJE) and extend warm wishes to the marvelous graduate students of the "Curso-Taller: Bolivia en el Contexto Internacional" of UMSS-IDEI. I am grateful to Bolivian researchers who permitted me to attend their seminars: Lic. Fernando Mayorga, Lic. José Ortiz Mercado, Lic. Jorge Lazarte of the Facultad Latinoamericana de Ciencias Sociales in Bolivia (FLACSO), and Dr. René Antonio Mayorga of the Centro Boliviano de Estudios Multidisciplinarios. Maria Lohman of the Centro de Documentación Información y Biblioteca in Cochabamba made available publications of the center. Finally, I appreciated the hospitality of Darco Lazaneo and Dra. Carmen Molina de Lazaneo.

Closer to home, many Bolivianists and Latin Americanists have contributed to my efforts in some manner, either by their own work or by their encouragement: Robert J. Alexander, James M. Malloy, Herbert S. Klein, Christopher Mitchell, Laurence Whitehead, James Dunkerley, Jerry R. Ladman, Jennie K. Lincoln, Elizabeth G. Ferris, Abraham F. Lowenthal, and Heraldo Muñoz. For generously sharing research and publications, special thanks are due Fred Parkinson, Melvin Burke, Charles W. Arnade, Kevin Healy, Virginia Bouvier (formerly of the Washington Office on Latin America, WOLA), and Eduardo A. Gamarra. Guillermo Delgado P. and Grady Hillman kindly made available the wonderful translations of Quechua poetry, for which I am grateful. The assistance of several friends and colleagues at the University of Central Florida deserve particular mention: Dr. Jerome J. Donnelly, professor of English, has served as informal newspaper "clipper" throughout this project; Dr. José B. Fernández of the Departments of History and Foreign Languages has helped resolve all questions of translation and language; and Dr. Allyn MacLean Stearman of the Department of Anthropology has unstintingly contributed her Bolivian experiences and the photographs of the eastern lowlands included in this book. I owe an academic and personal debt to my mentor, John F. McCamant, professor at the Graduate School of International Studies (GSIS), University of Denver, for teaching me a love of all things Latin American and comparative. I have been grateful for the help and camaraderie of two former students, Renzo Nastasi and John F. O'Doherty. The secretarial assistance of the office staff of the Department of Political Science, provided by Rosemary Monroy and Susan Devor, and the editorial guidance of the editors and staff of Westview Press—Ronald Schneider, Barbara Ellington, Mick Gusinde-Duffy, Jane Raese, and Christine Arden—have been indispensable.

Waltraud Queiser Morales

Acronyms

ADN	Nationalist Democratic Action (Acción Democrática Nacionalista)
AP	Patriotic Accord (Acuerdo Patriótico)
APDH	Bolivian Permanent Assembly of Human Rights (Asamblea Permanente de Derechos Humanos de Bolivia)
BAMIN	Mining Bank of Bolivia (Banco Minero de Bolivia)
CBF	Bolivian Development Corporation (Corporación Boliviana de Fomento)
CEB	Bolivian Bishops' Conference (Conferencia Episcopal de Bolivia)
CEPB	Bolivian Confederation of Private Entrepreneurs (Confederación de Empresarios Privados de Bolivia)
CIA	Central Intelligence Agency
CNTCB	National Confederation of Peasant Workers of Bolivia (Confederación Nacional de Trabajadores Campesinos de Bolivia)
COB	Bolivian Labor Central (Central Obrera Boliviana)
COMIBOL	Bolivian Mining Corporation (Corporación Minera de Bolivia)
CONADE	National Committee for the Defense of Democracy (Comité Nacional de Defensa de la Democracia)
CONDEPA	Conscience of the Fatherland (Conciencia de la Patria)
CORACA	Peasants' Agricultural Corporation (Corporación Agropecuaria Campesina)
CSTB	Confederation of Bolivian Workers (Confederación Sindical de Trabajadores de Bolivia)
CSUTCB	Sole Unionist Confederation of Peasant Workers of Bolivia (Confederación Sindical Unica de Trabajadores Campesinos de Bolivia)

DEA	Drug Enforcement Administration (U.S.)
DIN	National Office of Investigations
DRU	Unitary Revolutionary Direction (Dirección Revolucionaria Unitaria
ELN	National Liberation Army (Ejército de Liberación Nacional)
ENAF	National Smelting Company (Empresa Nacional de Fundiciones)
FIB	Front of the Bolivian Left (Frente de Izquierda Boliviana)
FPN	Popular Nationalist Front (Frente Popular Nacionalista)
FPU	Front of a United People (Frente del Pueblo Unido)
FRB	Bolivian Revolutionary Front (Frente de la Revolución Boliviana)
FSB	Bolivian Socialist Falange (Falange Socialista Boliviana)
FSTMB	Bolivian Mine Workers' Federation (Federación Sindical de Trabajadores Mineros de Bolivia)
FUB	Federation of University Students of Bolivia
FUDP	Democratic and Popular Unity Front (Frente de Unidad Democrática y Popular)
GDP	gross domestic product
GNP	gross national product
GSA	General Services Administration
IMET	International Military Education and Training
IMF	International Monetary Fund
ITA	International Tin Agreement
ITC	International Tin Council
IU	United Left (Izquierda Unida)
LAFTA	Latin American Free Trade Association
LEC	Legion of Veterans (Legión de Ex-Combatientes)
LIC	low intensity conflict
MIR	Leftist Revolutionary Movement (Movimiento de Izquierda Revolucionaria)
MIR-NM	MIR–New Majority (MIR–Nueva Mayoría)
MNR	Nationalist Revolutionary Movement (Movimiento Nacionalista Revolucionario)
MNRA	Authentic MNR (MNR Auténtico)
MNRH	Historic MNR (MNR-Histórico)
MNRI	MNR-Left (MNR-Izquierda)
MPC	Popular Christian Movement (Movimiento Popular Cristiano)
MRTKL	Tupac Katari Revolutionary Liberation Movement (Movimiento Revolucionario Tupac Katari de Liberación)

NPE	New Economic Policy (Nueva Política Económica)
OAS	Organization of American States
PCB	Bolivian Communist Party (Partido Comunista de Bolivia)
PDC	Christian Democratic Party (Partido Demócrata Cristiano)
PDCR	Revolutionary Christian Democratic Party (Partido Demócrata Cristiano Revolucionario)
PIDYS	Comprehensive Plan for Development and the Substitution of Coca Cultivation (Plan Integral de Desarrollo y Substitución)
PIR	Party of the Revolutionary Left (Partido de la Izquierda Revolucionaria)
POR	Revolutionary Workers' Party (Partido Obrero Revolucionario)
PRA	Authentic Revolutionary Party (Partido Revolucionario Auténtico)
PRI	Institutional Revolutionary Party (Partido Revolucionario Institucional)
PRIN	Revolutionary Party of the Nationalist Left (Partido Revolucionario de la Izquierda Nacionalista)
PS	Socialist Party (Partido Socialista)
PS-1	Socialist Party–One (Partido Socialista Uno)
PSD	Social Democratic Party (Partido Social Demócrata)
PSOB	Socialist Workers' Party of Bolivia
PURS	Party of the Republican Socialist Union (Partido de la Unión Republicana Socialista)
RADEPA	Reason of the Fatherland (Razón de Patria)
SES	Special Security Services
SIDERSA	Bolivian Iron and Steel Corporation (Siderúrgica Boliviana, S.A.)
SOUTHCOM	Southern Command
UCAPO	Union of Poor Campesinos (Unión de Campesinos Pobres)
UDP	Democratic Popular Unity (Unidad Democrática y Popular)
UMOPAR	Mobile Rural Patrol Units, or "Leopardos" (Unidad Móvil de Patrullaje para el Area Rural)
UNCTAD	United Nations Conference on Trade and Development
UNP	People's Nationalist Union (Unión Nacionalista del Pueblo)
USAID	United States Agency for International Development
USIA	United States Information Agency
YPFB	Bolivian State Petroleum Enterprise (Yacimientos Petrolíferos Fiscales Bolivianos)

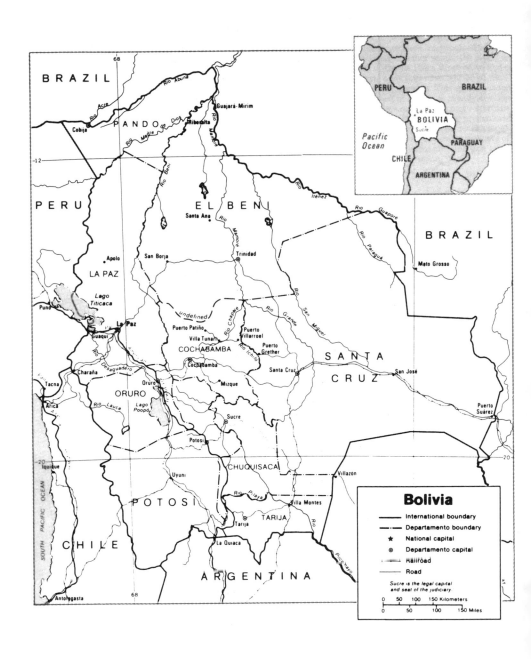

Bolivia

— International boundary
—·—·— Departamento boundary
★ National capital
⊚ Departamento capital
▦ Railroad
— Road

*Sucre is the legal capital
and seat of the judiciary.*

0   50   100   150 Kilometers
0   50   100   150 Miles

Introduction

Bolivia is essentially its people—a people buffeted by the most awesome geographical, political, and social forces in the nation's history. The most powerful force of all has been revolution. Bolivia is a people crucified by revolution, its victims, its perpetrators, and its heroes. Revolution and cocaine may sum up what the average individual knows about Bolivia—if even that. The country is largely unknown and ignored, misunderstood and ridiculed. No less than Russia, it appears to be "a riddle wrapped in a mystery inside an enigma." This country profile of Bolivia centers on the people and their tenacious struggle for a better homeland through liberating revolutionary change. Its pages chart a voyage toward understanding that the essence of the Bolivian, as well as the human, condition is unflinching human struggle.

Diversity and complexity characterize the Bolivian reality. From its perpetually snowcapped mountain peaks above 21,000 feet (6,500 meters) to its inaccessible Amazonian jungles, Bolivia is a land of great physical contrasts. Social contrasts are equally extreme. A popular travelogue, which has described Bolivia as a beggar on a throne of gold, best captures the irony of desperate poverty alongside fantastic riches. Bolivians are among the poorest people in Latin America, yet their country is rich in mineral and natural resources of gold, silver, tin, nitrates, petroleum, natural gas, and precious woods.

Bolivia also holds the record for many enviable and not so enviable Latin American "firsts." The ancient Indian civilization of Tiwanaku is the oldest in Latin America, predating even the Incan; and the Aymara descendants of Tiwanaku have been recognized as the first civilized people of South America. Lake Titicaca is the world's highest navigable lake, and La Paz the highest capital in the world. The first indigenist intellectual movements and the first social revolution in South America took place in Bolivia. And Bolivia reputedly has witnessed as many as

1

200 often violent changes of government since independence—perhaps another record.

Bolivia is a land with immense problems and few simple solutions. Each facet of Bolivian historical experience represents in microcosm the intractable problems of Latin America: underdevelopment, economic dependency, external intervention, political instability, authoritarian rule, ethnic and regional divisions, class conflict, and national identity crisis. Bolivia continues to struggle with these problems. After almost two decades of military rule and massive political corruption due to cocaine trafficking, Bolivians fervently desire representative government and an economic system that promotes development and social justice. The people need national unity to heal the divisive regionalisms of highland and lowland. Now, more than forty years after the 1952 National Revolution, the Bolivian political system has yet to solve the fundamental problems that initially propelled the country into social upheaval.

This is not to say that the problems of four decades earlier are exactly the same today; indeed, they may be worse. One reality has not changed since the revolution: the people's persistent struggle for their rights. The Bolivian character has generally been criticized in erudite social commentary, in the casual remarks of tourists and foreign diplomats, and in the internationally known work, *Pueblo enfermo*, by Bolivia's Alcides Arguedas. Was Arguedas correct in suggesting that Bolivians are an "infirm people" prone to violence and instability, to destruction rather than creation? Or are they a tenacious people who, despite torture, death, and betrayal, hope and struggle for a better life? Revolutions may continue to ravage Bolivia until the people are heard and their needs are satisfied; only then will the historic words of the great South American liberator Simón Bolívar—that the Bolivians are an ungovernable people—take on a more subtle heroic meaning.

Several themes guide this profile: the past and future course of national revolution; the complexity of a country that is a microcosm of global underdevelopment; and the uphill quest for political democracy and national sovereignty.

Chapter 1 reveals the diversity of Bolivia's topography, people, and culture. Chapters 2, 3, and 4 describe the grandeur of ancient Aymara and Incan civilization, the foibles of Bolivia's bloody dictators, and the euphoria of the National Revolution. Chapters 5 and 6 trace postrevolutionary society and economy, and Chapter 7 summarizes Bolivia's external relations. Highlighted throughout these chapters are central contemporary issues and problems posed by the revolution and its legacy, such as chronic military rule, endemic political corruption, the seemingly insurmountable debt crisis, the rapacious cocaine traffic, and the desperate diplomatic struggle for a seacoast. Finally, the Conclusion reviews the political dilemmas of revolutionary change and considers the possible lessons to be learned from Bolivia's experience for Latin America and the Third World.

1

Diversity of Land, People, and Culture

May my name and that of this country never perish.

Simón Bolívar

Bolivia is the heartland of South America. Christened in honor of Simón Bolívar, the most famous of the South American liberators, Bolivia lies in the geopolitical center of the continent, bordering five Latin American nations. To the northeast, southeast, south, southwest, and northwest of Bolivia lie Brazil, Paraguay, Argentina, Chile, and Peru, like spokes radiating from a central hub. From colonial to modern times Bolivia has functioned as a geographical buffer to the westward push of Brazil and the northern thrust of Argentina. Bolivia (along with Paraguay) divides the continent into northern tier and southern cone. Because of its centrality, Bolivia interacts within the three major regional subsystems of South America—the Rio de la Plata, the Andean, and the Amazonian.

GEOPOLITICAL FORCES

Since independence in 1825, territorial dismemberment by its neighbors has reduced Bolivia to half of its former size. Today Bolivia, with 424,152 square miles (1,098,581 square kilometers), is the sixth largest country of the Latin American republics—twice the size of France, or larger than Texas and California combined. Yet despite its size, Bolivia is sparsely and unevenly populated. Its estimated 7 million people represent one-fifth of the population of comparably sized Colombia, or the total population of Massachusetts.

With the loss of its Pacific coast in 1879, Bolivia became one of the two Latin American countries without a seacoast. (The other is Paraguay.) Bolivia has indirect access to the Pacific and Atlantic oceans

4

via the Peruvian ports of Tacna and Matarani, the ports of Antofagasta and Arica in Chile, and the Bolivian ports of Puerto Suárez and Puerto General Busch on the navigable headwaters of the Paraguay River. The Pacific route is linked by railway lines over high Andean passes and is used mainly to ship mineral ore. The Atlantic route, serving agricultural exports, makes its way 1,000 miles downriver to the sea.

Bolivia's essentially landlocked condition has hampered economic development and strongly influenced both Bolivian history and the national psyche. Without the coast, the Bolivian population retained its inward orientation—isolated from international currents and migrations, and dependent on its neighbors for access to the sea. The loss of the coast became a national stigma that has propelled Bolivia to war, embittered its regional diplomacy, and monopolized its national energies. The century-long struggle to regain an "outlet to the sea" continues, still a main source of national unity and hope for a country divided on many other issues.

Strategically, Bolivia is important for its vast mineral resources, many of which remain untapped. Bolivia is the major source of tin in the Western Hemisphere, producing about 16 percent of annual world production. It is also a major world producer of antimony, second after South Africa.[1] Other important industrial minerals include tungsten, lead, zinc, copper, iron, wolfram, bismuth, manganese, asbestos, and sulphur. Silver and gold are largely depleted but in colonial days were so important that the Spaniards may have extracted an estimated $1 billion of silver from the mines of Potosí alone.[2] Petroleum is no longer as plentiful, but natural gas deposits continue to be extensive.

Regionalism is a central geopolitical reality for Bolivia. Geography and the traditions of localism inherited from colonial Spain contribute to Bolivian decentralization. Geography has been the more potent force, splitting the country in half, into "a land divided." Communications and transportation systems have overcome neither the barrier of the high Andes Mountains cutting through the heart of the country nor the northeastern pull of the vast lowland rivers away from the highland and toward the undeveloped Amazon and Brazil. Nature itself seems in league with regionalist forces as this intricate system of waterways "leads from nowhere to nowhere."[3]

Extreme topographical diversity encourages intense racial and cultural division between the Andean highlands and the eastern, tropical lowlands. Highlanders and lowlanders are aliens in each others' world. The Bolivian highlander has more in common with highlanders from Peru or Chile, and the Bolivian lowlander with his counterparts in Brazil or Argentina. Politics, economics, and transportation ensured that until the mid-1960s the lowlands, representing 70 percent of Bolivian territory, were virtually ignored while the highlands, with 75 percent of the population, controlled national life. Regionalism explains why Bolivia, with two-thirds of its territory in the Amazon Basin, is still characterized as an Andean country.

The magnetic attraction of Bolivia's lowland population toward more developed and powerful Argentina and Brazil is another source of regionalism. Ignored or exploited by highland governments, lowland migrants have been drawn to greater social and economic opportunities in Brazilian and Argentinean border provinces. Because Bolivia has been unable to exert sovereignty in all the national territory, separatism has been strong. Lowlanders have learned to identify more closely with other countries than with their own. The southeastern department of Tarija was once Argentinean territory, and secessionist sentiment has surfaced there throughout Bolivian history. The eastern department of Santa Cruz was settled by Spanish explorers from Paraguay, and Cruceños (natives of Santa Cruz department) have historically identified with the Argentinean provinces of La Plata, launching secessionist revolts in 1920 and 1924.

Political and economic rivalry among the administrative divisions of the country should not be dismissed. Administratively, Bolivia is subdivided into nine regional departments: La Paz, Oruro, Potosí, Chuquisaca, Cochabamba, Tarija, Santa Cruz, Beni, and Pando. These regions, which correspond to different geographical and climatic zones, have traditionally vied for political and economic influence in the country. National influence and power have generally been linked to the economic wealth of the region and its importance to the national treasury.

For a time in the colonial era, the province of Chuquisaca and the capital, Sucre, served as the political center of the country. Sucre is still the legal and constitutional capital of Bolivia, although its national importance has long since declined. With the fantastic silver discoveries at Cerro Magnífico, the department of Potosí became the economic hub of colonial Bolivia and the departmental capital (also called Potosí) became the most populated city. When silver was depleted and tin replaced it as the backbone of the economy, political power shifted northward to the present de facto capital of La Paz and the mining centers of Oruro. After the mid-1960s, as economic and political power reverted to the lowland, the dominance of the highland provinces was challenged. With the oil riches of the 1970s and the cocaine traffic of the 1980s, the department of Santa Cruz became the main rival to the government in La Paz.

THE LAND AND ITS REGIONS

Bolivia is a country of great geographical and climatic diversity. The land and climate can be divided into three regions: the Andean, the transitional sub-Andean, and the lowland. Each region is characterized by distinct variations in climate and geography. The Andean region is composed of the arid *altiplano* highlands; the sub-Andean region consists of the mild to lush intermountain valleys of the *valles* and the *yungas*; and the eastern lowlands, or *oriente* region, includes subtropical grasslands and tropical rainforests.

The traditional centers of Bolivia's population have been located on the Altiplano, the high, inter-Andean plain at about 13,000 feet (4,000 meters) above sea level. Often compared to the Siberian tundras or the Tibetan plateau, the Altiplano lies between 18 degrees and 20 degrees and 30 minutes longitude. It extends approximately 500 miles (800 kilometers) in length and 80 miles (130 kilometers) in width between two main ranges of the Andes Mountains, the Cordillera Occidental to the west forming the border with Chile, and the Cordillera Real and Lake Titicaca along the border with Peru in the northeast. The Altiplano is a vast, landlocked water drainage system, the highest and largest of its kind in South America. In past geological eras it may have been a huge inland sea surrounded by mountains as high as 40,000 feet (12,000 meters) above sea level. Natural erosion has worn these peaks to heights of 16,500 to 21,000 feet (5,000 to 6,500 meters), depositing sedimentary rock and alluvial dust to great depths on the floor of the plateau. Lofty peaks still dominate the Altiplano landscape. Mount Sajama is an extinct volcano of 21,291 feet (6,520 meters) in the Western Cordillera. In the eastern Cordillera Real, the peaks of Illampu (21,500 feet or 6,550 meters) and Illimani (21,300 feet or 6,500 meters) loom over La Paz, the most populated city. La Paz itself is located in a deep rift of the Andes about 1,000 feet (305 meters) below the Altiplano.[4]

Lake Titicaca, the ancient and sacred lake of the Incas, is another geographical marvel. The largest and highest lake in South America, its sparkling, fresh waters extend 3,100 square miles (8,030 square kilometers) and reach estimated depths of 700 to 900 feet (200 to 300 meters). Among the dozens of islands that dot the vast lake, the largest and most sacred are the islands of the sun and the moon. Incan mythology holds that the sun god sent his son, Manco Kapac, and his daughter, Mama Ocllo, from the depths of the lake to found the Incan empire and civilize the surrounding Indian tribes. The royal couple were to cast their golden scepter into the air and establish the center of the new Incan empire where it landed. The scepter imbedded itself in Cuzco, Peru, and Manco Kapac and his sister became the first Incan rulers there.

The Desaguadero River, flowing 185 miles (300 kilometers) south-eastward, empties waters from Titicaca into Lake Poopó. Normally only 10 feet (3 meters) deep and 492 square miles (1,337 square kilometers)

The term *skyscraper* assumes special meaning amid the craggy lunar landscape of La Paz. The city is hemmed in by sheer rock precipices on three sides, permitting population expansion only upward or down along the winding path of the Choqueapu River to the valley's floor—hundreds of feet below the city's central plaza (photo by author).

in area, Poopó is the Altiplano's "dead sea" of extremely salty waters, which overflow into salt flats further south. Lake Poopó is believed to be evidence of two ancient lakes, Lake Ballivián and Lago Minchín, once part of the extensive inland sea. The immense saltpan of Uyuni (Salar de Uyuni), and the small salt flats in the south, may be the geological consequences of the long evaporated and lost waters of these ancient lakes. A conservative estimate of salt reserves in Uyuni yields 21 trillion tons (19 trillion metric tons). Indian workers transport salt from the great salt deserts, selling crude and refined forms in Bolivian cities.[5]

The climate on the Altiplano is frigid to temperate, but scanty rainfall, fierce winds, the rapid temperature inversion at sundown, and poor soil quality have made life on the high plateau rugged and harsh. Human settlements have concentrated along the more sheltered shores of Lake Titicaca, where the water (with its moderating influence on climate) and the more fertile soil permitted the cultivation of corn, potatoes, the potato-like *oca*, wheat, the highland grain of *quinua*, and garden vegetables. The potato originated in the Andes, where it has been cultivated since pre-Columbian times. In Bolivia some two hundred

Indian shepherds minding their flock of sheep on the arid and desolate Altiplano, which lies at an average 13,000 feet (4,000 meters) above sea level. The vast tundra-like plain has been home to the hardy Aymara and Quechua Indians of Boliva (photo courtesy of the Bolivian Embassy and General Secretary of Information).

varieties can be found. The potato and its frozen and dehydrated form known as *chuño*, as well as the hardy, high-altitude cereals of *quinua* and *cañahua*, are the staples of the highland Indian diet. These can be grown almost anywhere on the plateau except in the desert regions of the south.

The most exposed and higher expanses of the plateau support not only the herding of sheep, llamas, and alpacas but also the hunting of the nearly extinct *vicuña*. These last South American animals of the camel family are prized for their fine wool and lend a distinct picturesqueness to Andean Mountain landscapes. Because of the harsh climate and the dry rocky soil, vegetation is largely wild scrub grass (*paja brava*) and cacti. Mining, not agriculture, is the economy of the high plateau, and numerous mining centers such as Catavi (Llallagua) and Huanuni near the city of Oruro lie on the Altiplano and the higher mountain passes. The mining communities depend on food staples grown in Bolivia's more temperate and subtropical valleys.

The transitional, sub-Andean region of Bolivia almost defies categorization but includes at least two distinct zones. The first, the *valles*, consist of the wider, upper valleys of the central Andes to the east and southeast of the Altiplano. These steep but broad valleys and basins experience temperate and Mediterranean climate varying in rainfall in direct relation to altitude. The higher crests and ridges are colder and drier, with little vegetation or human settlement. Between 6,000 and 8,000 feet (1,800 and 2,500 meters) a wide variety of crops are grown, including corn (the staple of this area), peaches, plums, pears, wheat, barley, figs, olives, grapes, hardier citrus, and green vegetables. The departments of Cochabamba and Sucre are most representative of this area. The city of Cochabamba, once Bolivia's second largest, lies at 8,360 feet (2,550 meters) in the grain-rich Cochabamba valley. At a slightly lower elevation, the rainfall increases and the climate warms to support semitropical fruits: oranges, bananas, melons, papayas, avocados, peanuts, grapes, and the distinctive Bolivian custard apples, or *chirimoya*. The department of Tarija, with its capital in a broad valley at 6,250 feet (1,900 meters), and portions of Cochabamba and Santa Cruz departments form the semitropical subregion.

The *yungas*, lower and warmer valleys at an average altitude of 5,600 feet (1,700 meters), compose the second subregion. Yungas, an Aymara word meaning warm lands, has been applied by geographers to designate the entire sub-Andean system of valleys between the Altiplano and the Oriente lowlands. Bolivians commonly use the term to refer to the "mountain jungles" that lie deep in the narrow valleys and canyons that drop sharply off the northeastern slopes of the Cordillera Real. The highest elevations within this subregion differ little from the arid soil and hardy scrub grass of the Altiplano, but at middle ranges of 6,000 to 9,000 feet (2,000 to 3,000 meters) are found forests of pine, eucalyptus, laurel, cedar, and *quina* (a source of quinine).

The lower valleys are torrid, lush lands between 600 and 6,000 feet (200 and 2,000 meters) where the *coca* plant, used in the production of cocaine, has traditionally been cultivated from Incan times for markets on the Altiplano. Other semitropical and tropical agriculture includes coffee, tea, *ají* (hot pepper plant), *yuca* (sweet manioc), *camote* (sweet potatoes), mangoes, cacao, and pineapples. Although they constitute a rich agricultural zone, the North and South Yungas in the department of La Paz have relied on coca production because transportation costs made coca one of the few local products worth the arduous and expensive trip to La Paz. The 72-mile (115-kilometer) road from La Paz to Chulumani, the largest city in the Yungas and the capital of the province of South Yungas, is a seemingly endless series of precipitous curves that descend 11,000 feet (3,300 meters) in 50 miles (80 kilometers).[6]

Two-thirds or more of Bolivian territory fall within the country's third geographical region, the Oriente or eastern lowlands. The Oriente itself can be divided into three subregions: the plains, the northern tropical rainforests, and the dry scrub woodland of the Gran Chaco. With regional variations from north to south, the lowland climate is warm and humid. There is a distinct dry season from May through September and a wet season between December and February. Cold southerly winds from Antarctica, called *surazos*, may bring on a quick freeze and low temperatures from June through August.

The eastern plains are variously covered with grassland, palm, and river forests that extend from Bolivia's southeastern border with Brazil in the department of Santa Cruz north to the Río Beni in the department of Beni. The generally flat land is punctuated by rolling hills and inclines called *serranías* in the east. In the south begin the Plains of Grigotá and the drier Llanos de Chiquitos; and in the north, the wetter Llanos de Moxos, once the ancient inland sea of Lake Moxos. Small, round islands (*islas*) of thick forest and shrubs pepper the natural pastures and grasslands (*pampas* or savannahs) of the *llanos* (lowlands or plains) and border the undulating rivers and countless ponds and lagoons. Much of the northern plain is underwater several months of the year, forming marsh and swamp (*bañados*) and larger shallow lakes. The grasslands are ideal for cattle ranching, and hundreds of herds roam wild. The rich soil of the virgin forests, when cleared by slash-and-burn methods, yields sugar cane, dry rice, and cotton for local and export markets. Secondary crops include a wealth of semitropical and tropical fruits and, in some areas, coca bushes.

The most important city of the plains and of all the lowlands region is Santa Cruz de la Sierra, capital of the department of Santa Cruz. The ever-expanding city may already have overtaken Cochabamba as Bolivia's second largest. Santa Cruz increased in size after the oil boom that peaked in 1974 and became the lowland financial center for agriculture and drug traffic. The asphalted Cochabamba–Santa Cruz highway (completed in 1954), the railways connecting with Argentina and Brazil, and the international airport of El Trompillo link Santa Cruz with the highland and the world markets.

Tropical rainforests (*selvas*) dominate the most inaccessible and underpopulated Pando department, but they also extend into Beni and Santa Cruz, Cochabamba, and La Paz departments. Cattle ranching and tropical agriculture are important here. High jungle forests, especially in the northern Amazon basin, provide precious hardwoods, latex (natural rubber), and Brazil nuts. Tropical rivers team with fish and with lizards and caymans (crocodiles) valuable for leather. In this subregion lies the Chapare of Cochabamba department, where coca is cultivated extensively.

The main plaza of Bolivia's second largest city, Santa Cruz de la Sierra, which is the historic capital and thriving commercial center of the wealthy tropical department of Santa Cruz. The government of ex-general Hugo Banzer Suárez drew its support from this lowland center of economic and political power (photo by Allyn MacLean Stearman).

Most communication within this jungle and forest region is accomplished by the wide rivers meandering northward to the Amazon, although silting and rapids impede continuous navigation. The major cities are located on rivers for ease of communication. Trinidad, the capital of Beni, is situated along Bolivia's largest river, the Río Mamoré, which overflows its undefined banks in the rainy season, inundating the vast natural pastures and threatening the town. The city of Riberalta on the confluence of the Beni and Madre de Dios rivers serves as a port and transit center for lowland goods shipped to Brazil. Cobija, the capital of Pando, is on the Río Acre in the isolated northwestern corner of Bolivia between Brazil and Peru. Transport to the highlands is extremely difficult and costly. Until the Santa Cruz–Trinidad railway and the La Paz–Beni and La Paz–Cobija roads are built, air must remain the main link between the northern and central lowlands and the rest of Bolivia. With the exception of meat, which is flown by air transport to urban markets, products generally do not reach the highlands. But other Bolivian

A Camba woman (lowlander) and her child and their typical *pauhuichi* home thatched with palm leaves from the local *motacú* tree (photo by Allyn MacLean Stearman).

exports from the tropics reach the world market through Brazil, often as Brazilian goods.

Varieties of palms—the *totaí*, *chonta*, and *motacú*—figure prominently in lowland life and scenery. The totaí forms the coat of arms of Santa Cruz, and the motacú, sacred to the Indians, is used to thatch the roof of the *pauhuichi*, the distinctive lowland mud and wattle house. Numerous tropical animals are at home in the lowland: jaguars, pumas, peccary, deer, wild pigs, tapirs, poisonous snakes, monkeys, and hundreds of wild and rare birds. Only recently have extensive mineral riches of iron, manganese, river gold, and semiprecious and precious stones been exploited.

The third lowland subregion is the open scrub and woodland of the Bolivian Chaco, an extension of the Gran Chaco of Paraguay and Argentina. The Chaco lies in the southern and southeastern portions of Santa Cruz department and the eastern portions of Chuquisaca and Tarija departments. This region alternates between swamp for three months and parched desert devoid of rain for the other nine months of the year. The soil is extremely poor sand and clay covered with spiny shrubs, cacti, and dry forests of quebracho trees. The land is primarily used to graze wild cattle and goats. With proper irrigation, cotton, soybeans, and corn will grow in the subtropical to tropical climate. But because of the inhospitable terrain there are few cities in the Chaco; only small towns support the exploitation of petroleum and natural gas, and serve as way stations for the Santa Cruz–Villa Montes–Yacuiba railway into Argentina and the Santa Cruz–Roboré–Puerto Suárez rail link with the Brazilian border town of Corumbá on the navigable headwaters of the Paraguay River.

Geography has played such a central role in Bolivian life and history that geopolitical forces have taken on a life of their own. Overwhelmed, perhaps, by breathtaking and singular topography, Bolivians readily accept geographical determinism, or the "powerful mystic force which the land exerts upon its inhabitants."[7] Intellectuals have identified fiercely with the landscape. Franz Tamayo, Bolivia's philosopher-poet, immortalized the Andes with the words, "the spirit of these mountains is made man and thinks."[8] The Altiplano, the valleys, and the impenetrable tropical forests have contributed to the distinct, though confused, Bolivian identity. An asset in one sense, geographical diversity has nevertheless intensified social, racial, and cultural differences. The result is a complex ethnic mosaic that has been a formidable obstacle to national integration.

THE PEOPLE: AN ETHNIC MOSAIC

Bolivia is at heart an Indian country. It may have the highest percentage of Amerindians in Latin America.[9] More than 60 percent of the population is highland or lowland Indian, and nearly 30 percent are mestizos of mixed parentage. "Whites" make up only 5 to 15 percent, and other races and nationalities constitute a mere 1 percent. Racial and ethnic status poses problems in Bolivia, where race now means "social race"—the combination of physical characteristics, culture, language, and social mobility. Yet physiological appearance is often not a valid indicator of either race or social status. Bolivia is in reality an extremely heterogeneous society in which intermarriage between the indigenous race and the Spanish conquerors extended over 500 years. As a result, the racial term *white* largely refers to socioeconomic status.

The highland Indians—the Aymara and the Quechua—form the largest ethnic group in Bolivia.[10] The oldest are the Aymara, who make up 20 to 25 percent of the population (750,000 to 1 million Indians in the 1950 census). Their ancestors may be the most ancient of Andean peoples who in A.D. 600 founded the kingdom of Tiwanaku and created its architectural marvels hundreds of years before the Incan conquest. The ancient home of the Aymara lay along the shores of Lake Titicaca and the central Altiplano. Most Aymara speakers are concentrated there today. Aymara communities abound in the department of La Paz (where about 90 percent are located), but they are numerous in Oruro and Potosí as well. The Aymara are a fiercely independent people who were neither successfully subjugated by the Incas nor completely acculturated by the Spaniards. Before the 1952 Revolution, the Aymara lived as serf laborers (*pongos, colonos,* or *peones*) on the huge haciendas. Only the more isolated members of communities (*comunarios*) maintained their indigenous cooperative farms (*ayllus*).

The Quechua are the largest ethnolinguistic group in Bolivia and South America. These Indians, who speak Quechua, the official language of the Incan empire, are descendants of the Inca and the valley Indians who were subjugated and acculturated by Incan rule. Both historically and currently, Quechua communities have been most extensive in the departments of Cochabamba and Sucre, but they also exist in the valleys of Potosí, Tarija, La Paz, and Oruro. Quechua speakers may constitute as many as 37 percent of the population—as of 1950, more than 1 million people. Unlike the Aymara, who have the reputation of being taciturn and antisocial (*uraño*), the Quechua are celebrated in local lore as cheerful and sociable. They, too, formed ayllus and provided involuntary serf labor for Spanish haciendas and mines.

Few other highland Indians remain in Bolivia. The Uru lived around Lake Poopó, giving their name to the city of Oruro; the Chipaya came from the province of Charangas in the department of Oruro; and the Callahuaya, an Aymara subgroup who settled in northern La Paz department, were the medicine men and magicians for the Incas. The proportion of Indians from these groups who have survived as separate ethnic and linguistic groups is not known. Even within related Indian communities, wide differences in custom and dress persist. Within the Quechua nation, for instance, one can distinguish a variety of local groups: the Tarabucos, the Chayantas, the Laimes, the Ucumaris, the Calchas, the Chaquies, the Yuras Lipes, and the Tirinas.[11] A highlander can readily identify the region of the country and the community of an Indian by differences in dress, custom, and music.

Lowland Indian nations have also served an important role in the development of Bolivia and in the racial mixing of its people. This role is often underestimated because few lowland tribal groups have survived the forces of acculturation and deculturation. The ethnic diversity of Bolivia's lowlands is great, but appreciation of the region's cultural wealth has been eclipsed by popular and scholarly interest in the more highly developed highland communities. In addition, much less is known about the lowland peoples, even though they are the basic ethnic alloy in the racial melting pot of the Oriente. Ethnologists differ in their assessments of the contributions of lowland Indians to lowland society and racial stock. Some argue that there was little intermarriage between the Spaniard and the forest Indians, but others maintain that a thorough mestization occurred. Perhaps this confusion reflects the simultaneously successful process of assimilation and extermination of the lowland Indians.

Of the hundreds of pre-Columbian Indians, probably no more than 50,000 forest Indians survived in lowland Bolivia. The Indians were primarily nomadic hunters or gatherers, but some were sedentary agriculturalists. The two major Indian groups were the Guaraní and the Arawaks. Within the Guaranian nation (the larger of the two) were the fierce Chiriguano who resisted domination by both Incan and Spanish rule. The Chiriguano were sedentary farmers who had migrated from south of the lower Amazon to settle in Paraguay and then moved northward into Tarija and Santa Cruz departments. The tribe was one of the largest and most organized of the forest Indians. Perhaps most organizationally developed, however, were the Arawak group—especially the Moxos Indians, who developed a sedentary agricultural economy and whose villages and kingdom of Moxos were located on the Moxos Plains in Beni department. The Chiquitano, a tribe of Amazonian origin distinct from the Guaraní and Arawak linguistic families, controlled the lowland plains of Santa Cruz in the sixteenth century. They befriended the Spanish discoverer, Captain Ñuflo de Chávez, who had left the colonial city of Asunción in Paraguay to found the city of Santa Cruz de la Sierra.

Four linguistic groups (the Panoan, the Tacanan, the Moxoan, and the Guaranian) survived in lowland Bolivia. The Guaranian Indians were Christianized and organized in Jesuit missions (*reducciones*) until the Jesuits were expelled in 1767. Without the protection of the religious settlements, Indians were subject to massive exploitation and slavery. Either most communities were destroyed or their members fled into inaccessible jungle. A linguistic and governmental study in 1969 identified the Chiquitanos as the largest lowland Indian group with 19,000 members but, in fact, found only 5,000 Guarayos and 650 Sirionó.[12]

The traditional "white" population of Bolivia, the *blancos*, are not easily counted either. The 1976 Bolivian census employed three ethnic categories: Indian, mestizo, and white. Inasmuch as most upwardly mobile people claim white status regardless of actual racial background, it is as difficult to determine who is racially white as to decide who is an Indian. Demographic studies suggest that 5 to 15 percent of the population is white. Traditionally, whites encompassed the aristocratic upper class of Bolivia known as the *gente decente* or the *gente buena*, meaning the "better folk" or gentry who possessed wealth and European cultural refinement. Most also claimed to be pure descendants of the

Spanish conquerors and the original ruling families of the colonial era. These whites tended to remain aloof from the recent immigrants from England, Italy, and Germany. Although the latter were physiologically "whiter," they were socially inferior to the local elites.

The blancos of the eastern lowland boasted greater racial purity than the highland elites. And the typical Bolivian perceived the light-skinned Cruceñan or Tarijan woman as the classic beauty of the creole class (or *criollos*, the Spanish elites born in the New World). The lowlander aristocracy racially identified with the "European" peoples of La Plata (Paraguay and Argentina) and felt superior to their highland counterparts. Highlanders demonstrated greater physiological attributes of "whiteness" in the valley towns than on the Altiplano. But the simple reality was that most Bolivians, whether highlanders or lowlanders, were mestizos— the products of centuries-long racial mixing. White identity has been preserved by adherence to aristocratic values and lifestyle, not by "blue blood." Despite the 1952 Revolution, the blancos still perceive themselves as the embodiment of the best in Hispanic tradition, the refinement of European cosmopolitan cultures, and the guardians of conservative, elitist political beliefs.

The most ambiguous racial category in Bolivian society is that of the mestizo, or *cholo*. A transitional racial group, the mestizos have proceeded from the intermixture of European and native Indian parentage. In highland Bolivia the term *cholo* originally implied miscegenation between descendants of the white, Spanish colonizers and the highland Indians (both Aymara and Quechua). Before the revolution, however, *cholo* referred specifically to the respected mestizo middle class, and *chola paceña* to a mestizo lady of social standing and prosperity. The classic La Paz chola was distinguished by her intricate mestizo jewelry and dress—the richly embroidered Spanish shawl (*manta*), the lavishly gathered skirt (*pollera*), and the felt bowler hat or sombrero. This tradition has been appropriated by recently acculturated Indians—much to the annoyance of the older mestizo middle class.

In the cultural sense, *cholo* today refers to an upwardly mobile Indian. Since the 1952 Revolution, increased social mobility of the rural Indian broadened the usage of *cholo* to mean an Indian who adopted urban life, the Spanish language, and mestizo customs and dress. In response, the "new" mestizo middle class (either descendants of the old middle class or those who had recently come into money and property) often eschewed creole dress (*de pollera*) altogether for the modern fashions (*de vestido*) of the upper class, to preserve their eroding social position. Yet despite the current popularization of the term *cholo*, old social distinctions persist. Although many have claimed mestizo status, tra-

Chola women wearing the distinctive mestizo dress of Bolivia: the widely gathered skirt (*pollera*) and the felt bowler sombrero that was popularized in the twentieth century and fashioned by the prestigious Italian firm of Borselino (photo by author).

ditional cholas are few; in declining numbers, they represent the stricter social barriers and standards of earlier prerevolutionary days.

In the Oriente the lowland term *camba* describes the interracial mixing of the white settlers and the forest Indians. Initially *camba* referred to a lowland Indian, but it later came to mean a mestizo. In upper-class lowland society *camba* may still retain the pejorative connotation of "Indian," or person of low social status. In the last ten years, however, *camba* has also been employed with great regional pride to refer to all lowlanders, to distinguish them from the highlanders (*kollas*). The contrast is both regional and racial, given that kollas are of different ethnic stock and possess different cultural traditions. Originally, the term *kolla* referred to the Indians who lived in the north-central Altiplano from Lake Titicaca to Lake Poopó and, later, to the Indian descendants of the ancient Incan empire, the *Kollasuyo*. Today the term epitomizes the highland identity, as distinct from *camba*, the term of solidarity for the lowlander.

Recent immigration has also contributed to Bolivia's population. At the turn of the century, immigrants from Europe (especially Germany) came to Bolivia and were assimilated into the traditional "white" society. Recent immigrants since 1950 have been European, North American,

Asian, and Semitic. The whites in this second wave who have established themselves in the Bolivian social hierarchy were undoubtedly accepted as racially white. Other groups, mainly nonwhites, were categorized as "other" ethnic nationals and aliens in the country. European and North American nationalities included Dutch, Germans, Italians, Spaniards, Canadians, and Americans. The Dutch and German Mennonite colonies, each made up of several thousand people, have been an important presence in the Oriente. These settlers have successfully resisted racial and cultural assimilation in keeping with the special rights granted by the colonization pact with the Bolivian government. Jewish immigrants have represented many different European nationalities as well.

The less than 1 percent "other" category in the national census refers mostly to recent nonwhite immigrants. Among nonwhite groups are the seven hundred Japanese and Okinawan families who settled in 1956 and 1965 in Santa Cruz and Beni and intermarried with other Bolivians. A small number of Arab immigrants (predominantly from Palestine, Syria, and Lebanon) and Jewish Semitic people have also been readily assimilated. Brazilians of various races total more than 30,000 in the border regions, and black immigrants from Brazil are increasing in number. Ultimately, Bolivia's ethnic mixing has strained its national culture and identity.

CULTURE AND NATIONAL IDENTITY

Bolivians today are fiercely protective of their predominantly Indian cultural heritage. But this was not always the case. Until the philosophical movement of indigenism early in the twentieth century, only Europeanized white culture mattered; Indian traditions were ridiculed as barbaric. Hence Bolivia was split into two warring cultures: elite and popular. The first was progressive; the latter, backward. Contemporary cultural pride is generally the mature fruit of a postrevolutionary campaign to popularize indigenous folklore. But the struggle to incorporate the Indian heritage into Bolivian national life began at the turn of the century with the efforts of Bolivia's more enlightened intellectuals and philosophers.

Through culture and its main components—popular customs and social thought—early philosophers hoped to fashion an authentically Bolivian national identity and pride. Preaching social realism and in-digenism, these philosophers saw intellectual and moral value in the same Indian who had been ridiculed and abused for centuries as a slovenly, taciturn brute. Popular folklore would bridge the country's dual cultural heritage: the Indian and the Spanish, the ancient and the modern, the elite and the popular. The result of this intellectual revolution was

Chola women at a traditional *presterío* (religious festival) in the Altiplano town of Jesús de Machaca (photo by author).

cultural nationalism—the ideological and integrative force behind the 1952 National Revolution.

Folklore

The intricate ethnic tapestry of Bolivia is most apparent in the culture and folklore of the people. Each region of the country exhibits distinctive dress, music, cuisine, and local festivals. These customs often identify not only the district but the specific village of an individual. They also reflect the syncretic beliefs of Roman Catholicism and Indian mythology, and the extensive cultural exchange between Spanish and indigenous Indian festivals. Folkloric celebrations, dances, music, and social practices reveal the richness of this cultural exchange and the pervasiveness of the Indian heritage throughout Bolivian society. Typical cultural practices and events include the mestizo funeral service (*velorio*), the religious festival sponsored in honor of the town's patron saint (*presterío*), and popular folkloric holidays such as Carnival and the festival of miniatures known as *Alasitas*.

Though ostensibly Catholic, the mestizo funeral service incorporates the ritual mourning and hospitality found in ancient Indian cosmology and customs. In La Paz no expense is spared in the velorio. All the deceased's relatives and acquaintances gather to pray and feast in memory of the departed one. During the wake, incessant rounds of cocktails (*cocteles*), steamy pisco punches (*ponches*), beer, cigarettes, and coca leaves (accompanied by pieces of ash rock to neutralize the alkaline substance) pass down the file of mourners neatly seated along the four sides of the viewing room. At daylight, mourners and casket proceed to the cemetery for the internment ceremony. Threading past bereaved relatives lined along the cemetery gate, guests extend condolences (*pésames*) before leaving; some return to the obligatory funeral celebration. Immediate family and friends complete the funeral rites on the following day. Trekking to the Choqueapu River below La Paz, they ritually wash the clothes of the deceased. Mourners picnic until the garments are dry and then light the bonfire that will burn the cleansed clothing. This simple ceremony dispatches the soul of the deceased into the afterlife and soothes the sadness of those left behind.

National independence celebrations and hundreds of traditional festivals reveal the mestizo syncretism of faith and custom. The presterío, a social institution popular in the highlands and valleys, obligates a person of the community to sponsor and finance a festival in honor of the local saint or religious feastday. On August 6, national independence day, thousands of religious celebrations occur in La Paz alone; many more take place in other cities and towns. A popular religious and folkloric festival is the pilgrimage to the shrine of the Virgin of Copacabana on the shores of Lake Titicaca, a site sacred to the Aymara, Incas, and Christians alike. Other celebrated sites include the village of Tiwanaku near the pre-Incan archeological ruins, the shrine of the Virgin of Urquina in Cochabamba, and the Chapel of the Virgin of Socavón in Oruro.

Annually, a socially respected mestizo from La Paz sponsors a presterío in the small and isolated altiplano village of Jesús de Machaca to celebrate national independence and honor the Niño (Child Jesus), the town's patron saint. The sponsor, a descendant of Machaca's Aymara Indian community, is obligated to provide the finest celebration even if impoverished in the process. This customary leveling ritual affirms the ancient communal belief that by giving, one receives. The Niño is said to return threefold the fortune spent in his honor. The festival's sponsor gains social respect and status: Traditionally, the opportunity "to pass *preste*" (i.e., to serve as festival sponsor) is the crowning social honor an individual can achieve in the community.

The typical folkloric festival is a huge party. In Machaca the celebration opens with the religious procession of the Niño (*entrada*), his silver and gold treasures, and troupes of folkloric dancers around the main plaza into the colonial church. The next days' festival events include a ritual crossing of the nearby lake in Indian reed boats (*balseada*)

An August 6 celebration in the name of the Niño in the highland village of Jesús de Machaca, some four to five hours from La Paz by winding dirt road. After the dusty trip, arrival is a most welcome experience (photo by author).

and the nocturnal vigil (*víspera*) with dancing, fireworks, and warming ponches until dawn. Later, during a mock bullfight (*corrida*), a bull is released into the plaza to the delight or dismay of the spectators. Another favorite event is the *calvario* (calvary), which evokes both Christ's Crucifixion and certain Indian rituals wherein celebrants gather at the local hill to contract symbolic marriages and buy miniature houses and plots of land.

If the presterío is a success, guests are expected to help defray the costs of the celebration (a custom known as *arco*). Although good hosts see that liquor flows freely, beer can always be bought wherever vendors, who have descended upon the isolated town for the event, erect their makeshift stalls. The host's cooks, who must serve hearty food for hundreds of guests over several days, seem to be endlessly preparing meals. Another essential festival ingredient is dancing, provided by the festival-goers dressed in elaborate folkloric costumes adapted from fourteenth-century Spanish court attire.

Dances are among the most important and prolific aspects of Bolivian folklore, with more than 500 varieties. Ceremonial in nature, they represent important events and activities of the indigenous community: hunting, planting, weaving, harvesting, and worship. Traditional Hispanic dances, heavily influenced by acculturation and very popular at festivals, include the *diablada*, the devil dance, and the *morenada*, the dance of the black slaves.

The origins of the diablada have been traced to a medieval Spanish dance involving leaping, fierce devils who represent the seven deadly sins of Christianity. The Christian concept of the devil became confused with the Indian theogony of *Supay*, a pre-Hispanic spirit of evil and the lord of all mineral riches in the Andes Mountains. The mineworkers later believed in *El Tío* (meaning "the uncle"), their representation of the devil who inhabited the depths of the mines, and to whom they prayed against cave-ins and for rich mineral finds. The dance was performed in the pagan-Christian carnival celebrations before Lent during the viceroyalty, when Indian mineworkers were given a respite from their grueling work. The dance invoked the Virgin of *Socavón* (the mine), who represented the Christian-pagan deity of good in battle with the devil. The choreography consists of monstrous devils dressed in high red boots and leaping to music reminiscent of a European court gallop. The dance and the beliefs behind it are the main attractions during the mystical festival of the Virgin of Socavón held annually in the mining town of Oruro.

The morenada is a dance satirizing the black slaves (*morenos*) whom the Spanish imported by the thousands into Peru and Bolivia. The choreography builds on a side-to-side movement accompanied by a slow and monotonous musical rhythm mocking the courtly steps popular in the Spain of King Philip III. Dancers wear black masks and white court wigs while rhythmically swinging the *matraca*, a musical rattle of African origin. In addition to the morenada, post-Hispanic folk dances influenced by acculturation with European forms include the traditional Andean *cueca* and the *bailecito*, both performed with a scarf or handkerchief. The cueca is a popular and integral dance form in all mestizo and criollo celebrations, and is internationally associated with Bolivia and other Andean countries.

Among the pre-Hispanic dances, the *sarao* from Beni, the *trenzas* from Tarija, and *los tobas* from the lowlands are popular tropical dances. Highland favorites are the *tarqueada*, the dance that rewards the Indian communal authorities who have managed the community's land holdings during the year; the *llamerada*, which is the llama-herding dance; the *kullawada*, the dance of the Indian weavers; and the *wayño*, the favorite social dance of the Quechua and the Aymara. The wayño and kullawada have been incorporated into mestizo and creole dance, and are characteristic of contemporary Bolivian dance and musical culture.

Morenada dancers at a folkloric festival on the Altiplano. The Morenada satirizes the court dress and customs of the Spanish. Dancers show off colorful and elaborately beaded costumes as they swing musical rattles, the *matracas* (photo by author).

Musical instruments are another distinctive feature of Bolivian folklore. Flutes, trumpets, and clarinets were the principal pre-Columbian instruments. Well known is the *siku* or *zampoña* (the latter being the Spanish term for a series of vertical flutes much like the Greek and Tibetan Flutes of Pan). Another typical post-Columbian instrument of Bolivia is the *charango*. A cross between the mandolin, banjo, and guitar, the charango was adapted from a fifteenth-century European stringed instrument formed of wood. In Bolivia the soundbox of the charango was made from the shell of an armadillo, giving the instrument its distinct appearance and resonance.

Bolivia's festivals have encouraged and preserved the potpourri of Indian mythology and colonial customs. In La Paz the celebration of Alasitas commemorates an ancient harvest and fertility festival held by the Indians in October but changed to January by colonial edict to coincide with the feast of Our Lady of La Paz, patroness of the capital. Originally during Alasitas, which means "buy me" in Aymara, only items in miniature were sold: tiny cakes and sweets, toy-sized kitchen utensils, play houses, cars, wedding rings, and tiny figurines of the *Ek'eko*, the Aymara god of fertility. As the Ekeko ensured prosperity

These members of a typical amateur folkloric group demonstrate their skill on drums and *zampoña,* the vertical flutes that create the distinctive haunting sound characteristic of Andean Indian music (photo by author).

and luck for the coming year, the purchase of a figurine was like an amulet against bad fortune. To symbolize the realization of their aspirations, couples hoping to marry would buy a miniature ring, or those wanting a new house would buy a toy version. Alasitas today is a more commercialized national crafts fair, although the mix of Christian and Indian beliefs still characterizes the holiday.

The celebration of San Juan on June 24, popularly thought to be the coldest night of the year on the Altiplano, is another contemporary version of an ancient fertility ritual. In La Paz families light bonfires (*fogatas*) around which neighbors socialize and exchange hot pisco punches during the cold night vigil. The steaming punches not only ward off the chill but also represent a gesture of social respect and friendship for the recipients. During the San Juan celebration, the thousands of bonfires on the hills ringing the city create a constellation of lights as brilliant as the winter night's sky.

Pre-Columbian customs are practiced by Indians and non-Indians alike. It is not unusual for the average highlander to buy a *dulce mesa* at the witchcraft and folk medicine market in La Paz and to offer this preparation of sweets and colored baubles to *Pachamama,* or mother earth, the revered spirit of good and prosperity in Aymara and Quechua cosmology. The offering to Pachamama, like the votive candle used by Christians, intercedes with the deity to grant the supplicant's request. Even sophisticated Bolivians often observe the customary practices of respect for Pachamama, such as pouring a libation onto the ground to symbolize that one's worldly bounty comes from the earth. To remind them that it is the earth that gives and the earth that takes, the folk ceremony of the *ch'alla*, derived from an ancient propitiatory and fertility rite, "christens" or commends new possessions into the hands of Pachamama.

Philosophy and National Ideology

Indigenism, the philosophical movement of greatest impact on Bolivia, directly contributed to the nationalist ideology of the 1952 Revolution. The "apostle of nationalism" and earliest proponent of indigenism was Franz Tamayo, whose thought influenced the prerevolutionary military reformers and the nationalist ideology of the revolutionary party, the Nationalist Revolutionary Movement (Movimiento Nacionalista Revolucionario, or MNR).

In his widely read *Creación de la pedagogía nacional*, Tamayo argued that Bolivia must discover its true national character and culture in the Indian and in the land. He combined indigenism, the return to Indian roots, with tellurism, the belief in the mystical formative power of the Andean milieu on man. And he exhorted Bolivians to find their unique spirit: "There exists a Yankee soul and a Japanese soul which are quite distinct from the European. This same personality we must discover among ourselves. We must try to create the national character."[13] For Tamayo, the physical environment was fundamental: "The land makes the man; and it is in the land where the ultimate reason for his thinking, his deeds, and his morality must be sought."[14] Of greatest import in Tamayo's vision was the acceptance of the Indian as the heart of national culture and the greatest national asset.

The nationalist philosophy of Tamayo clashed with the elitist views of another Bolivian social thinker, Alcides Arguedas, who saw the roots of Bolivia's disunity, instability, and backwardness in the ethnic problem. In *Pueblo enfermo*, which achieved literary fame throughout Latin America and Europe, Arguedas charged that the racial mixture between Spaniards and the Indians had tainted society and created the hated mestizo, a hybrid who combined the bad traits of both races—the arrogance and despotism of the whites and the servility and savagery of the Indians. The only solution to the ethnic disease, he believed, was massive European immigration: Bolivians were a sick people and only outsiders could cure them.

Unlike Arguedas, Tamayo believed that racial mixing was the solution, not the problem, to Bolivia's racial and cultural identity. History had demonstrated to Tamayo that Indian vitality was Bolivia's salvation; the Indian, he wrote,

> continues to be the solid basis and strongest element of the nationality of which he is a part, because of the astounding vitality of his blood. And this survival is truly a victory. Indeed the Indian has reconquered his usurped position. The mestizo who constitutes the numerical and qualitative majority in our America is the superior and more valuable racial element; in his veins flows the victorious and unconquerable blood of the Indian.[15]

Nevertheless, the pessimism and realism of Arguedas was a necessary antidote to the optimism and romanticism of the liberal era. Liberalism was a foreign system that encouraged republican government and the founding of political parties in the 1870s: the Liberals, the Conservatives, and, later, the Republicans. As a social ideology, liberalism legitimized elitist politics with formulas of democracy and progress while practicing corruption and class oppression. Arguedas condemned this system, which in eighty years of independence had spawned twenty rulers, either tyrants or dreamers. Partisan feuds, personal avarice, and corruption were the political legacy of liberalism, he complained: "The situation has reached such a level of immorality that two Bolivians are unable to work together without the one cheating the other."[16] His solution for political immaturity was benevolent dictatorship.

Both Tamayo and Arguedas were essential precursors of more radical currents—Arguedas by routing complacency, and Tamayo by challenging racial prejudice. Tamayo later said: "I am the precursor of Mariátegui, Haya de la Torre, Valcarcel, Uriel García and other indigenists of this continent."[17] Indeed, his indigenism influenced a generation of "Indianists" such as Jaime Mendoza, Fernando Díez de Medina, Roberto Prudencio, Carlos Medinaceli, and Jesús Lara, who combined mystical faith in the land and ancient Indian tradition into today's national folklore and Indian cosmology. Roberto Prudencio popularized the new Bolivian man (the kolla, or descendant of the Inca) as well as the new Bolivia (or Kollasuyo), historically the southern kingdom of the Incan empire. Jaime Mendoza integrated Indian beliefs directly into popular culture: "The Indian is the land itself. He is the autochthon. He is the human personification of this entity which, although barely a speck of mud, shelters the secret of life. This is the source of the cult of Pachamama which in a way eclipses even the cult of the sun."[18]

Indian mythology was a foundation for Bolivian nationalism much like Nordic mythology was for Germany or the myth of the "cosmic" man was for Mexico. Indeed, indigenism made possible the home-grown ideology of the Bolivian National Revolution. In the words of an MNR political theoretician, Díez de Medina: "Bolivia must make its own path and attend to its internal social reality. Enough of Marxism and fascism. We need a new political synthesis, typically Bolivian . . . conceived in indigenous values, a socialist economy, and with a South American, not European, ethic and politics, rooted in the land."[19] Díez de Medina condemned the exploitation, inequality, and political corruption "which gives everything to a few, but doesn't extend even elemental necessities to the great majority; this problem of inequality is the origin of national discontent."[20] And despite his radical tone, he rejected Marxist class struggle for a Bolivian model of state corporatism and economic nationalism, both central elements of the MNR political program. His thought also provided the ideological foundation for the main postrevolutionary opposition party, the Bolivian Socialist Falange (Falange Socialista Boliviana, or FSB).

By challenging cultural colonialism, indigenism raised people's consciousness against political and economic colonialism. Revolutionary nationalism was one expression of this new social awareness; another was Marxism. In the footsteps of Peru's foremost Marxist and indigenist, José Carlos Mariátegui, Bolivian Marxists applied class analysis to the Indian problem. Influenced both by Mariátegui's *Siete ensayos de interpretación de la realidad peruana* and by the Aprista party critique of Manuel A. Seoane, *Con el ojo izquierdo mirando a Bolivia*, Marxists such as Ricardo Anaya, José Antonio Arze, and Arturo Urquidi formulated the political ideology of Bolivia's leftist parties and labor unions—the Party of the Revolutionary Left (Partido de la Izquierda Revolucionaria, or PIR), the Revolutionary Workers' Party (Partido Obrero Revolucionario, or POR), the Bolivian Communist Party (Partido Comunista de Bolivia, or PCB), and the Bolivian Mine Workers' Federation (Federación Sindical de Trabajadores Mineros de Bolivia, or FSTMB).

For the Marxists, indigenism was subordinated to international imperialism and capitalist exploitation. Oppression of the Indians was a special form of worker exploitation. The solution of the Indian problem would depend on the destruction of the capitalist economic system: nationalization of the mines and land to the tiller. Bolivian Marxists employed indigenism to justify a socialist Bolivia, arguing that the civilization of the Incas had been a natural communist society that contemporary Bolivia should emulate.

Although Marxist philosophy was rejected by the nationalist architects of the Bolivian Revolution, the Marxist goals of land reform and nationalization of the mines were adopted and became the heart of the revolutionary reforms. With the restratification of Bolivian society since the revolution, Marxism has become a more popular ideology among students, workers, and even elements of the progressive military. Despite the great shortcomings of dogmatism and factionalism, the Marxists provided philosophical indigenism with a socioeconomic content.

The weakness of Bolivian philosophy and political ideology is an elitist escapism that has failed to translate ideas into social action. Tamayo, the firebrand of nationalism, did not practice what he preached; and others contorted indigenism into an esoteric cult of native exoticism, and honest social criticism into a fad of anarchism and revolutionism. The Indians remained victims; and racism, social injustice, and political decadence, which the philosophers had condemned, continued.

CHALLENGES AHEAD

Is Bolivia a land divided, a geographical accident of independence? Are the divisions of geography, region, race, and culture discussed in this chapter too formidable? Or can Bolivia become one nation? Judging by the emotional intensity of Bolivian nationalism and pride, national unity appears attainable. But the social and economic record is disheartening. Despite the 1952 Revolution, the Indian question has not been resolved: Bolivia's majority is still psychologically, socially, and legally bereft of full citizenship, and Hispanic elitism remains the dominant myth. Why has Bolivian diversity, a potential strength, been reduced to fratricidal distinctions among race, region, and class? Why can't pride in who and what the Bolivians are as a people emanate from their dual historical heritage of ancient pre-Incan society and Spanish conquest?

NOTES

1. Thomas E. Weil et al., *Area Handbook for Bolivia*, Foreign Area Studies, American University (Washington, D.C.: Government Printing Office, 1974), pp. 60, 308–309.

2. Ibid., p. 58.

3. Harold Osborne, *Bolivia: A Land Divided* (New York: Oxford University Press, 1964), p. 32.

4. Altitudes vary widely with the sources. The figures here are based on Weil, *Area Handbook*, p. 50; cf. Osborne, *Bolivia*, p. 8.

5. Hugo Boero Rojo, *Enciclopedia Bolivia mágica*, 3rd ed. (La Paz: Editorial Los Amigos del Libro, 1978), p. 184.

6. Osborne, *Bolivia*, pp. 19–20.

7. Martin S. Stabb, *In Quest of Identity: Patterns in the Spanish American Essay of Ideas, 1890–1960* (Chapel Hill: University of North Carolina Press, 1967), p. 33.

8. Guillermo Francovich, *El pensamiento boliviano en el siglo veinte* (Mexico City: Fondo de Cultura Económica, 1956), p. 94. In Spanish, the poem reads: "El alma de estos montes / Se hace hombre y piensa. / Tramonta un ansia inmensa / Los horizontes. / Y en la luz huraña / Más de una sien transflora / Una montaña."

9. Jonathan Kelley and Herbert S. Klein, *Revolution and the Rebirth of Inequality: A Theory Applied to the National Revolution in Bolivia* (Berkeley: University of California Press, 1981), p. 49.

10. This section draws heavily from Weil, *Area Handbook*, pp. 81–86. Based on the 1976 census, Indian populations are smaller, inasmuch as language spoken is the main category used to assess population. That is, persons who speak only Aymara number 315,228; those who speak only Quechua, 568,707; and those who speak both Aymara and Quecha, 52,684. Persons who speak both Spanish and Aymara number 680,018; and both Spanish and Quecha, 864,774. To avoid this confusion, I have used the 1950 census here. See *Bolivia en cifras 1980* (La Paz: Instituto Nacional de Estadística [INES], 1981), p. 41.

11. Boero, *Enciclopedia*, p. 91.

12. Ibid., pp. 18, 77–78.

13. Franz Tamayo, *Creación de la pedagogía nacional* (La Paz: Editorial El Diario, 1944), p. 11.

14. Ibid., p. 172.

15. Ibid., p. 132.

16. Alcides Arguedas, *Pueblo enfermo: contribución a la psicología de los pueblos hispano-americanos* (Barcelona: Vda. de Luis Tasso, 1909), p. 104.

17. Fausto Reinaga, *Franz Tamayo y la revolución boliviana* (La Paz: Editorial Casegural, 1956), p. 85.

18. Francovich, *El pensamiento boliviano*, p. 76.

19. Fernando Díez de Medina, *"Siripaka;" la batalla de Bolivia, "anoika" ideario del pachakutismo* (La Paz: Editorial Artística, 1950), p. 10.

20. Ibid., p. 15.

2

Early History: The Pre-Columbian, Colonial, and Republican Eras

To an equal degree, both the precolonial history of Bolivia and its postcolonial history have been characterized by instability and violence. Never an easy people to subdue, the ancient as well as modern inhabitants of this highland nation have struggled against occupation and repression for many centuries.

THE PRE-COLUMBIAN ERA TO INDEPENDENCE (600–1825)

The first stage of premodern Bolivian history paints a sweeping panorama of glorious Indian empires, bloody Spanish conquests, and violent independence struggles. Only after sixteen years of bitter war was the new South American nation wrested from the embrace of Spanish colonial rule.

Pre-Columbian Civilizations (600–1532)

Shrouded in mystery and myth, the history of ancient pre-conquest Indian civilizations survives in artifacts and conflicting oral traditions. Neither the Incan nor the pre-Incan culture perfected a written language, but both civilizations have been studied through the elaborate pottery, carvings, weavings, and gold and silver ornaments they left behind. Ancient pre-Incan peoples inhabited the Peruvian coast and Andean plateau as early as 7500 B.C. By 1500 B.C. they had developed agriculture, farming corn in the lowlands and potatoes in the highlands. In the latter area they also domesticated the llama for meat and the alpaca for wool.[1] Several famous pre-Incan Indian settlements gradually formed. One was Tiwanaku, south of Lake Titicaca.

31

Bolivian archeologists have dated the beginnings of the pre-Ti-wanaku peoples and culture, established below Lake Huiñaymarka (Titicaca), as early as 1600 B.C. and the decline of their descendants with the rise of the Aymara and Incas around A.D. 1200.[2] The Tiwanakan civilization probably emerged between 100 B.C. and A.D. 100, but most anthropologists agree that by A.D. 600 the Tiwanakan empire dominated the Bolivian Altiplano.[3] The *Tiwanakotas* were believed to be the ancestors of the Aymara, the pre-Incan Indian-language group of some twelve "nations" that populated the Bolivian and Peruvian highland near Lake Titicaca and neighboring valleys of the La Paz Yungas. The empire of Tiwanaku predated the future grandeur of the Incan imperium as the first vast South American Indian empire, extending as far north as the Ecuadorean border with southern Colombia, along the Peruvian and Chilean coast, and into northern Argentina.[4]

In A.D. 300, the capital city, Tiwanaku, covered an area of about 4 square miles (11 square kilometers) and may have housed from 20,000 to 50,000 inhabitants. The Tiwanakan culture is believed to have influenced the religion of the Incas and other pre-Incan groups. Viracocha (also known as Pachacamac) was the great-creator god of the ancient Tiwanakotas; his shrine, 25 miles (40 kilometers) from the modern city of Lima, remained a sacred site to later Andean religions. The Tiwanakotas also discovered bronze by alloying copper and tin. This process required a high level of social and economic organization and an extensive system of roads and communications. The archeological ruins of their civilization near the present-day Bolivian town of Tiwanaku attest as well to their knowledge of architecture and astronomy.

The decline of Tiwanaku remains a mystery. Several oral traditions attempt to explain its demise by disaster. One legend recalls a great flood, another a great drought; and a third relates that Huyustus, the ancient mythical leader of the Kollas, razed it to the ground. Around A.D. 1200, the kingdoms of the Aymara followed the glory of Tiwanaku. In Bolivian history the Aymara and the Kollas are sometimes inter-changeably referred to as the immediate ancestors of the highland Indians before the Quechua conquest. One theory depicts the Aymara as an Indian grouping different from the rulers of Tiwanaku; but another links the cultures of the Tiwanakans, the Aymara, and the Kollas, arguing that the Aymara were the descendants of the Tiwanakan empire.

The Aymara were a large linguistic group that encompassed numerous "nations" and kingdoms on the Bolivian highland. And the Kollas were an Aymara nation that fought the Incas but were eventually incorporated into the Incan empire. The political organization of the Aymara encompassed the powerful military leaders (*mallcus*), the hereditary chieftains of large federations and districts (*curacas*), the local authorities (*jilakatas*), the religious wisemen and counselors of the state (*amautas*), and the venerated council of old wisemen (*aukis*). This system was most likely inherited from Tiwanaku and later adopted by the Incas.

Socially, the Aymara kingdoms were based on the unit of extended family and tribal farming cooperatives, known as the *ayllu*. Several ayllus formed a *marca*, or federation of ayllus. Economic organization centered around communal cultivation of the potato and diverse highland grains. Aymara religion and mythology drew from the symbols of nature: the sun, the moon, and the stars. Supreme deities were Viracocha, the creator; Pachacamac, the god of good; Khuno, the god of evil; and later Pachamama or mother earth, the god of fertility. Culture was highly developed; accurate historical records were kept using the *quipus*, which were colored and knotted cords of rope also adopted by the Incas.

By A.D. 1200, coterminous with the Aymara kingdoms of the central Andean highland, the Quechua empire of the Incas was founded near Cuzco, Peru. Originating north of Titicaca, the Incas extended their vast kingdom, the Tahuantinsuyo, over the Andean and coastal terrain once dominated by the Tiwanakans, thereby creating the second, culturally unified, Pan-Andean empire from northern Ecuador to Talco south of Santiago de Chile. This empire extended 4,000 miles (6,400 kilometers) in length and encompassed an area of 380,000 square miles (1,026,000 square kilometers).[5] The Incas conquered the Aymara around 1460 but were forced to repress many subsequent rebellions, including a major one in 1470. *Incas* was the name given the entire Quechua-Indian empire that the Spaniards were to conquer, although *Inca* (in the singular) referred only to the ruling echelon or the royal princes of the empire. The word may have been a corruption of *Intis*, meaning "sun worshippers" or "Children of the Sun," given that a major Incan deity was *Inti*, the sun.

The origin of the Incas is the subject of legends. One theory proposed by Bolivian historians is that the Incas were once part of the Aymara federation of Lupaca and the ayllu of the Ayares, a people who lived in the region of Puno in Peru and on the Bolivian shores of Lake Titicaca. When the Tiwanakan empire declined, the Aymara people dispersed and the Ayares migrated from Titicaca to Cuzco in Peru. The migration, according to Bolivian legend, was commanded by the *curaca* (chieftain) Manco Kapac and his sister-wife, Mama Ocllo, children of the sun. In Cuzco they established their kingdom, and the Ayares intermarried with more primitive Indian communities of the Quechua language family. With the addition of the Quechuas (or "people from the tropical lands") the Incan empire, based on the political and socio-economic system of the Aymara and Tiwanakotas, soon flourished. At the head of the empire of 8 to 10 million inhabitants stood Sapa-Inca (*sapa* means "supreme"), or the hereditary Inca—a theocratic despot, descended from Inti, the sun god.

By 1450, the Incan realm extended over what is modern Peru; and by 1527, it had achieved its zenith, divided into four geographical regions or *suyos*: Chinchansuyo in the north, Kollasuyo in the south, Antisuyo in the east, and Kuntinsuyo in the west—altogether, the Tahuantinsuyo, meaning in Quechua "unity," "empire," and the "four corners of the earth." The four suyos were subdivided into provinces composed of various markas, governed by the *humayus*; and the markas were formed by the allyus and their elected or hereditary chieftains, the curacas. Having adopted the administrative system of the Aymara, the Incas now perfected it.

The Incan social structure evolved into a rigid pyramid of classes that exploited agriculture. Land was held "in common" and could not be sold. The Incas established royal monopolies over the mines, forests, and vast flocks and herds. The produce of the land was divided into three parts shared among the Inca and ruling caste, the priests, and the ayllu agricultural cooperatives. Within the ayllu, land was collectively owned and divided into *tupus* (two-acre plots) and distributed according to a variable system—generally, one tupu for each male in the family and a half tupu for each female. Everyone cooperatively farmed not only the lands of the Inca and the priests but also the ayllu plots set aside for widows and orphans. Family plots were farmed by that family. The system of *mita* established a labor draft whereby all males, except for the very young and old, served in the army, on public-works projects to maintain imperial roads and irrigation systems, and in the mines.

Social organization at the apex of the system included the hereditary Inca ruler (Sapa-Inca) and his royal descendants; the imperial nobility, who were the principal military, bureaucratic, and religious officers; and the sons and daughters of the district aristocracy of chieftains. This regional upper class, the *orejones*, owned private property in the form of jewelry and slaves. Below it was a free but propertyless peasant class of *hatunrunas* and a slave class of *yanaconas*, usually captives from hostile tribes or peasant social offenders.

A powerful imperial army, organized along the model of the Roman legions, bound the territorial stretches of the empire together both militarily and politically. The colonization policy of the *mitimaes* (meaning "one sent to another part") further ensured loyalty to the capital city of Cuzco (which once encompassed some 100,000 inhabitants). Imperial policy dictated, first, that conquered peoples, even whole communities, be resettled in territories friendly and loyal to the Incas; and, second, that reliable Quechua tribes be sent to colonize strategically important zones such as the fertile valleys of Cochabamba and Sucre. The great

Incan rulers unified this diverse assortment of tribes into an imperial state integrated by one religion and body of laws, the Quechua language, and an extensive system of communication and material distribution. Depositories (*tambos*) along the imperial roads contained food and supplies for the royal messengers, the *chasquis*, who sped oral messages and the knotted message ropes (the quipus of the Aymara) to the central governmental archive in Cuzco along two parallel coastal and Andean highways traversing the empire from north to south.

This highly developed empire began to decline with internal feuding and local uprisings, particularly by the recalcitrant Kollas who had retained their Aymara language and cultural identity despite the extensive Quechua migrations. When the Spaniards arrived in South America early in the sixteenth century, the Incan empire was divided and easily subdued by a combination of Spanish treachery and firepower. After Francisco Pizarro and Diego de Almagro invaded Peru in 1532, Gonzalo Pizarro, brother of the Conqueror, incorporated highland Bolivia into the Spanish empire in 1538.

Spanish Colonial Rule (1532-1809)

The Spanish founded the major cities of colonial Bolivia in subsequent decades: Charcas (also La Plata, Chuquisaca, and later Sucre) in 1538, Potosí in 1545, La Paz in 1548, Cochabamba in 1571, Tarija in 1574, and Oruro in 1606. Spanish explorers from Asunción, Paraguay, moving westward under the leadership of Ñuflo de Chávez, discovered and founded Santa Cruz de la Sierra in 1561. The concentration of Indian population and, especially, the newly discovered mineral wealth, like the vast silver and mercury deposits of Potosí, made the central Altiplano and southern valleys the natural administrative seat of Spanish colonial rule in Bolivia. The Audiencia of Charcas (Upper Peru), a judicial and administrative division under the jurisdiction of the Viceroyalty of Lima, was decreed in 1559 and established in Sucre (Charcas) by 1561.

Mining dominated the colonial economy from the sixteenth to the eighteenth centuries, transforming the city of Potosí into the Villa Real of Carlos V. Potosí was the wealthiest and most populated city in the New World by the middle of the seventeenth century, with perhaps 160,000 inhabitants in 1650. Over time, the mercantile emphasis on intensive deep mining caused extensive population dislocations and agricultural strain on the land. More and more agricultural surplus was needed to supply the burgeoning mining and urban-commercial centers, where Spanish aristocrats lived in opulent splendor amid mass Indian poverty.

Life in Upper Peru did not change fundamentally for the indigenous people, who now were ruled by Spanish overlords instead of an Incan ruling caste. Although hardships were the common lot of the poorest classes under both systems, historians have criticized Spanish rule—especially the institutions of the *encomienda* and *mita*—as rapacious and exploitative. The encomienda was a colonial institution that served to consolidate the conquest by granting to loyal *adelantados* (Spanish governors of provinces) and soldiers of the crown the possession of land tracts and the power to administer the inhabitants of the territories. And the mita was a system of forced tribute labor by the Indians that assured the crown abundant free labor for state and private enterprises.

The encomienda served multiple functions under Spanish rule. The Spanish overlord, or *encomendero*, was entrusted to Christianize, administer, and protect a specific Indian population or community, the *colonos*. In return for his "civilizing" function to the crown, the encomendero was permitted to employ free indigenous labor in agriculture, cottage industry, and mining, as well as to tax all male Indians. There were two types of encomienda granted by the crown, the *yanaconas* and the *mitayos*. The yanaconas were serfs tied to the land and domestic service on the estate and in the household of the landlord; whereas the mitayos were Indians organized under the system of mita to provide free labor for a portion of the year in the mines. The mita combined the Incan system of tribute labor (also called mita) with the medieval peninsular custom of forced labor adopted in the New World. The Incan tribute-labor system was limited to the period between the harvest and the planting. The Spanish mita originally obligated indigenous people between eighteen and sixty years of age to provide three months of free labor in the fields or mines.

Widespread abuses soon developed in the mita and encomienda systems. The mitayos became a slave labor force tied to the mines without compensation or time limitation. Hundreds of thousands of Indians perished under subhuman conditions in the mines; as many as 2,500 to 12,000 died in any one year in Potosí alone. In addition, tuberculosis may have decimated some 15 percent of the highland Indian population in the first fifty years of the colony.[6] The encomienda, like the mita, also developed into a harsh system of colonial control and exploitation that reduced the Indians to serf labor for landowners who ultimately came to own Indian communal lands and exert complete command of Indian labor. Encomienda grants, initially intended for only one generation or two, became outright land grants by the eighteenth century. Encomiendas were gradually replaced by large haciendas of land privately owned by a wealthy colonial aristocracy. The Indians were now transformed into a vast class of serfs and sharecroppers permitted the use of a small subsistence plot in exchange for a portion of the harvest and voluntary labor service (*pongueaje*) to the landlord (*hacendado*). The landowning system represented a feudal or semifeudal society in which the hacendado exercised complete political, social, and economic power, often brutally.

After extensive administrative reorganization in the eighteenth century, the Audiencia of Charcas, consisting of Bolivia, Paraguay, and portions of Peru, Argentina, and Chile, was placed under the newly established Viceroyalty of Buenos Aires in 1776. This reorganization was intended to dilute the political autonomy of the Audiencia of Charcas. A system of eight intendancies was also established in 1782 to centralize the weakening Spanish control in the vast territory of the Audiencia.[7] Nevertheless, the Spanish social and juridical system, which permitted only peninsular-born Spanish individuals to occupy high governing positions and to own lucrative properties, had engendered bitter native resentment by the eighteenth century. Sucre, then called the "Athens of America," had developed into the major intellectual and educational center for the entire highland—La Plata region. Its University of San Francisco Xavier of Chuquisaca, founded in the seventeenth century by the Jesuits, disseminated the radical French enlightenment thought of Rousseau, Montesquieu, Locke, Voltaire, and other liberal philosophers. Soon liberal ideology, socioeconomic tensions, and Spanish misrule fueled highland-independence unrest among the mestizo and creole elite.

The obvious consequences of Spanish colonial misgovernment were the numerous bloody Indian insurrections of the eighteenth century. The most threatening were the uprisings between 1780 and 1783 of Tomás Catari, known as Tupac Catari, and of his brothers and followers in La Paz, Cochabamba, Charcas, and Oruro; and of José Gabriel Condorcanqui, known as Tupac Amaru, in Cuzco, Peru. These uprisings, which sought the extermination of the white man and proclaimed the reestablishment of the ancient Incan empire, pitched tens of thousands of Indians against equal or greater Spanish troops. Even following the brutal executions of the indigenous leaders, several years elapsed before the rebellions throughout the Andean highlands had subsided. The racial hatred and fear on both sides, however, persisted for decades after independence from Spain had been achieved.

Independence and Creation of Bolivia (1809-1825)

By 1809, the forces of disarray in Spain after Napoleon's invasion (1807–1808) and the colonial decay abroad had converged and the first cries of independence of Alto Perú and the Hispanic New World burst out in Bolivia. The insurrection of Chuquisaca on May 25 and the Revolution of July 15, commanded by Bolivian independence hero Pedro Domingo Murillo, rendered Bolivia one of the first colonies to rebel

against Spain, yet one of the last to be liberated. The 1809 rebellion in
La Paz established a popular citizens' council (*cabildo abierto*) and elected
a governing junta (*junta tuitiva*), which proclaimed the act of independence and self-rule. The viceroy of Lima, José de la Serna, dispatched
5,000 Spanish soldiers to repress the uprising of 1,000 patriots. As
battles were being fought, a reactionary internal coup in La Paz routed
the leaders of the new government, who fled but were ultimately captured.
The rebellion had failed. Murillo and key revolutionary leaders (whose
names still grace the avenues and streets of the capital) were executed
on January 29, 1810, in the main plaza of La Paz, today's important
Plaza Murillo. There a statue of the independence hero displays the
prophetic inscription: "Patriots, I may die, but the torch of liberty that
I have left burning can never be extinguished."[8]

With the declaration of independence in Buenos Aires on May 25,
1810, by the Viceroyalty of La Plata (which had jurisdiction over Upper
Peru, or "Alto Perú"), each of Bolivia's cities eagerly seized Murillo's
revolutionary firebrand and joined the Argentinean rebellion. In 1810,
uprisings erupted in Cochabamba on September 14 and in Potosí on
November 10; then in 1811, in Tarija on July 13 and in Santa Cruz on
September 24. Bolivia rallied to the independence armies of La Plata
dispatched by the revolutionary junta of Buenos Aires to liberate Alto
Perú from the royalist forces of General José Manuel de Goyeneche. In
the second revolt of Cochabamba on May 27, 1812, the defiant women
of the city battled the royalist armies when there were no men left to
fight. Their day of heroism became the traditional Mothers' Day in
Bolivia.[9]

One by one, four major Argentinean expeditions (by Juan José
Castelli, General Manuel Belgrano, General José Rondeaux, and Lieutenant
Colonel Gregorio Araoz de la Madrid) were defeated by the brutal and
wily Goyeneche. Fifteen years of violent revolutionary struggle followed
these initial uprisings as Spanish forces dispatched by the viceroys of
Lima and Buenos Aires attempted to subdue unruly Alto Perú. Bolivian
history terms this the Heroic Era of the Fifteen Years War (Guerra de
Quince Años), a protracted guerrilla insurgency by rural highland
republiquetas ("little republics") against the superior Spanish manpower
and weaponry in the royalist-occupied cities. But General Goyeneche
remained an immovable obstacle to highland liberation. As the revolutionary initiative shifted away from Alto Perú, Bolivian independence
had to await the victories of Bolívar, San Martín, Sucre, and Santa Cruz
in other arenas of the anticolonial struggle.

After 1820, as Venezuela, Colombia, Ecuador, Chile, Argentina,
Paraguay, and Uruguay became independent, royalist armies in South
America fell into disarray. Since Napoleon's invasion of the peninsula,

the royalists in South America had been divided into various governing factions, reflecting the complexity of political events in Spain. There were the absolutists versus the reformist liberals; the Bourbonists versus the Bonapartist appointees; the supporters of King Carlos IV versus those who rallied around his son King Ferdinand VII or Ferdinand's sister Carlota; and the monarchists versus the power of the central Spanish revolutionary junta (established in opposition to the French occupation or by 1820 against the liberal constitutionalists). In Peru the liberal Viceroy de la Serna was opposed by the absolutist General Pedro Antonio de Olañeta. The split in the royalist forces favored the independence revolution. Ironically, the political confusion in Spain meant that the Latin American creoles who struck for independence in 1810 did so while pledging loyalty to King Ferdinand VII. Divisions among the royalists led able military leaders such as Andrés de Santa Cruz to defect to the revolution.

The final stages of the independence struggle began after General José de San Martín, the liberator of Argentina, proclaimed the independence of Peru on July 28, 1821. In 1824, the Venezuelan Liberator of the North, Simón Bolívar, moved southward to consolidate the independence forces with San Martín and to challenge the last pockets of loyalist resistance: de la Serna in Lima and Olañeta in Alto Perú. With 10,000 troops, Simón Bolívar routed 16,000 royalist forces in the Battle of Junín on August 6, 1824; and the independence commanders, Andrés de Santa Cruz and Agustín Gamarra, won the Battle of Zepita near Lake Titicaca. General Antonio José de Sucre, commanding an independence army of 7,000 men, seized Viceroy de la Serna and soundly defeated the 10,000-man royalist force in the decisive Battle of Ayacucho on December 9, 1824. General Olañeta continued to hold out but was finally killed on April 2, 1825, in the Battle of Tumusla. The revolutionary wars were over, and Alto Peruvian independence from Spain was assured. The ultimate political destiny of the highland remained unclear, however.

The future of Alto Perú as an independent republic would depend largely on the decisions of Bolívar and Sucre. Bolívar never intended an autonomous Alto Perú. Believing that South America could offset the power of Europe and North America only through continental unity, he dreamed of a vast federation of states. He had already unified the northern South American states in the Gran Colombia federation, and in 1816 the Argentines had optimistically proclaimed the United Provinces of South America. The expectation, therefore, was that, as in colonial times, the former Audiencia of Charcas (Upper Peru) would be incorporated into either the Peruvian federation or that of La Plata. When the Argentineans challenged the influence of Lima after 1825 and the new Peruvian state came into territorial conflict with Gran Colombia, the idea of an independent Alto Perú as a buffer state to such rivalries became even more attractive.[10]

While Bolívar was being feted in Lima, Sucre was ordered to La Paz. Under the influence of patriots such as Casimiro Olañeta, José Miguel Lanza, and José Mariano Serrano, who were determined to create an independent highland republic, Sucre issued the Decree of February 9, 1825. This decree summoned an assembly of notables on July 10 to decide the fate of Alto Perú. Initially, assembly forces divided over three options: independence, incorporation with Lower Peru, and annexation by Argentina. When both Peru and Argentina passed resolutions supporting an autonomous Alto Perú as a buffer between Lima and Buenos Aires, the delegates in Sucre unanimously concurred. They resolved to create the Republic of Bolívar, naming the nation after the great liberator and appointing him as its protector and first president. These honors ultimately won Bolívar over to the independence of Bolivia. In commemoration of the liberator's victory at Junín, August 6, 1825, became the official date of the independence and creation of the Republic of Bolivia.

THE POSTINDEPENDENCE ERA (1825–1880)

Bolivia's postindependence years were characterized by violence and venality in government. Except for the ten-year rule of Santa Cruz, the country's political and economic fate hung upon the whims of a succession of corrupt dictators. The Pacific War shattered an already debilitated economy, reduced the national territory, and lost the country's direct access to the sea. The legacy of these bitter decades continues to haunt Bolivia's historical memory.

The Peru-Bolivian Confederation

After Bolívar's temporary presidency of several months, the young republic elected José de Sucre as its first constitutional president in January 1826. Sucre attempted to rebuild the war-weary and economically drained country. However, his reformist political and social policies proved no match for the decline in mining (the major fiscal support of the state) and the depopulation of the highlands. Despite more progressive designs, his government came to depend on a regressive head-tax system. The 800,000 Indians of the country accounted for nearly 60 percent of the official revenue. Even church properties were seized in an attempt to expand the monetary base of the state.[11] In August 1828, Sucre's rule came to an end. A mutiny within his 8,000-man Colombian army of occupation, an assassination attempt on his life, and the invasion of General Agustín Gamarra from Peru influenced Sucre to resign and return to his native Venezuela. Gamarra installed Bolivian General Pedro Blanco as his puppet president after Sucre, but Blanco lasted only five days before being assassinated. In the ensuing conflict between Bolivia and Peru, Gamarra became the Peruvian president; and on May 4, 1829, Santa Cruz became the new president of Bolivia.

The ten-year rule of Andrés de Santa Cruz (1829–1839) achieved political and economic stability and left an indelible mark on the institutions of modern Bolivia. His reforms included compiling Bolivian law into the first legal code of the newly independent republics, expanding higher education and public works, and balancing the fiscal budget. Santa Cruz reportedly claimed (as did the first president and dictator of Paraguay) that Bolivia was the only country in the Americas without a foreign debt.[12] By sound management, his government reduced the internal public debt from 3 million pesos to less than 1 million.[13] Politically, Santa Cruz believed in strong government despite the passage of a democratic constitution that superseded the more authoritarian first constitution of Bolívar. Santa Cruz assumed dictatorial powers and was the first of the military strongmen, or *caudillos*, who ran Bolivia for forty years after his exile in 1839. Unlike his successors, Santa Cruz balanced one-man rule with scrupulous public administration and true patriotism.

Born near La Paz of a Spanish father and a Quechua mother (Juana Basilia Calahumana, who claimed to be the direct descendant of the last Inca, Tupac Amaru), Santa Cruz dreamed of resurrecting the ancient Incan political order. President of Peru (1826–1827) until ousted by Gamarra, Santa Cruz remained drawn to Peruvian politics. Finally, he realized his long ambition in October 1836 and, by force, unified Bolivia and Peru into the Peruvian-Bolivian Confederation (Confederación Perú-boliviana). An 1834 treaty with beleaguered Peruvian President Luis José de Orbegoso invited Bolivian intervention in a three-way Peruvian civil war. The armies of Santa Cruz invaded and defeated the forces of the two rival caudillos, Gamarra and Felipe Santiago Salaverry. Peru was reorganized into the Confederation with the state of South Peru governed by Orbegoso, the state of North Peru under President Pío Tristán, and Bolivia administered by General José Miguel de Velasco. Santa Cruz became the "Protector," or dictator of the Confederation.

Political chaos within Peru meant negligible internal resistance to the grand designs of Santa Cruz. However, external reaction to the Confederation proved another matter. The unification of Lower and Upper Peru, although it brought political peace to a violent and faction-ridden Peru, tipped the precarious South American balance of power into all-out war with neighboring Argentina and Chile. An Argentine expedition sent by General Juan Manuel de Rosas was repulsed by Santa

Cruz, but Chilean troops under Diego Portales also attacked, and ultimately Chilean General Manuel Bulnes overpowered the Confederation forces in the decisive 1839 battle of Yungay. The Chileans, fearing future political and commercial rivalry by a powerful and reorganized Peru, cut short the Peruvian-Bolivian Confederation (1836–1839). Santa Cruz, one of the greatest Bolivian independence figures, was forced into exile in France, where he died a disillusioned man. His dreams of Bolivian grandeur through unification of ancient Incan lands and territorial expansion ended—as would other Bolivian expansionist attempts—in defeat.

The Caudillos

The fall of Santa Cruz initiated a period of great political turmoil during which Bolivian military officers and generals vied with one another for control of the state. A pattern of rule by caudillos was firmly established with the governments of Belzu and Cordova and consolidated during the presidencies of Generals Achá, Melgarejo, and Morales. The Ballivianista, or Red Party (Partido Rojo), of the Linares and Ballivián administrations arose in opposition to militarism. Serving as a precursor to the great civilian political parties of the 1880s led by silver magnates, lawyers, and intellectuals instead of generals, it established a new pattern of political rule for the twentieth century.

The Age of the Caudillos began with an internal power struggle between Generals José Ballivián and Velasco and the imminent threat of a second Peruvian invasion by President Gamarra. In 1840, a Bolivian Congress named Velasco president, but by June 1841 an uprising by General Sebastián Agreda ended the Velasco government. Agreda, attempting to return Santa Cruz to power, had been only 102 days in office when General Ballivián revolted and assumed the presidency. Capitalizing on Bolivia's political chaos, Peru invaded and occupied La Paz. Ballivián rallied the disorganized Bolivian forces and defeated Gamarra on November 18, 1841, in the heroic Battle of Ingavi. This battle consolidated Bolivian independence from future Peruvian conquest. Rebellions by a young Colonel Manuel Isidoro Belzu and Generals Agreda and Velasco forced Ballivián's resignation and the establishment of a ten-day interim government. In 1810 General Velasco became president for the fourth time, only to be overthrown by General Belzu in December.

Belzu served first as interim and then as constitutional president (1848–1855). A mestizo, he was affectionately called "Tata Belzu" by the masses. He was also hailed as Bolivia's first populist caudillo because his policies favored the Indians and oppressed classes. Belzu's government instituted beneficial reforms such as the nationalistic Mining Code and protectionist economic legislation, the new 1851 Constitution (Bolivia's fifth), and the 1854 national census of Bolivia's 2.3 million inhabitants. Nevertheless, Belzu was a typical military autocrat of the times addicted to excesses and terrified of assassination and rebellion by the rival caudillos Mariano Melgarejo, Agustín Morales, and José María Linares— all future presidents and dictators.

In March 1855, a national congress elected as president General Jorge Cordova, the official candidate and Belzu's son-in-law. Belzu reportedly commented: "I'll leave this one in office, but he won't last."[14] Two years later the undistinguished and conspiracy-prone government was overthrown by General Agreda and José María Linares, Bolivia's first civilian president. The rule of Linares (1854–1861) brought sweeping fiscal, administrative, and judicial reforms, which antagonized traditional power elites and aggravated the chronic unrest. Linares turned to harsh dictatorship to thwart the incessant coup plotting by ex-presidents and generals who refused to stay retired. But before he could organize national elections, a military coup by members of his own cabinet overthrew him in January 1861 and soon brought the minister of war, General José María de Achá, to the presidency.

Although Achá's term differed little from that of his predecessor, it became known as "the most violent of the nineteenth-century governments" because of the infamous "Massacre of Loreto," an execution of seventy opposition politicians.[15] In addition, the dispute with Chile over the guano and nitrate riches discovered in Mejillones on Bolivia's Pacific coast erupted in 1863. Before Achá could organize Bolivian resistance, he was deposed on December 28, 1864, by Melgarejo, the most infamous of Bolivia's tyrants.

Mariano Melgarejo, an illegitimate mestizo, is remembered as the *caudillo barbaro*, a brutal and dissolute despot who squandered state funds on drunken orgies and mistresses. Two of his more traitorous acts were the sale of 40,000 square miles of Bolivia's rich Matto Grosso lands to Brazil and the loss of Bolivia's rights to valuable nitrate deposits in Atacama province. Melgarejo hastened the War of the Pacific between Bolivia and Chile by making secret deals and concessions to Chilean nitrate companies for personal gain. The 1866 Mejillones Treaty permitted Chile greater control over Bolivia's coastal territories, ceding everything below the 24th parallel to Chile and exempting from future Bolivian taxes mineral exports leaving Pacific ports.

Disliked by the traditional upper classes, Melgarejo's social and economic policies supported free-trade capitalism and the new mining oligarchy. An unpopular 1866 land decree, which seized and sold communal Indian lands, alienated his populist peasant base and provoked bloody peasant uprisings. Merciless repression of enemies and near political anarchy further characterized his six-year rule (*sexenio*). Overthrown in January 1871 by General Morales, he was soon killed by the brother of his mistress in a quarrel.

General Agustín Morales annulled the agrarian reform and renegotiated the more unequal foreign agreements. His rule, however, was as authoritarian and erratic as the rest. Like his predecessors, he died violently riddled by bullets—in this case, from his nephew's pistol. An interim presidency of the distinguished civilian politician, Tomás Frías, preceded the election of Adolfo Ballivián in May 1873. Frías, once the private secretary to Sucre and a doctor of law, became president again in 1874 upon Ballivián's sudden death. These civilian governments struggled to negotiate the seething territorial disputes with Chile and to prepare the nation in the event of war. However, the civilian constitutionalists, or Rojos, were powerless against the hawkish army and the angry opposition to the international agreements of Melgarejo. Preempting scheduled elections, Hilarión Daza seized power. He was the last of Bolivia's military caudillos before the outbreak of the Pacific War.

The tenure of Daza is unforgettable to Bolivians and more tragic than Melgarejo's sexenio because it marked the loss of the country's Pacific coast. Daza presided over the passage of the 1879 Liberal Constitution (Bolivia's ninth), which, though modified in 1880, remained the basic parliamentary document until the Chaco War. Daza's government and the 1878 national assembly passed an infamous ten-cent tax on nitrate exports by the British-Chilean Nitrates and Railroad Company of Antofagasta. This action provided Chile with the long-awaited pretext to initiate the Pacific War against Bolivia and Peru. By the time of Daza's overthrow in December 1879, Chile already controlled the entire Bolivian coastal territories.

The War of the Pacific and Loss of the Littoral

Despite the blame against President Daza, the causes of the War of the Pacific (1879–1884) were complex and long-standing. Historians have argued that this war may have been inevitable given the powerful underlying political and economic conditions affecting Bolivia at the time. Certainly one of these was the chronic political instability of the country. The heartland of Bolivian political and economic life was the Altiplano. The new republic, taxed by revolts and by corrupt and inept leaders, was unable to exert state control over its distant coastal lands. Until the discovery of fertilizer riches there, the provinces were sparsely populated and generally ignored by La Paz. Even after the discovery, the stagnation in the Bolivian economy and the poverty of people and government alike generated little domestic capital for exploitation of the guano and nitrate riches. Bolivian political and economic weakness was therefore an important underlying cause of the war.

In contrast, Chile had been experiencing a period of political and economic expansion since 1830. Locked in a fierce commercial rivalry with Peru, Chilean entrepreneurs, in cooperation with British capital, were best equipped to exploit the guano and nitrate deposits in Bolivia's Atacama Desert. Economically, Chile saw the great riches of the coastal region not only as a solution to the 1878 financial crisis but also as a way to balance its budget and finance further national expansion. As the Chilean Minister Abraham Koening explained in 1900, "the area is rich and worth many millions," for which reason Chile sought to control and keep it.[16] Geopolitically, Chile was intent on dominating the Pacific coast as the logical culmination of rivalries with Peru and Argentina. Chile, excluded in 1878 by Argentina from influence in the Atlantic via Patagonia, was intent on achieving hegemony along the Pacific coast.[17]

Bolivia's claims to the Atacama region were based on the principle of "uti possidetis juris of 1810," whereby the territory that had been under the jurisdiction of the Audiencia of Charcas was inherited by the newly independent Bolivian state. Bolivia's claims were not seriously disputed by its neighbors, especially the Chileans, until the discoveries and commercial successes of the guano and nitrate deposits as natural agricultural fertilizers in 1840. An October 1842 Chilean law claimed territory as far north as the 23rd parallel south latitude, whereas Bolivia claimed as far south as the 27th parallel. In 1857, the Chileans launched an unsuccessful attempt to seize the guano-rich Mejillones area and in 1863 occupied the territory. Although the Extraordinary National Assembly of Oruro authorized the Bolivian government to declare war, the Bolivians were unable to enforce their sovereignty.

The delicate territorial negotiations were left to the Melgarejo regime, which was patently favorable to Chilean interests. The Treaty of 1866, the First Treaty of Limitation between Bolivia and Chile, which Melgarejo signed, in part precipitated the outbreak of war in 1879. In the treaty, which Bolivian historians have denounced as a "give-away," Bolivia renounced its maximum claim of territory to the 27th parallel south latitude and Chile its claim to the 23rd parallel. The treaty fixed the boundary at the 24th parallel. However, a problematical area between the 23rd and 25th parallels became the shared zone of mineral and nitrate exploitation.

The Bolivians sent a mission in 1872 to modify the boundary interpreted as prejudicial to Bolivia, but the Chileans were not interested. With negotiations stalemated, the new Bolivian president-elect, José Ballivián, signed a secret defense treaty with Peru in 1873. This treaty later became the Chilean pretext for the fierce conduct of the war against Peru. Another excuse for the war was the Treaty of 1874, which again fixed the boundary at the 24th parallel but ended the zones of shared economic exploitation and exempted Chilean companies from new taxes in Bolivian territory for the next twenty-five years.

In 1878, the Bolivian Congress, influenced by President Daza, levied a ten-cent tax on each hundred pounds of nitrates exported from Bolivian territory in violation of the 1874 Treaty. Bolivia temporarily suspended collection of the tax and canceled the contract of the Nitrates and Railroad Company of Antofagasta when this British-Chilean company refused to pay the tax. In response, the Chileans sent a battleship, which seized the Bolivian port of Antofagasta on February 14, 1879, and gave Bolivia a twenty-four-hour ultimatum to accept arbitration. When Bolivia refused compliance with the ultimatum as long as its port was being held, the Chilean government instructed Colonel Sotomayor to occupy Antofagasta and the entire Pacific coast south of the 23rd parallel on March 9, 1879. Only on April 5, after all coastal occupations had been completed, did Chile declare war on Bolivia and Peru.

Bolivia was easily defeated in the land war because of the unpreparedness of its troops and the irresponsibility of its military leaders. President Daza was notorious in his misconduct of the war. Generally inebriated, he ultimately deserted in the defeat of Camarones, leaving the Peruvian army to fight the Chileans alone. Chile's superior naval forces and disciplined army easily seized Bolivian and Peruvian ports. Most of the naval war was turned against Peru in order to capture Peruvian mining centers on the coast and destroy its military power. By 1880, a spent Bolivia withdrew from actual combat in the war. Peru doggedly fought on until it signed a separate peace with Chile. The Treaty of Ancón in October 1883 ceded Peru's province of Tarapacá to Chile and permitted Chilean occupation of Tacna and Arica for ten years. Bolivia was forced to sign a pact of truce on April 5, 1884, leaving Chile in control of all the occupied Bolivian coastal territory. A final treaty of peace was not signed until 1904, and even this treaty is disputed.

The loss of Bolivia's littoral stemmed from causes deeper than the venality of its civic life. The War of the Pacific was in part the natural consequence of the expansion of foreign and international capital and the Chilean drive toward geopolitical hegemony in the South Pacific region. Nevertheless, Bolivian governments clearly hastened this ignominious end to the caudillo era. As a result of the defeat in the War of the Pacific, military governments were discredited and the rise of civilian political parties became both desirable and possible.

REPUBLICAN GOVERNMENT (1880–1930)

The era of Republican government represented a major shift in Bolivian political life. Civilian political parties, organized around shared political and economic interests, replaced military strongmen. The new politicians created a system of limited franchise and alternation of state power among elitist factions of personalistic leaders. The political parties protected the economic interests of a new ruling class composed of the tin mining elite and remnants of the old landed aristocracy. Government from 1880 to 1930 was of, for, and by the new mining plutocracy, "a state that tin owned." This ruling system had fallen into decline by 1930 with the onset of the Great Depression and Bolivia's tragic involvement in the Chaco War. Nevertheless, for fifty years Republican rule provided the political stability needed for economic growth.

The Founding of Political Parties

Two major political parties were formed over continuation or cessation of the War of the Pacific. In its classic party program of 1883, the Liberal Party of General Camacho proposed to press the war effort and reject the peace settlement with Chile. Led by Mariano Baptista, the Conservative Party advanced the antiwar position and a national policy of peace, traditionalism, and order. The Conservatives represented the interests of the silver mining oligarchy and dominated Bolivian politics until 1899 in the "era of the conservative oligarchy." The Liberals, victors of a brief civil war in 1899, supported the rise and empowerment of the new tin mining elite, which came to dominate politics for the next twenty years.

Liberals represented secular and federalist rule, and Conservatives supported the traditional role of the Roman Catholic church in society and unitary government. Yet despite these ideological distinctions, both political parties were fundamentally alike in class background and policy, and agreed "on the need for civilian dominated government" as a precondition for economic development. Liberal and Conservative Party rule from 1884 to 1920 was simply an alternation between one branch of the privileged class and another for control of the government. As Herbert Klein has explained, "both groups came from the white upper classes, which sought to lead the nation into a new era of peace and prosperity through constitutional government, and the aims of both were stability, national unification, and the stimulation of economic activity."[18]

Post-1880 parties reduced, but did not eliminate, the violence and instability of Bolivian politics under the military caudillos. Despite the

1880 constitution, which provided for the legal transmission of power, a contained electoral violence between the political party in power and the party out of office replaced the more widespread violence of post-independence military rule. Electoral violence became inevitable because Bolivians lacked a political culture of compromise. Politicians were dependent on the spoils of government for personal enrichment and social advancement. Nevertheless, the elitist rules of government and the limited electoral franchise (2 to 3 percent of the population) permitted the party in government to grant opposition parties relative freedom of expression and substantial representation in the national assembly. Elections during this era were more often manipulated by the ruling party than they were free and fair. As long as the political parties represented the establishment interests of the silver and tin barons, a certain degree of political infighting and instability was permitted and, indeed, harmless.

Presidents in the early Republican era were generally civilians and members or representatives of the silver mining and entrepreneurial elite. The irresponsible government of Daza was replaced in January 1880 by the provisional presidency of General Narciso Campero, elected to a four-year constitutional term in June. Reflecting the interests of Bolivian army leaders and the prowar civilian politicians, General Campero, along with his chief of staff, General Eliodoro Camacho, organized the Liberal Party in 1883. In 1884, however, a pacifist, pro-mining candidate seized the presidency from the Liberals.

Gregorio Pacheco, of the Democratic Party, a small third party in sympathy with the conservative position, won the election by 11,760 votes. A close runner-up was Aniceto Arce of the Conservative Party, with more than 10,000 votes. The Liberal candidate, General Camacho, lost. The election of Pacheco and the strong vote for Arce were significant indicators of the political shift that had occurred after the War of the Pacific. Both Pacheco and Arce were silver mining industrialists; Pacheco was the first of this new economic elite to serve as president. Arce soon came next, followed by Mariano Baptista, a famous lawyer for the silver miners, vice-president under Pacheco, and leader of the Conservative Party.

When a parliamentary law in 1898 retained Sucre as the national capital, a civil war, the "Federal Revolution," erupted. The silver mining and landed elite of the Conservative Party, based in the southern cities of Sucre and Potosí, opposed the rising tin mining and industrial-commercial elite of the Liberal Party, centered in the northern cities of Oruro and La Paz. The violent transition that elevated the winning Liberal oligarchy to power reflected a transformation of the Bolivian economic elite, latent regional rivalry, and Liberal frustration over repeated electoral defeat. Unable to gain the presidential palace through constitutional means, the Liberal Party resorted to revolt. General José Manuel Pando (1900–1904) was the first president of the Liberal era. And party control was consolidated under the two presidential terms of Ismael Montes (1904–1908, 1913–1917), the great Liberal leader of the day.

A turning point in Liberal rule came in 1920 with the overthrow of the party by disaffected Liberals who had earlier formed the Republican Party. In the "Republican Revolution" of July 12, José Gutiérrez Guerra, a noted financier and the last in the line of Liberal presidents, was deposed. The political fragmentation of the traditional elitist parties, the Conservatives and the Liberals, coincided with the apogee of the great tin empires built at the turn of the century.

Creation of the Tin Empires and the Rosca

Mineral exploitation since the Spanish conquest of Alto Perú had been the mainstay of the Bolivian economy and the basis of social stratification and political rule. The Imperial City of Potosí was the principal New World source of silver until a decline occurred around 1783. Between 1810 and 1850, the decapitalization of mining and the slump in silver production intensified as a consequence of pre- and postindependence turmoil and general economic stagnation. Silver mines were abandoned for lack of capital, cheap labor, experienced technicians, and specialized recovery machinery. Prohibitive transportation costs owing to the absence of railways, export-import taxes levied on overland and seaport routes, and protectionist government policies further burdened the silver mining industry.[19]

In the end, new political, economic, and technological developments supported the final resurgence of silver mining between 1873 and 1895— the age of silver. Between 1850 and 1860, advanced mining technology (such as the steam engine) revived the Altiplano mining economy as thousands of flooded mines were reopened at reasonable cost. The expansion of Peruvian and Chilean mining and Bolivia's valuable Caracoles silver mine on the Pacific coast introduced further technological innovation into the highland. With the increase in the world price of silver, foreign capital and international mining enterprises expanded into the area—especially after 1870, in the wake of internal capitalization from 1850 to 1860 by the merchant class of the Southern interior cities of Cochabamba and Sucre. Bolivian entrepreneurs, generating sufficient surplus capital from agriculture to invest in mining, established three major silver empires in Potosí by the mid-1850s: the Huanchaca Mining Company of Aniceto Arce, the Real Socavón Mining Company of the Carlos Aramayo dynasty, and the Guadelupe mines of Gregorio Pacheco. State- and private-sponsored infrastructure, such as construction of the railway from Oruro to the Pacific port of Antofagasta in 1895, facilitated the transport and export of ore. Relative political stability after 1884 completed the conditions necessary for Bolivia's entry into the modern era of mining. The nineteenth-century silver age had made possible the transition to industrial mining and the rise of the tin empires of Aramayo, Hochschild, and Patiño.[20]

Sharp declines in the global price of silver in 1870 and again in 1893, as European nations shifted to the gold standard, coincided with the growing demand after 1880 for industrial metals: copper, lead, zinc, wolfram, antimony, and especially tin. The year 1900 initiated the tin boom as prices more than doubled from 1898 levels and rapidly reached their zenith by 1927. Few silver magnates survived the transition to tin. They were replaced by a new group of Bolivian and foreign entrepreneurs. Of the big three tin barons, only the Aramayo family had been influential in silver, whereas Hochschild and Patiño represented the new tin elite associated with international capital.

With a 25 percent share of Bolivia's tin production, the Carlos Aramayo holdings were based in Bolivia and operated as essentially Bolivian capital despite heavy European investments. With a similar share of tin production, the holdings of Mauricio Hochschild (of European Jewish ancestry) were managed from Bolivia, where Hochschild lived for most of his life. The most extensive holdings, contributing nearly 50 percent of national tin production, were those of Simón Patiño. A mestizo, "white-collar" mine employee of nondescript origins, Patiño struck it rich in a seemingly worthless Uncía mine in Potosí and quickly consolidated the largest mining empire by buying out the British Uncía Mining Company in 1910 and the Chilean Llallagua Company in 1924. Patiño Mines, owned solely by Bolivian capital, ultimately acquired vast European holdings in both nonmining and mining-related investments, such as the British Williams, Harvey and Company, a major smelter of Bolivian ore. Until his death in 1940, Patiño enjoyed cosmopolitan life in Paris and New York, while managers for Patiño Mines dictated policy to the Bolivian government. As Bolivia's most powerful capitalist, who had often extended vast private loans to the government for tax concessions and political favors, Patiño held a virtual veto power over the state.[21]

The tin era brought increasing dependence of the Bolivian economy on the three tin magnates who controlled production and on the vagaries of the global market. The economy during the heyday of tin suffered the typical Third World dilemma of "declining terms of trade," whereby a country exporting primary raw materials could not amass sufficient trade revenue to pay for expensive manufactured and luxury imports. Bolivian governments kowtowed to the economic program of the tin interests: economic liberalism and free trade. The state subsidized the mineral export sector, providing inexpensive transportation infrastructure and shipping, and permitting an unregulated foreign exchange. The economic consequences of these policies were chronic budget deficits, with the government providing the bulk of development costs while recovering a pittance from perfunctory taxes on mining. As the state was entirely dependent on tin profits for fiscal operating revenues, development projects in agriculture and other economic diversification schemes not central to mining were ignored. Although tin profits enriched only a small group of Bolivian capitalists and their foreign stockholders, the economic imbalance was tolerated because tin was the principal source of wage labor, foreign exchange earnings, and government budgets.

Despite immediate criticism of the government's servility to big mining interests, reforms were impossible so long as most governers were the hired political representatives of the mining industrialists. The Rosca is what the Bolivians termed this interconnecting political and economic web of the big three mining companies and the sociopolitical establishment that catered to them. The ruling establishment of the tin oligarchy connected the traditional landed elites, the new urban class of entrepreneur importers, and the clique of lawyers and bureaucrats (*políticos*). The latter, professional politicians and administrators of the state who ruled in the name of tin, were protected by the conservative military. In short, the economic influence of the mining interests overpowered the machinery of the state, thereby creating a mining superstate.

Sensitive to international fluctuations in demand and price, the tin industry followed a boom and bust cycle that threatened government stability and resources. The 1929 Wall Street crash and the subsequent Great Depression devastated the open Bolivian economy. Tin prices never again reached pre-1929 highs, and fiscal revenues in 1932 dropped to approximately 17 percent of 1929 receipts. The tin crisis left the state treasury bankrupt. The money that accrued during the brief economic recovery in 1932 was quickly siphoned off to finance the costly and tragic Chaco War. As tin had been the economic catalyst that consolidated twenty years of Liberal rule during the Republican era, its collapse in 1929 speeded the demise of the traditional two-party system and the ascendancy of a new third party.

The Republican Party and the Coming of War

The Republican Party's seizure of power in 1920 marked the beginning of the end of an era. Politics was changing from relatively stable two-party, oligarchic rule to a less stable and more populist multiparty system. The dissension within the Republican Party between

1920 and 1930 influenced this political transition and brought Bolivia nearer to the outbreak of the Chaco War.

In 1914, the Liberal Party split and its leading intellectuals and statesmen—Daniel Salamanca, Bautista Saavedra, General José Manuel Pando, and José María Escalier—founded the Republican Party. Although the Republican platform was preoccupied with the recovery of Bolivia's lost maritime territories and typically demanded more morality in government, the program differed little from traditional Liberal Party fare. In 1917, the Republicans ran party candidates for national office but were defeated in the Liberal-controlled elections. Charging fraud, the young party grabbed power in a bloodless coup on July 12, 1920. Once in control, the Republicans split into two factions, each headed by highly personalistic political bosses, both of whom coveted the presidency: Salamanca of the Genuine Republican Party (Genuinos), and Saavedra of the Socialist Republicans (Saavedristas).

The two strongmen differed in personality, political style, and electoral base. Saavedra, a self-styled populist, represented middle-class Liberals and resented the old party's close ties to the powerful tin barons. His appeal to urban middle-class artisans, small merchants, and laborers generated a nonestablishment political base and a new class consciousness. Frightened, the urban upper class and traditional rural and regional elites rallied around Salamanca, a Cochabamba landowner and old-style patrician. Deep personal animosities and competitive strategies of the bosses aggravated the underlying class conflict that the party rift had generated. For the first time in Republican history, social problems were used to alter the rules of the political game and to divide the oligarchy against itself.

As president (1921–1925), Saavedra enacted progressive social and labor codes and doubled government taxes on mining. Though more concerned for the underprivileged classes, Saavedra blatantly manipulated his populist support. Unable to control the popular dissatisfaction that his policies encouraged, he violently repressed the Indian uprising of 1921 in the highland village of Jesús de Machaca, the first general workers' strike in 1922, and the 1923 miners' strike or "Massacre of Uncía." While the economy dipped and climbed with the volatile price of tin, Saavedra negotiated millions of dollars in private loans from Wall Street bankers at disadvantageous terms. He encouraged the entry of foreign capital and protected the operations of companies, such as Standard Oil of New Jersey, that were drilling for oil in the lowlands.

To discredit Saavedra and his Socialist Republicans, the Genuinos of Salamanca and the new Nationalist Party of Hernando Siles denounced the political repression, economic mismanagement, and "sellouts" to foreign interests perpetrated by Saavedra. Siles, the Socialist Republican presidential candidate for 1925 and Saavedra's opponent within the party, was forced to support the "Saavedrista" party line in order to win the elections and become president. Intending to free himself from Saavedra's political hold, he formed his own Nationalist Party in January 1927. The deepening economic depression forced President Siles to contract additional foreign loans under extremely onerous terms. His unpopular plan to amend the constitution and extend his presidential term aroused universal opposition. Then the death of a student in an antigovernment demonstration touched off a student rebellion. Soon the army, opposition political parties (Liberals, Socialist Republicans, and Genuine Republicans), and economically depressed urban workers joined the students. Ironically, the Siles government, champion of the 1928 university autonomy reforms, was toppled by a bloody student revolt on June 25, 1930.

The 1930 "constitutionalist" revolt was indicative of future changes in Bolivia's political life. Since 1930, students have continued to be a major force in the making and unmaking of Bolivian governments. Moreover, the upheaval demonstrated the power of mass action and popular street revolt over the classical palace coup. Unfortunately, the uprising also rid the people of the ruler who had stood between the presidency of Daniel Salamanca and the catastrophic Chaco War.

After interim military rule and a constitutional prohibition of consecutive presidential terms, Salamanca was elected president. He soon became unpopular. His personality was rigid, and he was unable to solve Bolivia's extreme economic crisis. He repressed all opposition—traditional parties, labor, students, and the leftist parties founded in the 1920s—and became obsessed with foreign relations. As a cure for grave domestic ills, he pursued the aggressive Bolivian colonization of the Chaco. A steady increase occurred in the number of border disputes with Paraguay over control of the inaccessible southeastern territory. In 1931, Salamanca escalated a border incident into full-scale war. The era of Republican government, begun in 1880 in the aftermath of one war, failed to survive the next war. The Chaco War would be the catalyst and harbinger of the 1952 Revolution.

NOTES

1. Helen Miller Bailey and Abraham P. Nassatir, *Latin America: The Development of Its Civilization*, 3rd ed. (Englewood Cliffs, N.J.: Prentice-Hall, 1973), p. 64.

2. Hugo Boero Rojo, *Enciclopedia Bolivia mágica*, 3rd ed. (La Paz: Editorial Los Amigos del Libro, 1978), p. 94.

3. Herbert S. Klein, *Bolivia: The Evolution of a Multi-Ethnic Society* (New York: Oxford University Press, 1982), pp. 13–14, 271.

4. Bailey and Nassatir, *Latin America*, p. 64.

5. José Fellmann Velarde, *Historia de Bolivia*, 2nd ed., vol. 1 (La Paz: Editorial Los Amigos del Libro, 1978), p. 62. The extension of the Incan empire is also given as 3,000 miles and 350,000 square miles in J. Alden Mason, *The Ancient Civilizations of Peru* (London: Penguin Books, 1968), p. 121.

6. Fellman, *Historia*, p. 107.

7. Thomas E. Weil et al., *Area Handbook for Bolivia*, Foreign Area Studies, American University (Washington, D.C.: Government Printing Office, 1974), p. 19.

8. Alfredo Ayala Z., *Historia de Bolivia en cuadros sinópticos*, 2nd ed. (La Paz: Editorial Don Bosco, 1980), p. 71. The full text in Spanish reads: "Compatriotas, yo muero, pero la tea de la libertad que dejo encendida, nadie la podrá apagar."

9. Ibid., pp. 75–77.

10. Klein, *Bolivia*, pp. 98–101.

11. Ibid., pp. 104–111.

12. Bailey and Nassatir, *Latin America*, p. 563; see also Weil, *Area Handbook*, p. 23.

13. Ayala, *Historia de Bolivia*, p. 105.

14. Boero, *Enciclopedia*, p. 126.

15. Klein, *Bolivia*, p. 133.

16. Juan Siles Guevara, *Bolivia's Right to the Pacific Ocean* (La Paz: Fundación Manuel Vicente Ballivián, 1960), p. 68.

17. Ibid., pp. 60–62.

18. Herbert S. Klein, *Origenes de la revolución nacional boliviana: la crisis de la generación del Chaco* (La Paz: Editorial Juventud, 1968), pp. 22–23, 24.

19. Klein, *Bolivia*, pp. 101–107.

20. Ibid., pp. 124–132, 141–143.

21. Ibid., pp. 165–166.

3

Contemporary History: The Chaco War to the Revolution (1930–1952)

Most historians of the 1952 Bolivian National Revolution have described the Bolivian defeat by Paraguay in the Gran Chaco War as a major cause of the revolution.[1] Through the war the Bolivian government had hoped to win a quick victory, gain an outlet to the Atlantic Ocean, and revitalize national pride.

THE CHACO WAR: A PRECURSOR OF REVOLUTION

Conflicting claims by Bolivia and Paraguay to the Gran Chaco territory—a "desolate waste area in the heart of South America" of a quarter-million square miles (675,000 square kilometers)—dated back to the sixteenth century. The boundary issue had remained dormant until the late 1920s, when the foreign policy of Salamanca and rumors of extensive oil deposits reactivated the dispute. Unsubstantiated charges blamed the war on the instigation of the U.S. and British oil companies, Standard Oil and Royal Dutch Shell.[2]

President Salamanca's hawkish role was undisputed. The Bolivian Chaco policy had been his brainchild and was supported by the ultranationalist clique around him. In the 1920s, Salamanca had popularized the slogan: "We must take a firm stand in the Chaco." While in political opposition, he had criticized the Hernando Siles government for cowardice and inaction in the boundary conflict. As president, despite severe economic constraints, Salamanca allocated extensive defense spending for military penetration of the Chaco. On July 1, 1931, he severed diplomatic relations with Paraguay over a minor border clash. A year later, on July 18, 1932, a Bolivian attack on Fort Santa Cruz near Laguna Chuquisaca (or Pitiantuta), a vital and strategic source of water in the barren region, was deliberately escalated into open war by Salamanca despite the objections of the general staff and the pacifism of many Bolivians and Paraguayans.[3]

Soon the euphoria of speeches, parades, and quick victory faded as the Chaco campaign bogged down in defeats: the fall of Fort Boquerón and Fort Arce in September and October 1932, and the battles of Nanawa in July 1933 and El Carmen in November 1934. In the spring of 1935, Paraguayan forces threatened Bolivia's oil centers, the regions of Tarija and Santa Cruz (up to the very foothills of the Andes), and the Chaco command center in Villamontes. The Paraguayans, deep into Bolivian territory, were overextended. In a desperate defense of home territory, the Bolivians drove them back and recaptured the oil region by May. At this critical point the war stabilized. On June 12, 1935, a protocol of peace and cease-fire was signed in Buenos Aires, to take effect in forty-eight hours, but the final peace treaty was not signed until July 21, 1938. The three-year war was over; the postwar crisis was just beginning. How would Bolivia deal with defeat?

Moreover, why had Bolivia lost the war when most statesmen in Latin America had expected a decisive win? Who was to blame for defeat? In 1932, Bolivia possessed 21,000 soldiers and a trained reserve of 10,000 noncommissioned officers and 300,000 men against a total Paraguayan manpower of 3,321 troops and no trained reserves. Bolivia also had three times Paraguay's population and outgunned its opponent by as much as ten to one.[4] Yet despite this superiority, Bolivia lost the war because of corruption, political dissension, inept commanders, and loss of national morale.

Military-civilian conflict and incompetence were to blame for blatant misconduct of the war. From the start, the military high command had balked at Salamanca's war policy. On the eve of hostilities, the general staff had resigned, complaining that Bolivia was ill-prepared for war; but the president had ignored the advice of the military then and later. Had Salamanca planned war? Or had he miscalculated, intending to bully the weaker Paraguayans into territorial concessions? Officers at the front had been inept, corrupt, and cowardly. There had been four commanders in three years, and three armies were destroyed in the field. Bitterly, Salamanca had complained to his military: "I gave you money, soldiers, arms, honors. . . . Everything, everything I gave you. . . . The only thing I could not give you was brains."[5] The animosity and mistrust on both sides festered until November 1934, when the army arrested Salamanca at Chaco headquarters in Villamontes. Vice-President and Liberal Party Leader José Luis Tejada Sorzano became president in the middle of the war. The November coup ended the worst of the civilian-military bickering and chronic political factionalism and unrest back in La Paz, all of which had plagued the Salamanca administration. Yet it was too late to salvage the war effort.

The costs of defeat were substantial. Perhaps as many as 60,000 Bolivians and 50,000 Paraguayans had died,[6] and the Bolivian national debt reached 500 billion pounds.[7] The social and political consequences of the Chaco defeat were even more devastating—indeed, revolutionary. As Robert Alexander observed in his classic study of the Bolivian National Revolution:

> The Chaco War was the catalyst that started the process of undermining the traditional social system of Bolivia. Arousing the spirit of nationalism and the social consciousness of the youth of the upper and middle classes of the cities, it also had disintegrating effects on the life of the Indians, who were the great majority of the population.[8]

The war, by shattering the social and economic equilibrium of the old order, led to widespread political mobilization and intellectual ferment. More than 200,000 men—about 10 percent of the population—had been mobilized to the front. Most were Indians who did not return to agricultural or mining communities but, instead, crowded into the fast-growing cities. By exposing the extremes of ineptitude and inequality of the traditional political and social system, the war created both the psychological and structural conditions for radical change. Although the process of social ferment begun by the Chaco War "made the Revolution of 1952 inevitable," the most immediate product of postwar ferment was an era of reform from 1936 to 1939.[9]

THE POSTWAR REFORMERS (1936–1939)

Out of the postwar reconstruction, a new political coalition of veterans, unionized labor, organized peasant syndicates, and student groups was formed. And led by the young military reformers, Colonels David Toro and Germán Busch, a new political order was attempted. Without a clear ideology or program, the reformers sought social justice and equality, popular participation in politics, and the vindication of Bolivia's new nationalism. Central to this new nationalism was economic independence from foreign capital and the tin interests that had controlled the government for half a century. The reformers envisioned a strong Bolivian state that would be the leader of national development, not the captive of private economic interests. Although they failed, their goals inspired the 1952 Revolution.

Toro and the Expropriation of Standard Oil

After the truce in 1935, the political scene assumed a false calm quickly disturbed by the agitation of the four traditional parties (the Liberals, Genuine Republicans, Socialist Republicans, and Nationalists) over the presidential succession. The presidency of Tejada Sorzano, extended by Congress in February 1935, was to expire in August of that year; but amid considerable dissension, his term was continued to August 1936. He never completed the term. The mood of the country was changing, and disgust with the civilian politicians held culpable in the Chaco defeat was growing. "If the civilians are incapable of ordering their ideas," one La Paz newspaper warned, "then at least the army will impose some order."[10] Political normalcy continued to elude the country as the May 31 presidential elections neared.

On May 17, 1936, predictions of a coup became reality. Colonel David Toro and Colonel Germán Busch, supported by Saavedra's Republican Socialist Party and the new Socialist Party (an offshoot of the Nationalist Party), seized the government. As president of the civilian-military junta, Toro explained that "the political chaos and socioeconomic problems" were impossible to resolve "within the traditional political system." The army had been forced to intervene "to defend the interests and rights of the working classes and the veterans." The new government intended to establish a "system of state socialism" that would "return Bolivia to economic sovereignty" and "correct a situation of misery and poverty."[11]

Initially, the military government was accepted by most political groups. Its proposed program of national reconstruction, social justice, economic development, nonviolence, and veterans' aid placated the diverse political tendencies. President Toro's promise to effect "an evolutionary socioeconomic coup," not a "political revolution," reassured conservatives and reformers. However, the government's legislation, the preferences given to veterans, and plans for an official mass party panicked the conservatives. Dissension within the pro-government Socialist Party further contributed to political unrest. Under the ambiguous rubric of "socialism," the party encompassed disparate ideological groups and individualistic political leaders. Within its ranks were the traditional Republican Socialists of Saavedra (who was masquerading as a radical reformer), the leftist syndicalists of Waldo Alvarez, and Marxists such as Ricardo Anaya and José Antonio Arze. Attempts to oust Saavedra from the coalition sparked open feuding. Busch, representing the military institution, became restive and threatened to take over. To forestall a coup, Toro confiscated Standard Oil of Bolivia on March 13, 1937, and created the Bolivian State Petroleum Enterprise (Yacimientos Petrolíferos Fiscales Bolivianos).

This expropriation was the first seizure of a North American company in Latin America, predating a similar Mexican action by one year. Although the legal process had been initiated by Liberal President Tejada Sorzano, the actual confiscation of Standard Oil without indemnification characterized the postwar economic nationalism of the military reformers. Toro and Busch were opposed to the liberal economic system that had subordinated the Bolivian state to the private interests of the tin barons. During the wartime emergency, the state had imposed unprecedented economic regulation; but in the postwar economic crisis, the tin interests attempted to reassert private control. The military reformers resisted with a new economic and political model best termed *corporatism*, a distinctly Bolivian form of national "socialism."

The reformist military was soon beseiged on both sides—the tin oligarchy on the "right," and the socialists who wanted a Marxist solution on the "left." Although Toro was more radical than Busch in economic policy, neither was decisive in dealing with the economic power of the mining industrialists. Toro had imposed currency controls, tax reforms, and state-subsidized food stores and rationing. Busch had revoked, reinstituted, and again revoked these measures in an attempt to stabilize the economy and balance the opposition of the capitalists against strikes by labor for wage increases and price controls. Expropriation of Standard Oil, however, was one economic policy supported by the majority of Bolivians, conservatives and radicals alike. Standard Oil, implicated by the people in the Chaco defeat, symbolized foreign economic imperialism and anti-nationalism.

Busch and the Constitutional Convention

The Busch coup, which came on July 13, was a reaction not to Toro's economic policies but, rather, to his failure to insulate the military from partisan rivalries. However, the conservatives believed that Busch would dismantle Toro's state socialism and supported what they interpreted as a "restoration" of the old order. Busch did not dispel this view, explaining in a message to the nation that his would not be "a government of class" or "of political sects." He sought to harmonize the interests of capital and labor and to avoid imposing a new ideology (such as the previous government had imposed); his program would emphasize nationalism and Bolivianism.[12] But Busch upheld the oil nationalization. He also assembled the constitutional convention (proposed earlier by Toro) to institutionalize the social, economic, and political reforms that Toro had implemented under the program of the Revolution of May 17, 1936.

Political exiles of all party affiliations were allowed to return home to elect candidates to the national convention of March 1938. A functionalist representation scheme (based on a corporatist model) was used, allotting dominant representation to the Legion of Veterans (Legión de Ex-Combatientes, or LEC) and to the new labor and miners' unions, which had also been the backbone of popular support for Toro. The delegates, controlled by "progressive" groups, elected Germán Busch and Enrique Baldivieso as president and vice-president on May 27, 1938. The election and convention represented "a major breakthrough in postwar political development for the left."[13]

From May to October the conventionists worked feverishly on the new constitution, which would be remarkable for its social progressivism. They institutionalized into law economic independence from both internal and foreign capital. The constitution made explicit direct state control over the economy and introduced a new property law that emphasized the social and collective function of ownership: "The inviolability of private property" was protected "as long as it fulfills a social function." The constitution did not preclude future land reform but threatened the expropriation of unproductive farms and their redistribution to the peasantry. No binding legislation on Indian rights was passed; the more radical delegates had attempted to abolish the system of involuntary Indian labor and to legally protect communal landholdings. An educational reform, promising free and universal education, encouraged the founding of rural Indian centers such as the noted Warisata school.[14]

The 1938 constitution guaranteed the rights to unionize and to strike; but it was the Labor Code, also called the Busch Code (Código Busch) after its major proponent, that most effectively advanced protective labor legislation. Enacted on May 24, 1939, the code was hailed as "a decisive step in the improvement of worker conditions" and as a "major triumph for the Bolivian labor movement." In part, these laws were the result of increasing unrest by Bolivian workers who had formed the Confederation of Bolivian Workers (Confederación Sindical de Trabajadores de Bolivia, or CSTB) after the war. Major general strikes had occurred in May 1936 and July 1937; the miners had struck in April 1937 and in March and June 1938, and had held a national congress in August 1939; railway workers also struck in 1937 and 1939.

The constitutional convention was terminated in October 1938 by the government, which found itself unable to control the radicalizing forces of the left and the constant attacks of the right. Although reformist and leftist parties experienced unprecedented growth and organization under Busch, his government ultimately undercut the civilian reformers by refusing to join the parties of the left. Busch attempted to circumvent parties and politics altogether but found himself alienated from organized civilian support. He appealed directly to the masses and in April 1939 made himself "dictator" because of the country's "economic, social and moral crisis." He explained that "the actual situation of the nation oscillates between one of financial privilege which now as in the past attempts to absorb total state power and extremist tendencies which aspire to radical overthrow of institutions."[15]

Thus economic nationalism remained the heart of his military reformism. His decree of June 7, 1939, nationalized the Mining Bank and established tight state control over the Central Bank in order to protect the state's economic independence from mining interests and its right to control the nation's mineral wealth. The mining companies were required to sell all foreign exchange earnings from mineral exports to the Central Bank at the government-controlled exchange rate, lower than the free market price. Overnight, the government's tax revenues from the mining sector increased by 25 percent. "The slogan of my government," Busch maintained, is the "economic emancipation of my country"; then Bolivia can enjoy its own riches and use them to develop its industries and agriculture.[16]

In the end, political polarization undermined Busch's reforms and the experiment in military socialism. Busch and Toro confronted the typical reformer's dilemma. Their nonviolent constitutional reforms (a "revolution from above") were met at every turn by the aggressive opposition of both conservative reaction and leftist extremism. Moreover, Busch's record invited great controversy: To his enemies he was a fascist, although his government allowed thousands of German Jews into the country; to his supporters he was a forerunner and hero of the 1952 Revolution. Busch's rule ended abruptly with his suicide on August 28, 1939, but the popular belief that he was murdered by the tin interests persists today.

FORMATION OF RADICAL POLITICAL PARTIES

Attempts to reform the system from within continued. Despite the resurgence of the oligarchy after Busch's death, the new and radical postwar political parties continued the struggle. The Chaco experience had indeed changed men and undermined old political allegiances; there was a crisis of political legitimacy. The men who returned "charged the traditional parties with responsibility for the war and disclaimed any connection with them." Traditional "norms and patterns had no validity for a majority of the politically active population. The system had failed in a crucial hour, and that failure compromised it forever."[17] Four radical political parties—two nationalist and two Marxist—were formed in the postwar political vacuum. The Nationalist Revolutionary Movement and the Bolivian Socialist Falange were made up of nationalists; and the Party of the Revolutionary Left and the Revolutionary Workers' Party were made up of Marxists. As the key protagonist of the 1952 Revolution, the MNR was especially important.

The Nationalists

The Nationalist Revolutionary Movement (Movimiento Nacionalista Revolucionario, or MNR) was not founded until January 25, 1941, after the experiment in military socialism had ended and the oligarchy had regained control.[18] Nevertheless, the MNR had roots in the pre- and post-Chaco political ferment—especially in the Socialist Party, which had supported Toro and Busch. The Socialist Party, established in the spring of 1936, developed from a 1934 party program and the Revolutionary Socialist Cell, itself an offshoot of the old "Silista" Nationalist Party. Led by Enrique Baldivieso (once personal secretary to President Hernando Siles) and Carlos Montenegro (later an important MNR theorist), the Socialist Party espoused a nationalistic and corporatist ideology.

The Socialist Party later split into factions; one, the Independent Socialist Party, became the direct precursor of the MNR. In its ranks were major future MNR leaders including Víctor Paz Estenssoro, Augusto Céspedes, Hernán Siles Zuazo, and Walter Guevara Arze. During the 1938 constitutional convention, the Independent Socialists were an influential element of the leftist political grouping. Many of the MNR's founders were student activists, war veterans, and journalists of the middle class. The radical newspaper, La Calle, founded in 1936 by charter members of the MNR, was the political voice of an anti-imperialistic nationalism that singled out the big mining capitalists of Aramayo, Hochschild, and Patiño (the Rosca) as class enemies of the workers and popular groups. This anti-imperialism became central to MNR ideology.

On May 10, 1941, the founders of the MNR formalized the new party under the leadership of Víctor Paz Estenssoro in a document that described the group as "a patriotic movement of socialist orientation directed toward the defense and affirmation of Bolivian nationalism."[19] The basic principles of the party were approved on June 7, 1942: (1) opposition to a "sellout" democracy; (2) opposition to "pseudo" socialism, the instrument of a new exploitation; (3) support of revolutionary nationalism; (4) consolidation of the state and security of the nation; and (5) the economic liberation and sovereignty of the Bolivian people.[20] Notably missing from this program were land reform and liberation of the Indian.

The Bolivian Socialist Falange (Falange Socialista Boliviana, or FSB), founded on August 15, 1937, was the oldest of the radical political parties that remained important after 1952. The falangists originated in Chile, where Bolivian students and exiles had been influenced by the

Spanish fascism of Primo de Rivera and the Chilean Nazi party. Important leaders of the Bolivian falangists were Carlos Puente, who founded the Bolivian Nationalist Action, and Oscar Unzaga de la Vega, who established the FSB. The two groups merged in 1940, when, after Puente's death, de la Vega became undisputed leader of the movement until his own death in 1959.

FSB supporters were drawn from student activists of the Catholic high schools of Cochabamba. The ideology of the FSB was eminently pro-church, nationalistic, and elitist; it repudiated liberalism and communism for a national socialist model of state corporatism, then popular in Germany and Italy. The "Program of Principles" of the FSB "demanded in its internal organization a rigorous concept of discipline and the conscious subordination of the individual to the realization of collective ends, and a hierarchical system based on the selection of the most capable."[21] After 1952, the FSB was the only organized opposition to the MNR and represented conservative anticommunist interests.

The Marxists

The most important of the postwar Marxist parties was the Party of the Revolutionary Left (Partido de la Izquierda Revolucionaria, or PIR), founded on July 25, 1940, by José Antonio Arze and Ricardo Anaya. The PIR had antecedents in the Marxist student groups of 1928, the 1931 Confederation of Workers' Republics of the Pacific, and the Front of the Bolivian Left (Frente de Izquierda Boliviana, or FIB), which Arze organized in April 1939 while exiled in Chile. Members of the PIR included a radicalized middle-class elite and labor organizations such as the Confederation of Bolivian Workers and the railway workers' and teachers' unions.

The PIR, described as "the first truly leftist national party," professed a Stalinist-Marxist ideology but proclaimed itself independent of the Comintern.[22] The party was divided into two tendencies: the internationalist wing with pro-Soviet leanings and the nationalistic indigenist wing. Suspicious of the fascist political groups, including the MNR, the PIR allied with the oligarchy in the 1940s. Of the Marxist parties, the PIR platform represented a "moderate" left position that envisioned a nationalist bourgeois revolution (not a socialist revolution, which would come only much later), and a multiclass political coalition. The program called for the nationalization of the mines and petroleum, agrarian reform, and state control of the economy. As the only party to challenge the official candidate in the 1940 presidential elections, the PIR won more than 17 percent of the vote and rose to national prominence. In the early 1940s, the PIR, with its firm roots in the radical labor movement, was the dominant party of the left.[23] But by 1950, after its antirevolutionary accommodation with the traditional parties, the PIR was split and politically bankrupt.

The Revolutionary Workers' Party (Partido Obrero Revolucionario, or POR) was more radical ideologically than the PIR, but less successful politically. Led by Tristán Marof (the pseudonym of Gustavo Adolfo Navarro, a Marxist intellectual of international reputation) and José Aguirre Gainsborg, the POR was "the first of the major postwar radical parties." It was established in December 1934 at a conference of leftist exile groups held in Córdoba, Argentina. The roots of the party were in the socialist left of the 1920s and the writings of Marof, who as early as 1926 coined the rallying cry of the radical revolutionaries of the 1940s: "Mines to the state, land to the Indian." Marof represented the transition between the prewar and postwar generations of leftists.[24] The Revolutionary Workers' Party, despite its name, appealed more to university students and middle-class Marxist intellectuals than to Bolivia's workers. Many members of the POR (like those of the MNR and the PIR) had been activists in the 1928 university reform movement and were present at the creation of the Federation of University Students of Bolivia (FUB). Immediate antecedents of the POR were the Tupac Amaru Revolutionary Group, a leftist antiwar protest group of Marof in Argentina; the Bolivian Left of Gainsborg in Chile; the Group of Exiles of Peru; and, later, Gainsborg's Beta Gama Socialist Action group.

From the beginning there were two different ideological tendencies in the party. After its Second National Congress in October 1938, the POR split into two factions: the Marofistas and the Gainsborg Trotskyists. The Marof group represented a populist socialism of the left that combined indigenism and Marxism in a synthesis like that of José Carlos Mariátegui in Peru. The Gainsborg group included radical revolutionaries who believed in the Leninist model of takeover by an elite party as the vanguard of the proletariat, and in the establishment of a socialist state of workers and peasants. The majority of Marofistas formed the new Socialist Workers' Party of Bolivia (PSOB), which disappeared in the early 1940s. The more radical group, after Gainsborg's untimely death in October 1938, fell into disarray until reorganized by Guillermo Lora. Although the Trotskyist POR lacked the political leverage of the PIR and the MNR in the 1940s, it became influential later among the radical miners in the Bolivian Mine Workers' Federation (Federación Sindical de Trabajadores Mineros de Bolivia, or FSTMB), organized in May 1944.

An important change in the prerevolutionary decade of 1940 to 1950 was the ferment and radicalization that occurred in party activity as major reformist and revolutionary parties of the left gained popular support. Indicative of this fundamental change was the unexpected electoral turnout for the PIR's José Antonio Arze in 1940. Arze's 10,000 votes (out of 58,000 total votes) represented significant protest against the traditional system. Seventeen percent of the vote for an unknown leftist candidate was remarkable, given that the franchise was less than 5 percent and the opponent was a national war hero backed by the power of the establishment.[25] In this decade, political turmoil intensified as parties formed strange and complex political alliances and vendettas based on similarities and differences in radicalism and international alignment in World War II. Thus the MNR (like the FSB) was notoriously pro-Axis; and the PIR (unlike the POR) was subservient to the Moscow party line and rabidly anti-fascist. Such external preoccupations distracted the radical parties from domestic problems and impeded the unification of revolutionary forces until after 1947.

RESURGENCE AND FALL OF THE OLIGARCHY (1939–1952)

Within months after Busch's death, a reorganized oligarchy began to dismantle his reforms. Jolted by military reformism and the inroad of leftist parties, the Rosca unified its political forces into a class alliance of the propertied establishment and conservative military. Politically, they formed coalitions such as the Concordancia (also known as the Democratic Alliance) in March 1939. This coalition united the traditional Liberal, Genuine Republican, and Socialist Republican parties. After the Socialist Republicans left the Concordancia in 1940, the Liberals and Genuine Republicans formed the Unified Socialist Party. The Marxist PIR and the traditional parties that supported the government created the Bolivian Democratic Union in 1944, and the Antifascist Democratic Front in 1945. These were desperate attempts to stem the radical tide. The conservative coalition also supported the presidencies of two distinguished military leaders, Generals Carlos Quintanilla and Enrique Peñaranda, in 1939 and 1940, respectively. Conservatives again turned to a military leader, General Hugo Ballivián, to save the old order in 1951.

After the Chaco War, military intervention in politics was frequent as class conflict and political struggle divided not only the military institution but also the rest of society. In 1936, the reformist military filled a political vacuum; the traditional parties were morally bankrupt, and the new radical parties were disorganized and lacked a governing majority. In 1940, a nervous oligarchy resorted to a conservative military takeover to roll back reforms and block the parties of the left from legal control. Military reformers, allied with several radical parties, seized power again in 1943. In 1951, the traditional military attempted to replay the 1939 takeover. With the army split, neither the oligarchy nor the reformers were powerful enough alone to govern successfully from 1940 to 1952.

The Oligarchy and Peñaranda

Violating the constitution, conservative General Quintanilla became provisional president on August 24, 1939, and blocked Enrique Baldivieso, Busch's socialist vice-president, from rightful succession. When presidential elections were announced for 1940, the choice soon narrowed between two military candidates: General Enrique Peñaranda, a traditionalist, and General Bernardino Bilbao Rioja, a reformist. Influential as commander-in-chief of the armed forces and as the leader of the war veterans, Bilbao Rioja was a threat to a conservative restoration and, before the March vote, was ambushed and exiled. As the candidate of the Concordancia, General Peñaranda was elected. The oligarchy had achieved legal power by criminal means.[26]

The conservative Peñaranda government established close relations with the United States in return for economic and military assistance. Bolivia was the major tin supplier in the Western Hemisphere; and as war broke out in the Pacific, the United States increased its influence over Bolivia's internal politics to ensure uninterrupted supplies of strategic metals. The Peñaranda government renewed payments on the external debt owed to U.S. banks since suspension in 1931. A tin agreement was signed with the United States to provide 1,500 tons monthly for the next five years. This agreement (denounced by the opposition as a "sellout") provided the United States with an important stake in Bolivia's political and economic stability. In 1942, shortly after Bolivia broke diplomatic relations with the Axis (January 1942), U.S. Secretary of State Sumner Welles announced that the Export-Import Bank was extending a $5 million loan to Bolivia. From this sum Bolivia had to indemnify Standard Oil a total of $1,750,000 for the confiscation of its properties. The Peñaranda government declared war on the Axis on April 7, 1943, after the early April visit of U.S. Vice-President Henry Wallace.[27] In May, Peñaranda visited the United States and returned with more loans and military assistance.

The radical parties, especially the MNR, opposed increasing U.S. influence in Bolivia. Politics in the National Assembly became chaotic as radical opponents of the regime challenged its every policy. Peñaranda was forced to constitute five cabinets in less than three years. Two incidents characterized the extreme political unrest of his term. The first was the controversial "Nazi Putsch," which was used as a pretext to discredit the MNR and defuse opposition to the compensation of Standard Oil. On July 18, 1941, the U.S. ambassador denounced a Nazi plot of the MNR and the German minister in La Paz to seize power. As a result of this fictitious incident, which had been fabricated by the U.S. government and political conservatives, the German minister was expelled and many Germans were arrested and harassed; members of the MNR were repressed, and affiliated party newspapers such as *La Calle* closed down; the conservatives and the PIR formed the Antifascist Democratic Front; and the government imposed martial law.

The Catavi Massacre on December 13, 1942, in the Catavi Mine near the city of Oruro, was the cause célèbre that contributed to the fall of Peñaranda a year later.[28] In the highland mining centers, wildcat strikes for higher wages and better working and living conditions ended in a bloody confrontation between the army and the miners that left hundreds dead and wounded. The incident forged an alliance between the miners and the MNR. In Congress, opposition political parties (especially the MNR) demanded an inquiry by the government. The United States sent a special commission (the Magruder Commission) to investigate the crisis; its report was extremely critical of inhuman conditions in the mines.

Economic crises in other trades led to labor militancy and the strikes by railway workers, postal workers, and the teachers' union. The labor movement found political support among the radical delegates in Congress, while in the streets strikes repeatedly achieved pay increases and benefits. The Busch labor reforms made it difficult for Peñaranda and the Concordancia to halt the militancy of the labor movement, and official repression and security laws proved counterproductive. Catavi, and incidents like it, became rallying symbols in the struggle. Between 1940 and 1943, a "new era of political party-labor cooperation" was born, establishing a broader political base for the first MNR administration.[29]

The MNR and Villarroel

On December 20, 1943, Lieutenant Colonel Gualberto Villarroel seized the government. Villarroel was supported by both the MNR and Reason of the Fatherland (Razón de Patria, or RADEPA), a nationalistic military lodge of young Busch-style reformers. Secret military societies, influenced by Masonry and fascist ideology, were organized by lower-ranking officers who had discovered this solidarity in the prisoner-of-war camps in Paraguay. Military unrest among the young officer corps had been brewing during the Peñaranda administration: Only a few weeks after Peñaranda first assumed office, a rising had been put down; several others had failed later. The December 20 coup, called the "Revolution of the Majors" inasmuch as none of the five officers who led the revolt were above that rank, was not unexpected. The coup plotters had simply acted before the government could round up and exile them. After four years of failed attempts, the reformers were back in power.

The record of the first MNR-RADEPA government was mixed. The RADEPA, which was divided into two opposed tendencies, a fascist-right group and the more leftist-leaning elements allied with the MNR, exhibited all the confusion of previous military reformers. The United States (and all Latin American countries except Argentina) withheld recognition for six months until the more visible members of the MNR, such as Víctor Paz Estenssoro, Augusto Céspedes, and Carlos Montenegro, were removed from the cabinet. The United States further urged elections; these confirmed Villarroel as constitutional president in August 1944 and returned many MNR deputies to Congress. The United States, the Marxist PIR, and the oligarchy sought to discredit the Villarroel government as "Nazi," but this label was both unfair and simplistic. Given the growing economic dependence of Bolivia on the United States, the reformers saw in fascism a universal doctrine of national sovereignty and independence against foreign intervention.

The RADEPA was more attracted to fascism than were the Busch reformers, and some of its forces did not hesitate to use violence to repress political opponents, especially the PIR. José Antonio Arze, leader of the PIR, was attacked and almost killed when he ran for the presidency against Villarroel in 1944. The harsh government treatment of rebels in a November 1944 coup attempt proved a major embarrassment. The nine leaders in the plot were shot by firing squads. Circulating soon thereafter in antigovernment circles were rumors that more than sixty had been killed, tortured, and mutilated. The incident provided an opportunity for José Antonio Arze (then teaching in the United States) to ask for U.S. intervention on behalf of democracy in Bolivia. Opposition parties in Congress used the incident, as the MNR and miners had used the Catavi Massacre, to propagandize and spread discontent. This action rallied the oligarchy and the PIR in the formation of the Antifascist Democratic Front in 1945. Just as Catavi had brought down the Peñaranda government, the *fusilamiento* (shooting) of prominent members of the ruling class was the beginning of the end for Villarroel.[30]

At the same time, however, government policy favored the dispossessed: miners, Indians, and labor. The Villarroel-MNR administration encouraged unionization and was supportive in organizing the powerful mine workers' union, the FSTMB, in early June 1944. The new union was controlled by the MNR and Juan Lechín Oquendo of the POR, who became its secretary general. The FSTMB successfully rivaled the influence of the PIR in the CSTB, a union of the urban labor movement. The

PIR's Stalinist program and policies of accommodation with the oligarchy ultimately compromised its credibility with labor. Through its control of the labor ministry, the MNR promoted the formation of other trade unions for unskilled workers. The government passed new labor reforms guaranteeing voluntary retirement, job security, and social benefits for workers. A housing and rent law and family reforms to protect the lower classes were other achievements.

In May 1945, the government sponsored the first Indian Congress in Bolivia's history, thereby threatening the large estates, the last stronghold of traditional power. Previous social reforms had concentrated on the urban and mining proletariat, ignoring the rural fiefdoms of the elite and the widespread racial prejudice against the Indian peasants. Organization of peasant cooperatives (such as Cliza in Cochabamba) had occurred, but the reform governments had taken mostly symbolic measures. The Indian Congress abolished the feudal practices of involuntary servitude (*pongueaje* and *mitanaje*) but did not propose land reform. The occasion provided an opportunity for Villarroel to speechify about justice for all Bolivians and for Hernán Siles Zuazo to remind the thousand delegates that the "greatest problem was the problem of the land." Indeed, the main achievement of the Congress was the hope it gave the Indians—an achievement more substantial than its empty decrees, which were not enforced until after 1952. Now united, however, the Indian *campesinos* (peasants) began to take matters into their own hands.[31]

Because of international and internal pressures, relations between the MNR and the Villarroel military officers were becoming difficult; ultimately, the MNR was forced to leave the government. Like Busch, Villarroel was left to govern only with military support, which itself was divided between the junior and senior officers. On June 13, 1946, a coup attempt failed, but on July 21 popular demonstrations escalated into the overthrow of Villarroel. Striking teachers and railway and constructions workers, student unrest, and the agitation of the conservative Antifascist Front led to the confrontation. Villarroel resigned; but when he refused to leave the presidential palace, mobs attacked it, killed the president and his closest associates, and hung the bodies from the lampposts of the main plaza. The army did not intervene to protect one of its own—and thus another experiment in military reformism ended tragically. Whatever the successes and failures of Villarroel, like Busch he entered the pantheon of Bolivian heroes for his struggle to achieve Bolivia's economic independence.

Civil War

The fall of Villarroel started the "Sexenio" or the last six years of oligarchic government before the revolution. Immediately, a provisional civilian-military junta assumed control until the January 1947 elections. Two very conservative candidates ran for office: Enrique Hertzog of the Republican Socialist Union (PURS), which represented the many factions of the old Republican Party, and Tomás Manuel Elío of the Liberal Party. Hertzog won by 44,700 votes against 44,300, of which 13,000 were for exiled Paz Estenssoro and the persecuted MNR.[32] Back in power, the oligarchy formed the National Conciliation, an unlikely coalition of conservative political groups and the leftist PIR. This opportunistic cooperation with the oligarchy destroyed the PIR and led to the founding of the Bolivian Communist Party (Partido Comunista de Bolivia, or PCB) on January 17, 1950. Although most of the PIR's members defected to the Communist Party or joined the growing ranks of the MNR, only a few remained loyal.

Through its representatives in Congress, the MNR was able to continue its radical activism during this period, although major party leaders were exiled or in hiding. In the congressional elections of May 1949, the MNR emerged as a major legislative force despite the official repression of its members by the government. Its success was due in part to the close MNR-labor alliance and to the formation of the Miners' Parliamentary Bloc (Bloque Parlamentario Minero), which promoted the candidates of the MNR, the POR, and the FSTMB in the 1947 and 1949 elections. The inefficiency and repression of the government also helped the MNR's cause, making the party a martyr for political freedom. As the economy worsened in 1949, there was widespread labor unrest, especially in the mining centers where thousands were dismissed. The conservative PURS government became more violent and reactionary, opposing even the modest reforms already achieved by labor and the middle class. This intransigence served only to further radicalize the MNR and labor.

In November 1946, at a special union meeting in Pulacayo, the miners adopted the "Central Thesis of the FSTMB," known as the "Thesis of Pulacayo." This document, formulated by Guillermo Lora, elaborated the ideology of the FSTMB. The program's Trotskyist belief in "permanent revolution" stressed the necessity of the armed class struggle led by the workers—the only truly revolutionary class in Bolivia. Accommodation with democratic regimes was out of the question; the goal was an immediate socialist revolution and worker state. This program of violent class struggle was at odds with the multiclass strategy of the MNR and amounted to a declaration of war against the Rosca.[33] When the miners struck in January 1947 to support the adoption of the Pulacayo program, the PIR labor minister ordered in the troops. This action established a pattern of more confrontations and deaths. During a strike in Catavi in June 1949, 2 North American technicians and 200 to 300 Bolivians were killed.[34] And with the exile of Juan Lechín, an MNR senator in the legislature and leader of the FSTMB, there was more violence between the army and the miners.

On August 26, 1949, the MNR launched an insurrection against the government. The civil war, which had been organized by Siles Zuazo and other MNR leaders with some military support (mostly retired officers), lasted only twenty days. Premature discovery in La Paz and other grave errors doomed the revolt, although the strong resistance in some regions, especially the mines, came as a surprise to the government. The MNR had hoped for a quick coup, but the military remained loyal to the government and the masses were never mobilized and armed. The brief civil uprising had affected major areas of the country, and the rebels had held out for a time in Cochabamba and Santa Cruz. Having appropriated funds from the national banks and planes from the Bolivian national airline, they escaped into exile on September 15. Many of those who did not escape were imprisoned on the island of Coati in Lake Titicaca. The civil war, despite its failure, had indeed demonstrated both the broad-based MNR support and the power of the MNR-labor alliance.[35]

After order was restored between September and October, President Hertzog resigned in favor of his vice-president, Mamerto Urriolagoitia, who had been directing the government since May in any case. Urriolagoitia, more decisive and willing to use repression, officially remained president until August 1951. But after the spectacular MNR victory in the May 1951 elections, he panicked and transferred the reins of state over to the military, the last resort of the oligarchy. This illegal action was the immediate pretext for the 1952 uprising.

Revolutionary Accelerator: The 1951 Election

Between 1940 and 1951, important structural and attitudinal changes occurred in the political system. Most important was the consistent erosion of middle- and upper-class support for the traditional political parties and the gradual creation of a multiclass voting bloc for the MNR.[36] From the extraordinary protest vote for the PIR in 1940 and the congressional elections of 1942, 1944, 1947, and 1949, to the 1951 presidential election, the strength of the MNR and other radical parties had grown. The ideological base of the system had also evolved and radicalized with events and shifting political coalitions. The confused socialist and fascist tendencies between 1936 and 1946 had crystallized into two clear political blocs: supporters versus opponents of the status quo. The MNR had matured into a multiclass party of the democratic left, with a clear revolutionary slogan: Land to the tiller and mines to the state. But neither the bayonets of the military reformers, nor the fierce rhetoric and decrees of the radical congressional delegates, nor the incessant labor militancy had achieved structural change. The annulment of the 1951 election was final proof that the Rosca would not preside over its own reform.

In the presidential election of May 6, 1951, only 126,000 people voted—about 4–5 percent of a population of 2.7 to 3 million. Despite the restricted electorate, the clout of the government, and the money of big mining, Víctor Paz Estenssoro, forced to run from exile in Argentina, received 43 percent of all votes cast, a 5 to 3 plurality over the official candidate, Gabriel Gosálvez.[37] The conservative parties had unwisely split their vote over five different candidates, whereas the radical parties had unified behind the Paz Estenssoro–Siles Zuazo ticket. Votes for the official candidate roughly balanced those for Paz; but if the conservative coalition had voted for a unified ticket, they could have won. Despite the real threat of electoral defeat, the disintegration, factionalism, and opportunism chronic to Bolivian political parties impeded a solid conservative front.

Because none of the six candidates had an absolute plurality (51 percent) for victory, the final decision was referred to the National Congress according to constitutional provisions. Although the conservative parties outnumbered the MNR two to one in Congress and were most likely to win, President Urriolagoitia precipitously resigned to prevent even a remote MNR victory and left the government to General Ovidio Quiroga, chief of the army. Denouncing the MNR as communist, General Quiroga annulled the elections and appointed a military cabinet and General Hugo Ballivián as interim president of the country. Blatantly unconstitutional and alternately conciliatory and repressive, the new military government was never able to consolidate its power. Internal and external forces undermined the weak eleven-month rule. Opposition parties, including the conservative Liberals, criticized the government unmercifully; the political climate was chaotic. A dispute with the United States over tin prices and a halt in tin sales in late 1951 heightened the economic crisis. And the government itself and conservative parties joined the MNR-led chorus against U.S. economic imperialism—a fitting setting for the MNR revolt.

The Revolutionary Takeover

The Bolivian National Revolution of 1952 was primarily a proletarian, urban-based revolution instigated by the MNR. It was a replay of the 1949 civil war, but with more good fortune and fewer mistakes. On the eve of April 8, the MNR leaders in La Paz (Hernán Siles and

La Paz, Bolivia's de facto (administrative) capital and the center of political life for most of the twentieth century. During the 1952 National Revolution armed miners and workers commanded the heights above the city and thus won the "Battle of La Paz" (photo by author).

Juan Lechín) secured the support of General Antonio Seleme, the minister of Internal Security and chief of the National Police. Opening up the armories, the militarized police distributed arms to the MNR and the workers. Then, on the morning of April 9, fighting broke out in La Paz. Soon the center of the city was being held by the revolutionaries. The army regrouped below the rebel positions and in the heights above the city, planning an encirclement. After the first day, the army was winning, causing General Seleme to panic and seek asylum in the Chilean Embassy. The MNR rebels began to debate a compromise with the government but kept fighting. The situation was reversed dramatically on April 10, when miners from Milluni, ten miles north of La Paz, seized the air force base and prevented the bombing of rebel positions. Converging on El Alto (the heights above the city), the miners trapped the army from behind. In Oruro, about seventy miles south on the Altiplano, the MNR cadres and miners prevented army troops from reinforcing La Paz and trapping the Milluni miners between the two armies.

After some of the heaviest fighting in the revolt, the army commander, General Humberto Torres Ortiz, signed a truce on April 11 and fled with the top officers into exile. In three days, the Battle for

La Paz had virtually won the revolution. Casualties numbered 552 dead and 787 wounded.[38] On April 15, Víctor Paz Estenssoro arrived in La Paz from Buenos Aires amid a huge public demonstration, and on April 16, 1952, he was sworn in as the first revolutionary president.

NOTES

1. Historical sources for the prerevolutionary period include the following: Robert A. Alexander, *The Bolivian National Revolution* (New Brunswick, N.J.: Rutgers University Press, 1958) and *Bolivia: Past, Present and Future of Its Politics* (New York: Praeger, 1982); Robert Barton, *A Short History of Bolivia* (La Paz: Editorial Los Amigos del Libro, 1968); Porfirio Díaz Machicao, *Historia de Bolivia* (multiple volumes, publishers, and dates); Herbert S. Klein, *Origenes de la revolución nacional boliviana: la crisis de la generación del Chaco* (La Paz: Editorial Juventud, 1968), *Bolivia: The Evolution of a Multi-Ethnic Society* (New York: Oxford University Press, 1982), and *Parties and Political Change in Bolivia, 1880–1952* (London: Cambridge University Press, 1969).

2. Alexander, *The Bolivian National Revolution*, p. 22; and Augusto Céspedes, *Sangre de mestizos: relatos de la guerra del Chaco*, 2nd ed. (La Paz: Editorial Juventud, 1969), pp. 24, 222–225.

3. Klein, *Origenes*, pp. 152, 157, 167–175; Klein, *Bolivia*, pp. 188–193; and José Félix Estigarribia, *The Epic of the Chaco: Marshall Estigarribia's Memoirs of the Chaco War, 1932–1935*, edited and translated by Pablo Max Ynsfran (Austin: University of Texas Press, 1950), p. 3.

4. These force levels are based on Paraguayan sources and could be exaggerated. See Luis Vittone, *Las fuerzas armadas paraguayas en sus distintas épocas* (Asunción: Editorial El Gráfico, 1969), p. 185; and Estigarribia, *The Epic of the Chaco*, pp. 13–14.

5. Fausto Reinaga, *Franz Tamayo y la revolución boliviana* (La Paz: Editorial Casegural, 1956), p. 105.

6. Klein, *Bolivia*, p. 194; José Fellmann Velarde, *Historia de Bolivia*, 2nd ed., vol. 3 (La Paz: Editorial Los Amigos del Libro, 1981), p. 210; and Mariano Baptista Gumucio, *Historia contemporánea de Bolivia, 1930–1978*, 2nd ed. (La Paz: Gisbert, 1978), p. 72.

7. Edgar Avila Echazú, *Revolución y cultura en Bolivia* (Tarija: Universidad Autónoma Juan Misael Saracho, 1968), p. 30.

8. Robert A. Alexander, *Prophets of the Revolution: Profiles of Latin American Leaders* (New York: Macmillan, 1962), p. 199.

9. Alexander, *The Bolivian National Revolution*, p. 22.

10. Waltraud Queiser Morales, "A Comparative Study of Societal Discontent and Revolutionary Change in Bolivia and Paraguay: 1930–1941" (Ph.D. dissertation, Graduate School of International Studies, University of Denver, 1977), p. 206.

11. Ibid., p. 208.

12. Ibid., pp. 214–216.

13. Klein, *Parties*, p. 278.

14. Ibid., pp. 284, 287–290; Morales, "A Comparative Study," pp. 277–278; see also Agustín Barcelli S., *Medio siglo de luchas sindicales revolucionarias en Bolivia, 1905–1955* (La Paz: Editorial del Estado, 1957), p. 149.

15. Morales, "A Comparative Study," pp. 222, 278.

16. Ibid., pp. 276–277; Klein, *Bolivia*, p. 208.

17. Klein, *Bolivia*, p. 203.

18. Political party histories are drawn from Luis Peñaloza C., *Historia del movimiento nacionalista revolucionario, 1941–1952* (La Paz: Editorial Juventud, 1963), pp. 20–41; Augusto Céspedes, *El dictador suicida: 40 años de historia de Bolivia* (La Paz: Juventud, 1968), pp. 261–270; Manuel Frontaura Argandoña, *La revolución boliviana* (La Paz: Editorial Los Amigos del Libro, 1974), pp. 77–78; and Baptista, *Historia contemporánea*, pp. 79–137.

19. Peñaloza, *Historia*, pp. 38–39.

20. This is a direct translation of the program found in Céspedes, *El dictador suicida*, p. 267.

21. Alipio Valencia Vega, *El pensamiento político en Bolivia* (La Paz: Editorial Juventud, 1973), p. 271.

22. Klein, *Origenes*, p. 397.

23. Klein, *Bolivia*, p. 214.

24. Ibid., p. 198; Klein, *Origenes*, p. 219; Baptista, *Historia contemporánea*, p. 79; Guillermo Lora, *Historia del movimiento obrero boliviano, 1933–1952*, Vol. 4 (La Paz: Editorial Los Amigos del Libro, 1980), p. 138; and Liborio Justo (Quebracho), *Bolivia: la revolución derrotada* (Cochabamba: Editorial Serrano, 1967), pp. 101–103.

25. Klein, *Bolivia*, pp. 211–212.

26. This section is based on Alfredo Ayala Z., *Historia de Bolivia en cuadros sinópticos*, 2nd ed. (La Paz: Editorial Don Bosco, 1980), pp. 259–276; Baptista, *Historia contemporánea*, pp. 123–129; and Fellmann, *Historia*, vol. 3, pp. 241–247.

27. War was declared by a national decree of April 1943 but was not ratified until December 4, 1943. See Ayala, *Historia de Bolivia*, p. 274.

28. An official government interpretation of the Catavi events is Juan Manuel Balcázar's *Los problemas sociales en Bolivia, una mistificación demagógica: la "masacre" de Catavi* (La Paz: n.p., 1947); a labor interpretation is Barcelli's *Medio siglo*, pp. 161–164.

29. Klein, *Parties*, pp. 344, 349; Morales, "A Comparative Study," pp. 281–284.

30. Baptista, *Historia contemporánea*, pp. 153–156.

31. Ibid., pp. 160–162.

32. Ibid., p. 171.

33. Lora, *Historia del movimiento*, pp. 435–496.

34. Ibid., pp. 646–649.

35. Peñaloza, *Historia*, pp. 195–232.

36. Klein, *Bolivia*, p. 216.

37. The total vote was reported as 125,339, of which Paz received 54,049; Gosálvez, 39,940; and the four other opposition parties combined, 31,350. The

remaining candidates were Guillermo Gutiérrez Vea Murguía for Acción Cívica Boliviana, a new coalition representing the tin interests; Tomás Manuel Elío, Liberal Party; José Antonio Arze, PIR; and General Bilbao Rioja, FSB. See Christoper Mitchell, *The Legacy of Populism in Bolivia: From the MNR to Military Rule* (New York: Praeger, 1977), p. 31, and note 39, p. 37; Thomas E. Weil et al., *Area Handbook for Bolivia*, Foreign Area Studies, American University (Washington, D.C.: Government Printing Office, 1974), p. 34; and James M. Malloy, *Bolivia: The Uncompleted Revolution* (Pittsburgh: University of Pittsburgh Press, 1970), pp. 151–153.

38. Mitchell, *The Legacy of Populism*, p. 33. Fellman, *Historia*, vol. 3, p. 339, gives a total of 1,500 dead in the struggle in La Paz and Oruro.

4

The Bolivian National Revolution and the Political System

Social revolution engulfed Bolivia in 1952 primarily as a result of frustrated reformism. After the Chaco War, military and civilian reformers alike had attempted to institute radical change but had been thwarted by the power of the Rosca and the influence of the United States. The Bolivian masses cried out for reform. Politically mobilized and fed up with postwar economic hardships, record numbers of middle- and lower-class activists beseiged the bastions of public affairs for the first time. By 1952, they were unwilling to leave or sanction a conservative restoration. If peaceful reforms were impossible, then violent revolution became inevitable. Thus unbridled revolutionary populism elevated the MNR to state power and forged Bolivia's first truly nationalist political party.

REVOLUTION AND THE MNR IN POWER

Once in the Palacio Quemado (the "Scorched Palace," or seat of government), the MNR faced the insurmountable tasks of enacting its revolutionary program and rebuilding political and economic life. The core policies of the MNR's 1952 Revolution were radical: universal suffrage, nationalization of the mines, and land to the tiller. Although revolutionary legislation transformed the face of traditional Bolivia, the MNR emerged a house divided between "reluctant" and "radical" reformers. Assailed from without as well as within, the party failed to institutionalize the revolution; its legacy was factionalism and betrayal. In 1964, the new Bolivian army overthrew the MNR and ruled repressively for eighteen years. Had the legacy of MNR government from 1952 to 1964 incited military takeover and the subversion of the revolution?

77

The Program and Policies of the MNR

The original MNR program, drawn up by Cuadros Quiroga and issued in June 1942, was a vague and conservative document concerned with Bolivia's economic emancipation. The 1942 program called for state control over mining, not nationalization; the assimilation of the Indians, not agrarian reform; and nationalist consolidation of the state without explaining what this meant or how it would be implemented.[1] The alliance with labor, especially the miners, and the power struggle of 1947–1952 radicalized the MNR program. Its formal goals became indistinguishable from those of the 1946 Thesis of Pulacayo. In office, however, the MNR hesitated, but the more radical rank and file forced through their key class demands: For the miners it was nationalization of the mines; for the peasants, land reform; and for the urban masses, universal suffrage. Thus the revolutionary process and multiclass pressures shaped MNR legislation between 1952–1956.

One of the first reforms enacted was the electoral law. Issued on July 21, 1952, the sixth anniversary of Villarroel's overthrow, this law guaranteed universal adult suffrage, abolished literacy tests, and permitted all citizens of at least twenty-one years of age (eighteen years if married) to vote. The political impact was staggering. By the stroke of a pen the voting population expanded from around 200,000 to nearly 1 million.[2] Many new voters were illiterate Indian peasants, some 60 percent of the population. Before 1952, only 2 to 5 percent of the population could legally vote; and in the 1951 elections only 126,000 had voted, just 5 percent of a population of 3 million. By 1960, in comparison, there were 900,000 voters, or about 26 percent of the population of 3.5 million. In the 1978 and 1979 elections, there were 1.9 million and 1.8 million registered voters, or 38 and 36 percent, respectively, of the population of 5 million. Therefore, the enactment of the universal suffrage decree single-handedly replaced traditional elite politics with mass voting.

Signed in Catavi on October 31, 1952, the Act of Bolivia's Economic Independence nationalized the mining enterprises of Patiño, Aramayo, and Hochschild. The government created the state Bolivian Mining Corporation (Corporación Minera de Bolivia, or COMIBOL) and transferred control over "85 percent of the country's tin production, 95 percent of its foreign exchange receipts, and about 50 percent of the central government's fiscal receipts" from private into public hands.[3] Although the formal MNR program called for expropriation without compensation, in order to gain diplomatic recognition and desperately needed economic assistance from the United States, the MNR government vetoed the labor sector of the party and ultimately compensated the big tin barons. This decision compounded the severe postrevolutionary economic crisis by further decreasing depleted government resources. Although subject to currency and tax regulation by the state Mining Bank, medium and small mining companies remained in private hands, further allaying U.S. fears inasmuch as several medium-sized mines (not engaged in tin production) were American-owned.

The Agrarian Reform Decree, the last major policy act of the revolutionary government, was promulgated in Ucureña, Cochabamba, on August 2, 1953. The law reluctantly legalized a de facto situation of violent peasant takeovers of *latifundios* (large landed estates) in Ucureña (a bastion of peasant radicalism since the 1940s) and elsewhere. The reform confiscated only the excessively large estates, leaving the medium-sized properties (600–1,500 acres, or 240–600 hectares) intact. Former owners were compensated by twenty-five-year bonds at 2 percent interest, which new owners paid on the assessed land value. Especially important, the land reform decree abolished oppressive feudal debt servitude and restored to Indian communities the collective lands seized by unscrupulous *latifundistas* (wealthy landowners). Technical assistance, rural development capital, and an internal migration plan were additional, but often neglected, provisions of the reform.

Like the popular vote, the land reform marked a radical departure from the past. In 1950, some 72 percent of the economically active population were employed in agriculture, and 94 percent of the landowners held only 8 percent of the cultivated land. As a result of the land decree, by June 1970 one-third or 30 million acres (12 million hectares) of Bolivia's total agricultural lands of 89 million acres (36 million hectares) had been distributed to some 272,811 families.[4] Along the way, however, the reform encountered major problems. The recompensation policy did not always work because, once peasants had their land, payments to former owners ceased. And the agrarian reform did not prevent uneconomic *minifundios* (small subsistence farms), a severe decline in agricultural productivity, the chronic scarcity of operating capital, and irregular and slow transfer of titles. Nevertheless, the new policy broke the power of the traditional landed oligarchy dependent on the prerevolutionary hacienda system of captive peasant labor. Rural power and class relations were never quite the same again.

Other revolutionary measures addressed economic development, a main goal of the MNR's original political program and of the modernizing leadership now in power. On January 20, 1953, an educational reform law promised universal education for all, especially in the neglected countryside. The government began construction of major communication arteries (such as the Cochabamba–Santa Cruz road) and encouraged migration into the country's rich but underpopulated tropical and subtropical areas, especially Santa Cruz. Most development projects were realized through extensive infusion of U.S. economic assistance, primarily food aid ($5 million in July 1953 alone) under Public Law 480. Saddled with a bankrupt economy unable to finance development, the MNR grasped at foreign assistance despite the external interference it entailed.

Aid from the United States was conditioned on official moderation of the revolution's economic nationalism and, in one way or another, influenced the MNR to compensate the powerful tin barons in June 1953, to repay depression loans outstanding since 1931, and to approve a new petroleum code in October 1953. The latter sanctioned the development and exploitation of rich tropical oil resources by U.S. corporations. In 1955, Gulf Oil set up operations, and nine other North American oil companies followed. Because the Bolivian government was desperate for the technical skills and operating capital necessary to establish a national petroleum industry, U.S. aid exerted particular leverage in favor of private investment and against funding for the Bolivian State Petroleum Enterprise (YPFB). A massive aid package, which made Bolivia the largest Latin American recipient of U.S. foreign aid ($100 million by 1960), was tied to the International Monetary Fund's (IMF) draconian stabilization program of 1956.[5] If foreign aid guaranteed the shortrun survival of the MNR revolution, it was survival on U.S. terms. Thus the choice between revolutionary economic nationalism and liberal economic dependency became one of pragmatism. As more hard choices followed, the pattern of pragmatism over principle became second nature, ultimately destroying the MNR coalition and co-opting the people's revolution.

The MNR's Governing Style

The party's organization and penetration of key postrevolutionary interest groups—the army, labor movement, and campesinos—was equally critical to the character and future of the revolution. The question of what to do with the army was an early source of dissension within the MNR. The moderates favored reform; the radicals wanted it disbanded and replaced by the revolutionary militias that had formed somewhat spontaneously during the revolution and remained under nominal MNR control. President Paz decided to reorganize the traditional army but to shift military power to peasant and worker militias in an attempt to subordinate the military to civilian authority. The army was reduced in size and importance, and its overall mission was altered. Although pro-MNR officers who had retired after 1947 were reinstated, the officer corps was reduced by 20 percent and forces were cut from 20,000 to 5,000 men. Redirected into such developmental tasks as road construction, colonization, and agricultural production, the new Bolivian army became one of the first "civic action" militaries in Latin America.[6]

The MNR, well aware that a hostile army had kept it from power between 1947 and 1952, also began to politicize and proselytize the new army. Like other sectors of society, the MNR established party organizational cells in the military and favored pro-MNR officers in promotions and assignments. Although the army grew steadily after 1956, the coercive power of the government (when in party hands) lay in MNR popular militias until 1970. The frequent confrontation of progovernment and antigovernment militias was a normal, but divisive, consequence.

The MNR also organized and struggled to control grassroots centers of political power in peasant associations and labor organizations, or *sindicatos*. Through these organizations, many of which were linked to or even formed by MNR cadres, the party attempted to institutionalize the Bolivian Revolution in the manner of the Mexican Revolution. The MNR model hoped to consolidate the broad populist alliance of the middle class, peasants, miners, and unionized workers of the revolution into an MNR-dominant state, like the one-party dominant system of Mexico's Institutional Revolutionary Party (PRI). A key strategy in the governing plan was cogovernment (*cogobierno*)—that is, powersharing between the MNR and influential labor left. But cooperation between the moderate MNR and radical unionists proved too difficult in practice; and after 1956, when the MNR-labor alliance began to deteriorate, the MNR as a party began to unravel as well.

Labor was critical to political success. Days after the revolution, the Bolivian Labor Central (Central Obrera Boliviana, or COB) was created to represent the "general voice of Bolivian labor." Through the COB nearly all labor became affiliated with the MNR: the miners, and the factory, construction, white collar, and transportation workers. The largest single union within the COB was the mine workers' union, the FSTMB (with some 52,000 members in 1960), headed by Juan Lechín, the executive secretary of both the FSTMB and the COB. Though affiliated with the MNR, the COB remained independent; but so long as Lechín remained both influential with the unions and on good terms with the MNR (he was the MNR minister of mines from 1952 to 1956), the party could count on COB support. Moreover, in the first MNR cabinet each of the major unions controlled an appropriate government ministry: the mine workers controlled the Ministry of Mines; the factory workers, the Ministry of Labor; and the railroad workers, the Ministry of Public Works.[7]

The MNR hold over labor always remained partial—among other reasons, because party organization was weak at the local level. The party leadership consisted of several hundred members and a nine-member core group in the National Political Committee, the central executive organ. Party chapters on the regional level and departmental command centers controlled and coordinated the supporting interest groups of labor and campesinos. In the labor sector, party leaders were subordinate to union leaders who reported directly to national COB headquarters, thereby circumventing the MNR's functional command centers at the shop steward level. In the mines the parallel control structure of union leaders versus the MNR party organizers was most pronounced. At the root of this structural dualism was the COB's combative "class struggle" ideology and the radical influence of leftist political parties (PIR, POR, and PCB) within the Bolivian Labor Central. Labor radicals rejected the MNR's multiclass rhetoric and insisted that only true unionists would protect working-class interests against the encroachments of the MNR's middle-class mainstream. Party-labor co-government, therefore, meant labor autonomy vis-à-vis the government at all times. Depending upon political circumstances, this alliance might translate into warm support or bitter opposition. As one scholar observed, "through the COB, the labor left became a government within the government."[8] After 1956, as the MNR lost influence within the COB, its strategy of control sought to exploit ideological and class divisions within labor. In weakening labor, however, the party undermined its own sociopolitical base.

In contrast to the major difficulties for labor posed for the MNR, the new peasant landowners became a conservative political force easily manipulated by peasant leaders (caciques) and MNR rural organizers. The MNR, through the COB, loosed organizing teams onto the countryside to preempt activity by the radical PIR party, which had been influential in peasant unionization since the 1940s. In addition, the revolutionary MNR government founded and financed the National Confederation of Peasant Workers of Bolivia (Confederación Nacional de Trabajadores Campesinos de Bolivia, or CNTCB) and placed Ñuflo Chávez Ortiz, a member of COB and an MNR peasant organizer, as head of the new Ministry of Peasant Affairs. Through this ministry some 7,500 rural peasant syndicates were created by late 1960. Nevertheless, MNR penetration did not extend below the local administrative unit, and party cells reached only the provincial capitals. Although overlapping union and party leadership helped cement ties to the MNR, the peasantry at large remained inherently suspicious of political parties. The CNTCB seemed an instrument of government control rather than an effective lobbying organ for peasant demands.

Critics faulted the MNR for merely replacing landlords in the traditional patronage system with party men and government-sponsored syndicates. In short, the old patrimonial attitude toward the peasants persisted and was inherent in "new" structures formed from the top down. Peasant organizations, such as the labor unions, were affiliated with the MNR but remained basically autonomous. As with labor, interleadership struggles within the campesino movement were manipulated by the MNR to contain the potentially powerful peasant majority.[9] Whether the MNR's "corporatist" organizational style fragmented peasant solidarity or merely took advantage of an existing situation remains unclear. Nevertheless, by 1956 a divisive governing strategy appeared to be fundamental to the nature of the MNR and its populist politics gone awry.

As endemic divisions within the MNR surfaced during the economic stabilization crisis of 1956–1960, the conservatives of the party pitted one popular sector against another—campesinos against miners and labor, or labor against miners. When necessary, the party even turned labor against itself, manipulating the rank and file vis-à-vis the leadership or one labor union against another. This "divide and conquer" governing strategy, intended to maintain and control a loyal support base for the government, instead worked to fragment the MNR's heterogeneous class coalition. In a sense the MNR was the victim of its multiple personalities: one radical, socialist, and lower class; the other moderate, liberal, and middle class. If heterogeneity was a key MNR strength before the revolution, afterward it became a schizophrenia that tore the party in two.

The new electoral reforms contributed to the problem of stable and democratic party rule in that governments without a governing majority now became commonplace. The postrevolutionary "explosion of participation" brought mass politics, with its bubbling cauldron of popular demands—so different from the elitist, country-club system of the past. The MNR sought to keep its balance in this new, less predictable political game by means of a broad-based populist strategy and manipulative governing techniques. For example, the MNR "parceled out" government ministries to powerful interest groups to buy party loyalty. In this manner, job patronage—like organizational autonomy—worked to woo key interests. Yet despite such strategies, the MNR never built a cohesive party; it "simply supplied a party label which legitimized interest-group claims to fragments of governmental power."[10] If the MNR had succeeded in forging a united party out of its tenuous coalition of factions, the story of the revolution might have been different. But severely split itself, it became too weak to stem the political and economic chaos of fragmentation and too corrupt to forego the short-term opportunism of rule. In 1956, severe economic crisis, U.S. interference, and ideological and personality struggles brought an end to MNR populism and its system of largesse. As the pie of favors shrank and some interest groups prospered at the expense of others, the MNR coalition disintegrated. The presidency of Hernán Siles Zuazo and IMF stabilization marked this process.

Fragmentation of the MNR

From its founding, the MNR reflected three major tendencies and the personalities of key leaders: the more conservative nationalists identified with Hernán Siles Zuazo and Walter Guevara Arze; the more pragmatic activist reformers, with Víctor Paz Estenssoro; and the radical laborites, with Juan Lechín.[11] In order to appease all sectors of the party, a governing pact was worked out whereby each party personality would serve a presidential term. Paz held office from 1952–1956 and Siles from 1956–1960. Guevara Arze was promised the presidency in 1960 and Lechín, in 1964. Instead, because of a complicated series of events and the increasing fragmentation of the MNR, Paz was elected president in both 1960 and 1964. An irony of MNR history is that the continuation of Paz, accepted by the party majority in 1960 to prevent further fragmentation, actually split the party in 1964. A more immediate crisis was economic stabilization.

By 1956, inflation was holding the MNR hostage. The four years since the revolution had seen the money supply and the cost of living increase more than twenty times, severely restricting the government's ability to maneuver. Middle-class supporters of the party were especially hurt, whereas speculators were cashing in on the multiple money exchange. Party cross-pressures and U.S. influence convinced more conservative and pragmatic sectors of the MNR that an economic and political stabilization was essential to save the revolution. In August 1956, when Paz left the presidency, he created a Monetary Stabilization Commission advised by former U.S. banker, George Jackson Eder. Already directly financing Bolivian deficits, the United States refused to continue economic aid unless strict government controls on spending and other deflationary policies were introduced. With the IMF, the Eder mission imposed a stringent stabilization program that succeeded in cutting inflation within two years. The conservative, laissez-faire program reduced government spending, cut social welfare benefits and subsidies, trimmed bureaucracy, froze wages, and lifted all artificial controls on prices and monetary exchange. Although the MNR was an economic success, its political costs were insurmountable in the long run. Initially, the $25 million stabilization fund (provided by the United States) saved the MNR from a rightist coup by the FSB, but the price tag was further U.S. interference in Bolivian affairs.[12] Siles Zuazo, the new president, agreed to implement the unpopular economic plan when other MNR leaders expressed reluctance to become linked to economic austerity.

As Bolivians trudged to the polls in June 1956, four political parties sought victory—the MNR, FSB, PCB, and POR. But only the MNR's Siles and Ñuflo Chávez Ortiz (representing labor) had a chance. The FSB candidates (Oscar Unzaga de la Vega and Mario Gutiérrez Gutiérrez) did so well, however, that the FSB emerged as the second largest political party and the only viable opposition. The MNR attracted some 790,000 votes (83 percent) and the FSB, 130,000 (17 percent), with an especially strong showing among urban, middle class whites. During his term Siles worked to strengthen middle-class support for the MNR by making the middle class the greatest beneficiary of his economic stabilization. There was intense FSB-MNR competition for the small middle-class vote at the expense of MNR relations with the labor movement.

Siles's new governing strategy intensified factionalism and ultimately hurt the party. He turned the middle class, peasantry, and military against labor, especially the miners. He also abolished MNR-labor cogovernment and centralized party administration under loyal middle-class functionaries in La Paz. When the COB announced a general strike for July 1957 against IMF austerity measures (imposed in January), the government successfully divided labor so that progovernment unions (the Bloque Reestructurador) opposed the strike order of Lechín. Not only was the labor movement weakened overall by the split, but Lechín—the sole MNR influence over labor in the past—was besieged in COB as both radical unionists and conservative Silistas tried to unseat him. President Siles also tried to curb unrest in the mines by means of distinctive personal tactics (later to become his trademark)—hunger strikes and resignation threats. When these failed, he ordered the revitalized army in 1959 and again in 1960 to quell warring peasant militias. As the Siles "divide and conquer" strategy replaced the MNR's earlier "unite and distribute" policy, the party's mass support base continued to disintegrate.[13]

The dynamics of factionalism were inherent in the individualism of MNR politicians as well. Economic austerity and the crackdown on labor had simply encouraged the worst of these tendencies. In 1957, the National Political Committee denounced two newly formed MNR factions: the more conservative Action in Defense of the MNR (Acción de Defensa del MNR) and a radical anti-Lechín group, the National Left of the MNR (Izquierda Nacional del MNR). In 1958, Lechín and Chávez (vice-president until he resigned to protest economic stabilization) organized the Leftist Sector of the MNR (Sector Izquierda del MNR) as labor's opposition voice in Congress. Another party split occurred in 1960, when Walter Guevara Arze, unfairly passed over for the presidency, defected, formed the Authentic MNR (MNR Auténtico or MNRA, which later became the Authentic Revolutionary Party or Partido Revolucionario Auténtico, PRA), and ran as its presidential candidate. The MNR majority, however, supported the Paz-Lechín ticket to placate internal and external forces. Paz seemed the only viable candidate to bridge party dissension and maintain U.S. support; and to guarantee labor peace, it was necessary to offer Lechín the vice-presidency. Thus, in the 1960 elections the MNR leadership tilted leftward from the conservative Siles-Guevara axis to that of Paz and Lechín. In 1962, another MNR faction developed—the Front of Nationalist Unity (Frente de Unidad Nacionalista)—headed by José Fellmann Velarde, minister of education in the second Paz government.

The formation of the Sector Pazestenssorista, a personalist lobby to reelect Paz for the third time in 1964, opened a major party rift and ended in military intervention. A constitutional amendment in 1961 permitted an incumbent president to run again; but, according to the MNR leadership pact, Lechín was to be president in 1964. However, Lechín was unacceptable to the United States and to conservative MNR supporters. Moreover, the party leadership was already nervous about several coup attempts and the failed FSB revolt in April 1959. Personal rivalry proved critical in the final showdown, which many blamed on the excessive political ambition of Paz. Betrayed, Lechín deserted the party to form the Revolutionary Party of the Nationalist Left (Partido Revolucionario de la Izquierda Nacionalista, or PRIN). Siles also defected and organized the remaining anti-Paz factions into the Bloc for the Defense of the Revolution (Bloque de Defensa de la Revolución). Both Siles and Lechín boycotted the May elections. Abandoned by two-thirds of the party, Paz acceded to pressure from the military cell of the MNR to select as his running mate their leader, Air Force General René Barrientos Ortuño. Ninety days after both assumed office, Barrientos aborted the last revolutionary MNR government.

RESTORING THE REVOLUTION?
RETURN TO MILITARY RULE

The second presidential term of Paz Estenssoro did not end MNR factionalism. Paz continued the economic and political policies of Siles although he was allied with Lechín. Stringent economic measures and "fiscalization" of COMIBOL under the Triangular Plan—a precondition of $30 million in aid from the United States, West Germany, and the Inter-American Development Bank—provoked chronic unrest in the mines. The government declared a state of siege. Political party agitation by the FSB, Auténticos, and the POR aggravated the MNR confrontation with labor. Paz attempted to salvage the revolution with vigorous economic development programs financed by $205 million in U.S. economic assistance from 1961 to 1964. Official strategy counted on an increase in the economic pie to avoid bitter battles over distribution and on a new class of MNR technocrats (*técnicos*) to depoliticize competing class interests and impose administrative order.[14] However, when growing social unrest defied managerial expertise, the MNR relied increasingly on the military to guarantee social peace.

By 1964, the MNR had fully prepared the way for the return of the military to power. The party had decimated its mass base among the workers, alienated the middle class by incessant partisan bickering, and elevated the military to a new position of prominence. On November 3, 1964, General Alfredo Ovando Candia, whom Paz had appointed commander-in-chief of the army in August 1963, and Vice-President Barrientos moved against the splintered MNR government. Although Siles and Lechín supported the military coup, termed the so-called Restorative Revolution (Revolución Restauradora), within months both were exiled, as Paz had been. Of the original MNR revolutionary strongmen, only Guevara Arze and the Auténticos survived as a token of MNR complicity with the "Second Republic" of Barrientos.

Barrientos: "General of the People"

The military rationalized its tenancy of the presidential palace as protective guardianship of the revolution. The unpopular Paz reelection had united the diffuse opposition to MNR corruption and dictatorial tactics. Days before the coup, the political climate was agitated. On October 29, the miners of Huanuni-Catavi clashed violently with the army in Oruro and the government used force against striking teachers and students of San Andrés University in La Paz. The Cochabamba garrison—loyal to Barrientos—rebelled, and major army units around the country speedily backed them. On November 4, President Paz, deserted by the army and reluctant to raise the popular militias, chose exile in Lima. A military cabinet, which included Colonel Juan José Torres and Colonel Hugo Banzer Suárez (two important military figures for the 1970s), was sworn in on November 5. Barrientos, alone or alternately with General Ovando, headed the junta between 1964 and 1966, until Barrientos was elected constitutional president in July 1966.

Barrientos, a flamboyant Bolivian general, cultivated a direct, populist leadership style that won over the peasant masses, especially in his native Cochabamba valley. Fluent in Quechua, he spent half his time in the countryside culling rich personal alliances with powerful peasant leaders. In this way he replaced institutionalized MNR party populism with fiery charismatic populism formalized in the Military-Campesino Pact of 1966. This alliance of two powerful conservative forces (the military and the peasantry) constituted the bedrock of military rule well into the 1970s. To cement the pact, Barrientos and subsequent military presidents bought the loyalty of the military with lavish defense spending and special privileges, and that of the peasantry with public displays of land redistribution. Moreover, via the pact, the military guaranteed peasants the fruits of agrarian reform; and in return, peasant caciques, directly and personally linked to Barrientos, supported the military's national security policy against social unrest and leftist sub-version. A nominally independent campesino bloc, the Peasant Confed-eration (Confederación de Campesinos) of numerous autonomous and competitive organizations, unfortunately often served to intimidate the military government's political opponents.

Barrientos's rule was institutionally weak. His political coalition excluded labor and the MNR majority, and ignored the conservative FSB. He created a new political party, the Popular Christian Movement (Movimiento Popular Cristiano, or MPC), which lacked both ideological and organizational coherence. To broaden its popular base for the 1966 elections, the MPC temporarily incorporated the Peasant Confederation, the PRA, the PIR, and the Social Democratic Party (Partido Social Demócrata, or PSD) of Luis Siles Salinas, the vice-presidential candidate, into the Bolivian Revolutionary Front (Frente de la Revolución Boliviana, or FRB). The FRB polled 54 percent of the 1,265,750 votes, compared to 11 percent by the FSB coalition known as the Christian Democratic Community and 12 percent by two MNR groups, the MNR Pazestens-sorista and the MNR Andradista (the MNR Silista and the MNR Unificado abstained). Blank protest ballots cast by several leftist parties (the PRIN, the POR, and a sector of the PCB) were 5 percent of the vote. The leftist National Liberation Front received some 3 percent of the vote, and the old prerevolutionary reactionary parties, the PURS and Liberals, less than 1 percent. The bulk of Barrientos's support represented the rural peasant vote, with only 16 percent from urban areas.[15] Nevertheless, like most military rulers, Barrientos ultimately became frustrated by the multiparty system and decreed a unitary official party, the Partido Unico, in the summer of 1968; then, in December, he eschewed constitutional appearances altogether for open repression.

The Barrientos government encouraged the development of a new Rosca, or ruling class, of medium-mining entrepreneurs, industrialists, big importers, and agro-businessmen and their foreign allies. A new investments code in 1965 encouraged foreign investments by Gulf Oil and U.S. Steel. The Triangular Plan continued in the mines, where miners' real wages and benefits were reduced by half. While the military-run COMIBOL showed its first profit in 1966, this achievement was the result of bloody military-miner confrontations in March, May, and September 1965 and the infamous San Juan Massacre of June 1967 in the Catavi–Siglo XX mining complex. The new policy of "disciplining labor" decapitated union leadership and destroyed labor autonomy. More than a hundred activists, including Lechín, were exiled, and the FSTMB and the COB were "intervened," or placed under military administrative control. Although the economy grew by nearly 4 percent annually between 1965 and 1968, costs were high—namely, an unbalanced budget, increased foreign debt, and intensive exploitation of natural resources by foreign interests.

Politically, despite preservation of certain revolutionary reforms, Barrientos preferred conservative policies. The military institution, a product of U.S. counterinsurgency theory and training, treated all political opposition, whether leftist or not, as communist subversion. The counterinsurgency war against the Cuban guerrilla *foco* (center of guerrilla insurgency) established by Ernesto "Ché" Guevara in inaccessible southeastern jungles demanded close cooperation among the Bolivian military, the U.S. Department of Defense, and the CIA. After the death of Ché in October 1967, Barrientos's hold on the government slipped. If he had not died unexpectedly in a helicopter crash on April 27, 1969, some believed that he would have been removed by a military coup. In the interim months, civilian Vice-President Siles held office; but the next decade of Bolivian political history was one of military, not civilian, rule.

Move to the Left: Ovando and Torres

After the death of Barrientos, the political climate deteriorated rapidly as the political parties, especially a resurgent MNR and the FSB, struggled for influence with a restive military. Announcing "national pacification," General Alfredo Ovando Candia unseated President Siles on September 26, 1969. The silent power behind the throne, Ovando was the antithesis of Barrientos: A nationalist reformer intrigued by the Peruvian military model of "revolution from above," he organized a new civilian-military cabinet of the "national left." This government reversed the Barrientos policies. Labor unions were permitted to reorganize, miners were reemployed and their wages increased, and civil liberties were restored. Most important, Bolivian Gulf Oil Company, a subsidiary of U.S. Gulf Oil, was nationalized on October 17. These measures, though indisputably popular, created serious internal and external problems for the Ovando interregnum.

Except for the divided military, the Ovando government lacked a defined political base and never managed to organize its diffuse leftist supporters into a viable coalition. The military government relied on a group of young reformers who did not command the following of the major political parties: Marcelo Quiroga Santa Cruz, minister of mines; José Ortiz Mercado, minister of planning; Alberto Bailey Gutiérrez, minister of information; and Mariano Baptista Gumucio, minister of education. Suspicious of these civilian reformers, the military forced many to resign. Ovando became the reluctant mediator of the widening civilian-military rift. In July 1970, the needless deaths of nearly seventy university students, who had joined the National Liberation Army (Ejército de Liberación Nacional, or ELN) in an abortive guerrilla foco at Teoponte northeast of La Paz, further undermined Ovando's reformist experiment. Political party leaders complained because elections were postponed, and labor's hardline demands seemed excessive to military conservatives and private entrepreneurs already up in arms over economic nationalism and the seizure of Gulf Oil.

Opposition to the 1955 "Davenport" Petroleum Code was long-standing. Approved under the revolutionary MNR government to attract foreign capital investment in Bolivia's southeastern oil resources, the code distributed 11 percent of all profits to Santa Cruz department (where the wells were located) and 33 percent to the central government. This schedule was maintained under Barrientos even after the companies began exporting about 30,000 barrels daily via Chilean ports. As late as 1970, although similar agreements between Latin governments and foreign companies provided no more than a 50 percent profit remittance to national authorities, the code remained unpopular. The same profit schedule, approved by Barrientos for Gulf's natural gas exports, and a pipeline contracted to export gas to Argentina were fiercely opposed. In 1975, the U.S. Senate's MacKay Commission revealed that Gulf Oil contributions in 1966 had allowed Barrientos to acquire a helicopter. Gulf payoffs to Bolivian officials were believed to total $1.8 million.[16] Despite the justifiable nationalistic ire behind its takeover, Gulf (and the major oil producers) retaliated with a boycott of Bolivian crude. The Ovando government lost $14.4 million in oil revenues. The U.S. government, although it did not officially invoke the Hickenlooper Amendment, reduced aid to Bolivia by 75 percent between 1969 and 1970. In September 1970, shortly before his fall, Ovando pledged a generous $78 million compensation to Gulf.[17]

General Rogelio Miranda's abortive coup on October 4, 1970, led to President Ovando's resignation two days later. A conservative military triumvirate (which had refused to recognize Miranda) was established but rapidly stepped aside when radical supporters installed General Juan José Torres as the new president on October 7. The ten-month rule of Torres aggravated the basic dilemmas of military-led "revolution from above." The political system became polarized over Torres's socialist model of development and the capitalist model of Barrientos, Siles, and

Paz. At issue was the radicalization of the Bolivian revolution and a reduced U.S. role. The democratic opening to the left and the spontaneous mobilization of Marxist groups could not be contained within the structures of established parties and unions. Radicals in the new Popular Assembly urged Torres (much as the COB had earlier urged Ovando) to deepen the revolution. To the conservative wing of the military this "anomic" populism proved "communist" control over the Torres government and justified plots for its overthrow. Under conflicting political pressures, Torres moved to radicalize the revolution.

Torres pursued policy goals similar to Ovando's, but with greater zeal: economic nationalism, agrarian reform, industrialization, labor autonomy, and foreign policy independence. He established relations with the socialist bloc and in April pardoned imprisoned guerrillas (such as Regis Debray) of the Ché Guevara and Teoponte focos. On April 30, Torres cancelled the U.S. lease of the Matilda zinc mine. Finally, on May Day, 50,000 demonstrators opened the new Popular Assembly (Asamblea Popular) consisting of delegates from labor, peasant unions, and pro-Torres political parties.

The Assembly, dominated by labor radicals and leftists of many ideological persuasions, elected Lechín its president and adopted the Trotskyist program of Guillermo Lora's POR. The pro-Moscow and pro-Peking communist parties, Lechín's PRIN, a unified Siles-Paz MNR group, the Revolutionary Christian Democratic Party (Partido Demócrata Cristiano Revolucionario, or PDCR), which had split from the Christian Democrats, and two new parties of the left were all represented in the Assembly. The latter were the Leftist Revolutionary Movement (Movimiento de Izquierda Revolucionaria, or MIR) of Jaime Paz Zamora, a dissident group of the PDCR; and the Socialist Party (Partido Socialista, or PS), which under Marcelo Quiroga Santa Cruz united several left factions in a program of socialism, popular proletarian rule, and revolution of national liberation. The Assembly's June plenary session approved forceful resolutions to oust the U.S. Peace Corps, nationalize middle and small mining enterprises, reestablish worker control in the mines, and rearm peoples' militias. However, while the Assembly was wrangling over ideology and revolutionary purity, impatient workers took over private mines and a Maoist-influenced peasant group (Unión de Campesinos Pobres, or UCAPO) seized an agribusiness plantation in Santa Cruz. Kidnappings and violence, reportedly committed by the National Liberation Army, and the radical student takeover of the United States Information Agency's (USIA) Bolivian-American Center in La Paz emboldened the divided political opposition to unite and strike against Torres.

Hugo Banzer Suárez, head of the army's military college, attempted a coup in January 1971 but failed. The fragmented MNR also moved to the right and, after the Paz and Siles factions signed a unity pact in Lima, began to plot with the FSB and the anti-Torres military factions. Between August 19 and August 21, 1971, Colonel Banzer secretly entered Bolivia from exile in Argentina. As he was being taken to La Paz for questioning, a successful insurgency broke out in Santa Cruz. It was no accident that the Santa Cruz regiment initiated the revolt, given that the rebellion was financed by both Cruceño elites and Brazil. Cautiously, other regiments in the country fell into line. In La Paz, however, bloody worker and student resistance—perhaps the bloodiest since the revolution—had to be quashed by troops from the Miraflores barracks. On August 22, Banzer became the new president. Conservative military rule was back and the radical populist experiment finally over.

Move to the Right: Banzer

Seven years of Banzer's rule reintroduced conservative Barrientos-style policies, but under the unique condition of exceptional economic growth and prosperity. Just as Argentina's Perón and Bolivia's military reformers Busch and Villarroel were heroes for Barrientos, and Ovando and Torres were influenced by the Peruvian generals' "revolution from above," President Banzer patterned his rule on the model of the neighboring Brazilian military. In contrast to earlier military populism, Banzer's governing style was elitist and authoritarian. The government represented the new economic elites in mining, business, petroleum, and agribusiness. It repressed labor, peasants, and students. Politically, Banzer's rule relied on conservative military institutionalists and powerful external actors such as the United States and Brazil. The government had brief party backing from the Popular Nationalist Front (Frente Popular Nacionalista, or FPN)—a curious alliance of the Paz faction of the MNR and the FSB of Mario Gutiérrez. Nevertheless, by November 1974, a personalist dictatorship was in place. Banzer's ideology typified that of many frustrated military authoritarians who repressed all political life in the name of progress. Social peace and order, even by the barrel of a gun, were essential to Banzer's narrowly shared economic boom.

The social base of the Banzer government comprised the newly prosperous middle and upper classes represented by the National Association of Medium-Sized Mine Enterprises and the Bolivian Confederation of Private Entrepreneurs, as well as the powerful regional elites of Santa Cruz, who had grown rich in commercial rice, sugar, and cotton production. The government's capitalist sympathies were as obviously reflected in its economic policies as in its supporters. Private investors approved of regulations that froze wages but permitted prices to rise freely. Foreign investors welcomed lenient investment laws, especially the new Petroleum Code, which attracted fifteen U.S. companies to open new explorations. Foreign banks demonstrated approval with numerous hefty loans. And the United States, relieved by Bolivia's return to "responsible" economic management and social order, increased military and economic assistance to the Banzer government, doubling and tripling the amounts provided previous governments. On October 27, 1972, moreover, the United States approved the devaluation of the Bolivian peso, despite the subsequent labor repression it entailed.[18]

Repression complicated by growing economic crisis led to the ultimate downfall of Banzer in 1977. As long as there was economic prosperity, the middle class tolerated Banzer's authoritarianism; but the lower classes were initially cowed by force, and the military was preoccupied by internal divisions. Earlier, several coup attempts had been thwarted by heavy-handed measures, even murder and disappearances, such as the mysterious death of Colonel Andrés Selich in May 1973. Although the FSTMB congresses in December 1972 and November 1973 reelected Lechín as general secretary, the government would not permit the reestablishment of the COB. By early 1974, dissent had increased. In January, the Cochabamba peasant leagues blocked roads to protest high food prices. One hundred peasants were killed in that confrontation, termed the Massacre of Tolata, the first major bloodletting between peasant and military since 1952.[19] Thus, on February 12, the government hastened to renew the traditional Military-Peasant Pact, which had dominated the peasantry by pro-government leaders. In May, intellectuals heatedly protested the "sell-out" of Bolivian natural gas under a proposed agreement with Brazil. And on June 4, the Tarapacá Regiment of the capital launched an abortive predawn coup. Scores of younger officers were demoted or sacked. Nevertheless, on November 7, a final coup attempt marked Banzer's authoritarian clamp-down.

Political parties were also restive. With those on the left banned outright, what remained was only the unstable and unrepresentative FPN coalition composed of the MNR, the FSB, and the military. In policymaking, both the MNR and the FSB were basically ignored by the military; but to maintain this historically incongruous alliance intact, each party controlled its fiefdom of cabinet ministries. Both parties were seriously factionalized. When the MNR ousted Hernán Siles from a 1972 party congress, he formed his Chilean-based MNR-Left (MNR-Izquierda, or MNRI) from exile. In November 1973, Paz left the FPN and on January 8, 1974, was also exiled. Greedy for political spoils, other MNR factions sold out to Banzer; but in November 1974, all party activity was banned. The FSB split into a majority faction loyal to party chief

Gutiérrez and into Santa Cruz dissidents under Carlos Valverde. Although partisan bickering contributed to Banzer's "self-coup" (auto-golpe) of November 9, the parties had briefly provided the government a semblance of democracy.

After the "self-coup," the Banzer government ruled by naked military force. When textile workers and the FSTMB struck on November 11, troops occupied factories and mines and stayed four years. A Compulsory Civil Service Law forced out all popularly elected union officials and replaced them with government-appointed "coordinators." Only the miners organized effective resistance to military intervention, inasmuch as the government, fearing excessive bloodletting, had not removed their legitimate union officials. Strikes and unsanctioned union activism were banned. Despite troops in the mines, defiant miners struck in January 1975, June 1976, and December 1977.[20] Their heroic example soon spread to the rest of labor.

By 1977, political pressure for democracy had become intense. In Washington, the new Carter administration championed human rights abroad, especially in Latin America. At home, Banzer's foreign policy campaign in the Chile-Bolivia seacoast dispute had failed and no longer distracted public attention from the regime's domestic problems. Hoping for compromise, the government announced a partial amnesty in January 1977 and elections in 1980. But in November, unrest forced Banzer to promise to retire at the end of the year and to advance elections to July 1978. In early December, he decided against reelection in favor of the official candidate, General Juan Pereda Asbún. As opposition continued, broad national support for a hunger strike in the cathedral of La Paz, begun at the end of December by a handful of miners' wives and children, forced the government to reconsider amnesty. On January 24, 1978, Banzer's minister of the interior decreed complete unconditional amnesty for exiled or imprisoned political dissidents and labor leaders. Now the people could prepare for the polls.

THE MOVE TOWARD DEMOCRACY

In Bolivia elections can be major catalysts of change. By 1978, after eleven years without a constitutionally elected president, the demand for democratic elections was irrepressible. However, when elections in 1978, 1979, and 1980 were sullied by fraud and military intervention, advanced political decay set in. Cynically appropriating the mantle of the revolution, corrupt generals imposed one authoritarian government after another on Bolivia's social malaise. Military degradation culminated in the genocidal cocaine mafia of General García Meza. Militarism remained the dominant pattern until 1982, when Hernán Siles Zuazo assumed office as Bolivia's legally elected civilian president. Four chaotic years and nine presidents later, civilians returned to power. Unfortunately, the 1989 election of a third civilian president addressed few of the chronic problems confronting the country: debt, drugs, and death of the revolution.

Thwarted Elections

On July 9, 1978, twenty political parties, organized around seven presidential candidates, participated in elections; but two coalitions— the Peoples Nationalist Union (Unión Nacionalista del Pueblo, or UNP) of Pereda Asbún and the Democratic and Popular Unity Front (Frente de Unidad Democrática y Popular, or FUDP) of Siles Zuazo—attracted the majority of votes.[21] The blatantly fraudulent elections (according to international observers) gave Pereda 987,140 popular votes, Siles 484,383, and Paz Estenssoro 213,622 from the 1,971,968 total votes counted. Although Pereda had stolen the FSB-controlled lowland and southeastern departments, the highland vote was shared by Siles and Paz. Amid the vehement public outcry of fraud, the opposition parties and, surprisingly, the winner himself demanded that the National Electoral Tribunal annul the results. Apparently afraid that new elections and President Banzer's plans to hand the reins over to the military on August 6 could be the end of him, Pereda seized power on July 21 in a bloodless coup staged in Santa Cruz and Cochabamba. When Pereda promised elections in six months and then postponed them until May 1980, opposition parties rose up against his brief four-month rule.

General David Padilla Arrancibia, Pereda's commander of the army and supporter, launched a countercoup on November 24, 1978. Thus Pereda proved equally unpopular to both civilians and military. Siles and Paz acquiesced in the Padilla takeover and called off a threatened demonstration by the MNRI, MIR, PCB, and PS in Siles's Democratic Popular Unity coalition (Unidad Democrática y Popular, or UDP). Because young reformist officers in the Padilla cabinet seemed determined to protect the institutional integrity of the armed forces and to tolerate broader political participation, the only meaningful critics were a re-actionary FSB faction and the radical COB. Ultimately, Padilla's caretaker transition, having repulsed several coup attempts, ushered the country into the 1979 elections as promised.

The 1979 presidential campaign was tumultuous and violent. Plagued by daily speculations of postponement, on July 1 some 1,600,000 voters (out of the 1,800,000 registered) witnessed the first relatively free elections since 1964. Major electoral reforms enacted by Padilla prevented the scandalous voter manipulation of 1978. There were new registration lists, a uniform identity card, and color-coordinated party symbols on voting sheets. At first, fifty-seven political groups registered, but on election day there were eight slates and only three serious candidates: the UDP–Siles; the MNR Alliance–Paz; and the Nationalist Democratic Action–Banzer (Acción Democrática Nacionalista, or ADN). On July 30, the electoral tribunal reported the UDP with 528,696 votes, the MNR with 527,184, and the ADN with 218,587.[22] No candidate had an absolute majority.

Congress, dominated by the MNR, was left to choose the winner. Yet, because of partisan intransigence, Congress failed to marshal the 73 deputies out of 144 needed to elect a president. Between July 31 and August 9, the protracted electoral crisis embarrassed the country internationally. Foreign dignitaries from around the world, including the U.S. first lady, Rosalynn Carter, were forced to forgo the August 6 celebration of Bolivia's return to democracy. At last, on August 8, Walter Guevara Arze, the new president of the Senate and leader of the Authentic Revolutionary Party (PRA), emerged as interim president for one year. Unfortunately, Guevara, the first civilian president in ten years, lacked support from the parties and the military, and was overthrown within three months by Colonel Alberto Natusch Busch.

The coup of November 1, 1979, was a bloody affair in which more than 200 people died. Moreover, the brevity of the repressive fifteen-day military interregnum proved the fierce popular determination for civilian rule. Even the military split into rival pro- and anti-coup factions. Dismissed from his command, General Padilla publicly condemned the coup and urged civilian resistance. The political parties, the national congress (which Natusch had dissolved), and the 1 million–member COB joined in a massive general strike. Natusch tried to drum up international support with groundless charges of "communist intervention," but the Carter White House, displeased by the chaos and repression, suspended $27.5 million in military and economic assistance on November 2. The coup speedily collapsed, and on November 16 Lydia Gueiler Tejada, president of the Chamber of Deputies, was unanimously chosen as Bolivia's first woman president.

In the interim before the 1980 election, President Gueiler confronted critical political and economic conditions. The second devaluation of the peso since Banzer's earlier devaluation became necessary. Another threat was the military. A coup-prone faction led by General Luis García Meza, former commander of the army under Natusch and Gueiler's cousin, was restless. On April 14, these hardliners imposed the appointment of García Meza as army commander, reversing President Gueiler's November decision to remove him from that post. García Meza championed the military's resentment of a civilian investigation into army corruption and manipulated pervasive conservative attitudes that the military alone could save the country from the "communists." At the head of an extremely repressive security apparatus trained, and financed by the reactionary Argentine military and powerful regional drug barons, the García Meza group eyed the upcoming elections with apprehension. On June 7, the commander of the presidential guard attempted a coup and the assassination of President Gueiler. When this failed to postpone elections for a year, however, there was another coup attempt on June 17. Nevertheless, the June 29 elections were held as planned.

Voter turnout was impressive. Of the 1.5 million votes cast (72 percent of the eligible voters), Siles won nearly 39 percent (507,173); Paz Estenssoro, 21 percent (263,706); and Banzer, 17 percent (220,309). Marcelo Quiroga Santa Cruz of the Socialist Party–One (Partido Socialista Uno, or PS-1) received some 9 percent of the vote (113,309). But as often happened in Bolivian elections, no candidate had an absolute majority, and it was up to Congress once again. This time Paz supporters, disappointed by the confused outcome of the 1980 elections, threw their vote to Siles. The strong likelihood of a "leftist" victory touched off the notorious García Meza coup.[23]

Years of the Generals

The military acted swiftly and ruthlessly on July 17, 1980. Killing, torture, prison, and exile were the rule of the day. Marcelo Quiroga Santa Cruz was murdered; Paz Estenssoro was placed under house arrest in Tarija; and Lechín was imprisoned and later exiled. Paramilitary forces seized the COB headquarters and dispatched, dead or alive, recalcitrant labor leaders. Comparing himself to President Pinochet of Chile, García Meza tore into Bolivia's "Marxist cancer" with a frenzy. During his year-long rule, mining towns were bombed, labor leaders were exterminated, the press was muzzled, and the Church and foreign journalists were harassed. Human rights groups in La Paz reported that at least 300 people were killed. The drug connection was blatant: Both García Meza and his minister of interior, Colonel Luis Arce Gómez, were internationally implicated in trafficking. The governments of the United States, the Andean Pact, and other Latin democracies refused to recognize the unsavory regime. Most foreign assistance (except for Argentinean aid) dried up. Bolivia became a pariah nation ruled by a military-cocaine mafia. Desperate to mend Bolivia's tattered international reputation and to secure vital economic assistance, the military high command forced out García Meza on August 4, 1981.

In the next fourteen months, two generals—Celso Torrelio Villa and Guido Vildoso Calderón—failed to reestablish civilian confidence

Ex-president and general Luis García Meza, author of the July 1980 "cocaine coup," is being tried by the Bolivian courts for human rights abuses and for robbing the country of millions of dollars (photo courtesy of John Enders and the Associated Press).

in the military although they did normalize relations with the United States and the international community. General Torrelio took control from a military triumvirate on September 4, 1981, but he was soon replaced by General Vildoso on July 21, 1982. Torrelio's installment precipitated an institutional crisis as Colonel Faustino Rico Toro, closely associated with the disreputable García Meza, attempted to seize power on July 17. These rapid personnel changes were merely cosmetic. According to the popular quip, "Vildoso is Torrelio is García Meza." General Vildoso could not contain the popular pressure for the reestablishment of constitutional rule any more than his predecessors had done. Announcements of elections in 1983 further inflamed labor and the political parties as waves of general strikes immobilized La Paz and major cities during August. On September 7, 50,000 people demonstrated for the return to civilian government, and on September 17, after only fifty-eight days in office, General Vildoso handed the government to the 1980 Congress.

The bicameral Congress revalidated the 1980 elections on September 23 and overwhelmingly elected Hernán Siles Zuazo president on October 5. Of the 157 deputies, 113 voted for Siles and 29 for General Banzer.[24] More than 100,000 Bolivians thronged the streets on October 8 to welcome Siles to La Paz. Then, on October 10, 1982, Siles was sworn in as the first legally elected civilian president after eighteen years of military rule. The generals were in retreat; but because of their bitter legacy, the struggle for democracy, economic reconstruction, and social development proved a truly formidable challenge for successive civilian governments.

CIVILIANS IN POWER

Although Bolivia returned to civilian rule in 1982, the reestablishment of substantial democracy was short-lived. Entering office in October 1982, Hernán Siles Zuazo announced a progressive program of "populist democracy." Despite improvements in human rights and social welfare, Siles failed to contain economic collapse and political instability. With a military coup imminent, Siles "voluntarily" stepped down one year early to preserve civilian government. In June 1985, Víctor Paz Estenssoro became president for the fourth time. This historic election marked the first peaceful transition between elected civilians in twenty-five years and the first peaceful transfer of power between opposition parties since independence. Although Paz Estenssoro promised a new solution to the national crisis, he soon instituted his "democracy with authority," a euphemism for old-style repression and counterrevolution. In August 1989, ex-dictator Hugo Banzer Suárez lost his bid as Bolivia's third civilian president to ex-radical Jaime Paz Zamora. Nevertheless, Banzer remained influential in the new govenment. The unexpected Paz Zamora–Banzer pact and its policy of "new pragmatism" proved yet again that the principles of the 1952 National Revolution were ancient history.

Populist Democracy: Siles

The three abbreviated years of the Siles presidency (1982–85) were dominated by a single intractable national crisis—the massive $5 billion foreign debt inherited from the military.[25] The Siles mandate represented a lesson in the monumental task of reconciling debt, democracy, and stability. Foreign creditors imposed on the debt crisis traditional economic formulas that only further aggravated the acute economic and political instability. Following a severe drought and devastating floods in 1983 and an IMF austerity program in 1984, 1.7 million Bolivians faced outright starvation. The harsh repayment terms threatened Siles's goal to fully reestablish civil liberties. Under such extreme conditions of economic hardship, containment of one of the most politicized and militant labor movements in Latin America, within the structure and spirit of democracy, proved virtually impossible. An inevitable choice between capitalist austerity and socialist populism confronted Siles.

Although six cabinets and seventy-five ministers had already exited the political scene by January 1985, this instability was not entirely the president's doing. The conservative opposition, consisting of MNR-Histórico (MNRH) and the ADN, controlled the National Assembly and routinely blocked government legislation, thereby forcing Siles to rule by executive decree. Once law, the presidential initiatives were indirectly attacked by opposition delegates, who impeached cabinet ministers and fomented constant cabinet upheaval. In Congress, moreover, the right devised the creative "constitutional coup" whereby the ADN and the MNRH, supported by dissidents of the MIR and the military, planned to vote Siles out and decree new elections. On the left, the endless squabbling over power and patronage in the UDP's center-left coalition—the MNR, the MIR, the PCB, and the Christian Democratic Party (Partido Demócrata Cristiano, or PDC) paralyzed the government ministries. Soon Siles's own MNRI divided into three factions, thus neutralizing the executive's control of the cabinet and its influence in the legislature. Often at odds with communist cabinet ministers over economic policy, the PCB also split. The MIR posed a unique dilemma inasmuch as Jaime Paz Zamora, the nephew of Paz Estenssoro, served both as party leader and as Siles's vice-president. In January 1983, only three months after the UDP victory, the MIR deserted the coalition for open opposition and, after temporary reconciliation in April 1984, withdrew again in December. Despite the partisan rift, Paz Zamora remained vice-president, but it was rumored that he was conspiring with the military to unseat Siles and become president himself.

The military played a pivotal role in the civilian plotting. Factionalized into conflicting tendencies (institutionalists, constitutionalists, liberals, progressives, rightists, conservatives, and hardliners), military men openly backed civilian dissidents and instigated rebellions. In 1983–1984, hardliners behind two former army colonels (Faustino Rico Toro and Norberto Salomón) implicated in narcotics traffic plotted a "cocaine coup" to curtail Siles's investigation of the military-drug connection. In June 1984, a rebellion by 200 officers of the Cochabamba Army Command School against the liberal, pro-Siles army commander General Simón Sejas Tordoya, was quashed. Colonel Rolando Saravia, the corrupt commander of the elite "Leopardos" (a select antinarcotics enforcement unit trained by the United States, and also known as the UMOPAR) nearly succeeded in the removal of Siles on June 30. The president was kidnapped and held for ten hours until U.S. Ambassador Edwin Corr secured his release.[26]

The labor-left, initially the backbone of the Siles-UDP coalition, soon became its Achilles' heel. Union unrest punctuated each of the seven austerity programs imposed by the government between November 1982 and May 1985. Moreover, Lechín's tutelage radicalized the COB after the MIR and the PCB (which was in and out of the cabinet) lost influence with the rank and file. There were 250 industry-wide strikes in 1983 and 6 crippling nationwide strikes in 1984. Extreme vacillation marked UDP-labor relations as Siles alternately took a hardline stance but then caved in to worker demands. This cycle of confrontation and compromise would repeat itself over and over again as workers demanded favorable wage and price policies, a moratorium on repayment of the foreign debt, and worker-state cogovernment. It became popular among Bolivians to blame governmental immobility and a deteriorating economy on Siles's incompetence. In reality, however, stalemate was the inevitable consequence of the clash between two relatively equal but opposed socioeconomic interests—the labor COB and the private sector represented by the Bolivian Confederation of Private Entrepreneurs (CEPB). This class conflict became more pronounced under the Paz government.

From 1983 to 1985, Siles vainly courted the COB to enter the UDP coalition, but COB's price was cogovernment or worker-state management of public enterprises. Although Siles brandished the carrot of cogovernment whenever the stick failed, he ultimately never agreed to it, except in COMIBOL. In April 1983, the Miners' Union (FSTMB) seized COMIBOL and imposed worker management despite UDP opposition, including that of the two communist labor and mining ministers (who divided the PCB and labor supporters by their action). On May Day, the COB leadership mobilized 80,000 workers behind the defiant miners. The government finally acquiesced to the fait accompli and reorganized COMIBOL under majority union control in July. Until the end of Siles's presidency, the miners "occupied" the company.

This labor success marked a turning point, and despite numerous official maneuvers, no truly lasting concessions were realized in the next two years. In August, Siles rebuffed demands by Lechín and peasant leader Genaro Flores to introduce cogovernment to the cabinet and other state-run enterprises. This anti-labor line dominated government policy in the months after the more conservative, middle-class Christian Democrats bolstered the UDP coalition in September. However, both the November 1983 and 1984 peso devaluations, which prompted a hunger strike by 4,000 workers and a three-week general strike respectively, forced cogovernment to be hauled out again. In February 1984, when Siles agreed to minimal wage increases, the CEPB called a 48-hour strike—the first private-sector strike in Bolivian history. In May 1984, Siles conceded to the COB's pressure to halt repayment on the foreign debt; and after another prolonged general strike in March 1985, he offered labor a voice in Congress, a privilege that had been denied the unions since the fall of Torres in 1971. By the spring of 1985, these concessions were largely irrelevant and only bought time.

By November 1984, the political situation was desperate: Another massive general strike had occurred; there were daily calls for Siles's immediate resignation and fears of an imminent army uprising. The Catholic Church intervened and mediated the crisis in what pundits dubbed the "ecclesiastical coup." With all his support evaporated and a drug scandal swirling around him, Siles agreed to early presidential elections (in May or June) and became a lame-duck president. The political parties launched into an immediate frenzy of campaigning. Those on the left, discredited by the UDP failure, fragmented. The MIR split into three subparties (one boycotted the elections); and the PCB broke into two feuding halves. On the right, the MNR of Paz Estenssoro and the ADN of Banzer anticipated a tight presidential race.

"Democracy with Authority": Paz Estenssoro

Despite postponement, numerous irregularities, and betting odds that a military coup would preempt elections, Bolivians finally went to the polls on July 17, 1985.[27] As in the past, myriad parties, most minor or "taxi" parties (so-called because all their members could meet in a taxi cab), registered by the April deadline. But after final accreditation the seventy-four political groups and five multiparty fronts had dwindled to only eighteen, and of these only two were serious contenders: Banzer's ADN and Paz Estenssoro's MNRH. The parties of the left failed to unify and were represented by two fronts: Lechín's Unitary Revolutionary Direction (Dirección Revolucionaria Unitaria, or DRU), and the Front of a United People (Frente del Puebo Unido, or FPU). Both the ruling MNRI and the MIR participated. Nearly half (2.9 million) of Bolivia's total population of 6.4 million were eligible to vote, but only 1.9 million registered and some 1.7 million actually voted. The urban vote favored Banzer and the greater rural peasant vote preferred Paz Estenssoro; but with the vote split about equally between cities and countryside, Banzer was able to neutralize the campesinos. In the end, because of Bolivian electoral law, the ADN plurality (29 percent) over the MNRH (26 percent) was insufficient to elect Banzer (see Table 4.1).

The upshot was that Congress, as often before, indirectly selected the president and its choice represented a real upset. The left proved critical; its mood was best expressed by Simón Reyes of the PCB: "Nothing unites us with Víctor Paz Estenssoro, yet everything separates us from Hugo Banzer."[28] On the second ballot a coalition of center-left and MNR–splinter parties in Congress served as swing votes, giving Paz Estenssoro a total of 94 electors against Banzer's 51. Although Banzer undoubtedly felt cheated of his victory, a rumored deal promising him a clear field in 1989, U.S. and Latin American pressure, and his long-term political future dictated that he acquiesce to the results.

TABLE 4.1

Voting Results for General Elections, July 14, 1985

Parties	Votes	Percent	Seats
ADN	493,735	28.57	51
MNRH	456,704	26.42	59
MIR	153,143	8.86	16
MNRI	82,418	4.77	8
MNRV	72,197	4.18	6
Totals	1,728,365	100.00	

Source: Hoy Internacional, August 8, 1985, p. 3.

Siles's political pitfalls provided Paz Estenssoro a compelling lesson about what not to do. At his inauguration on August 6, Paz announced "government with authority, and without anarchy." First, he forged broad legislative and interest-group support for his new policies, appointing only three bona fide MNR members to cabinet positions and selecting the rest on the basis of their political usefulness. Paz's second planning minister, Gonzalo Sánchez de Lozada, had been president of the Senate and (although he served as an independent) was a prominent member of the private sector's CEPB and of Paz's special economic team masterminding economic austerity. Then, on August 29, he revealed the centerpiece of his government, the New Economic Policy (Nueva Política Económica, or NPE). When the COB launched an indefinite nationwide strike on September 9, the government clamped down with a state of siege on September 19. Two hundred union leaders were arrested and exiled to jungle detention centers. For the next eight months, despite sporadic strikes, Paz kept labor virtually cowed.

Issued as executive Decree Law 21060, the stringent new austerity policy bypassed the legislature altogether. An attempt in Congress to repeal the draconian decree was beaten back by the government's legislative majority in both houses (the first time in years that a democratic executive exerted such control). Instead, martial law was approved for ninety days. The final piece of the Paz governing strategy, the October 16 "Pact for Democracy" between the MNR and ADN, merely formalized this legislative alliance. The pact of "cooperative action" between the two major parties provided Paz powerful political leverage throughout his term and guaranteed him the vital legislative majority whose absence had severely hampered Siles. In sum, Paz's policy of "democracy with authority" translated into a Bolivian-style "imperial presidency." However, as with Siles in November 1984, a drug connection scandal shook the Paz cabinet in March 1987, and later that December the MNR experienced severe setbacks in municipal elections. MNR stalwarts began to fear that Paz's unpopularity would prejudice the party in the upcoming presidential elections. General Banzer's formal announcement on July 2, 1988, of his presidential candidacy (Banzer was the first to announce, well in advance of the other candidates) further weakened the ADN-MNR pact. On the pretext that the ADN had refused to extend voter registration, the MNR terminated the pact in February 1989. Moreover, repeated rumors that octogenarian Paz's health was failing hampered executive leadership.

For the rest of his term, Paz's relations with labor, the private sector, and middle-class supporters also became tense and complex. In the best of times, the government's policies were compared to the ineffective "wait and see" tactics of Siles; and in the worst, to draconian military rule. For example, on August 28, 1986, Paz was forced to impose another state of siege to control more than 7,000 striking miners on a protest march to La Paz. Some 160 labor leaders were arrested. Days before, the government had reorganized COMIBOL, closing eleven mines and cashiering 13,000 mineworkers. Although government repression, firings, and the tin crisis weakened and demoralized the COB (particularly the FSTMB), labor stoppages nearly every month disrupted economic recovery from mid-1986 to mid-1989. In March 1988, a nationwide strike of petroleum workers threatened a military coup, and unrest by students led to a police invasion of the university. Despite significant improvements in inflation and international credit, the NPE did not meet most ex-pectations. Indeed, the costs to social welfare and blue-collar workers were staggering, compared to the lesser impact on white-collar job seekers and the dependent urban middle class, because traditional job patronage continued to swell public bureaucracies despite austerity. Because of gross unfairness in terms of who paid and how much for the New Economic Policy, class inequality and conflict greatly increased. Under Paz Estenssoro the ideal of a popular, majoritarian, political democracy became nonsense before the authoritarian, minority-imposed, economic austerity.

"Liberal Revolution": Paz Zamora

As Bolivians again geared up for elections, the top candidates were becoming known around the world as the "three look-alikes." Some observers predicted the victory of the 62-year-old former general and ex-dictator, Hugo Banzer, whom a cabinet minister described as "a gentle, intelligent dictator."[29] Indeed, the economy—not human rights nor even cocaine—was the main domestic campaign issue, and most Bolivians remembered the golden prosperity of high tin and petroleum prices during Banzer's presidency. As one chola interviewee said, "In his time, there was work and there was peace. Those who were jailed were involved in politics."[30] The MNR's candidate and Paz Estenssoro's favorite was 58-year-old former planning minister and architect of the NPE, Gonzalo Sánchez de Lozada. Popularly known as "Gony," Sánchez de Lozada with his "gringo accent" seemed more American than Bolivian. He had been raised in the United States and graduated from the University of Chicago. Another very strong contender was 50-year-old Jaime Paz Zamora, leader of the social democratic MIR–New Majority and vice-president in 1983. The May 1986 Electoral Law of the MNR-ADN had clearly done its job—first, by narrowing the field of parties running candidates to only nine and, then, by concentrating power in the hands of only three.

The final tally of the May 7, 1989, elections placed Sánchez de Lozada in a precarious lead with 23 percent of the 1.6 million votes cast (out of 2.1 million registered voters), Banzer with 22.6 percent, and Paz Zamora close behind with 19.6 percent.[31] More than a million potential voters did not register or cast ballots. And despite statements by the U.S. Embassy that these were "most impressive" elections, numerous irregularities were found that annulled nearly 10 percent of the votes (see Table 4.2). Because no single candidate had received the necessary 50 percent of the vote, the final decision of who would be Bolivia's 111th president was once again decided by the newly elected Congress—as many observers had predicted would be the case.

Although the three candidates were not so very different (if campaign promises and programs were any indication), as in 1985 a tense period ensued during which no one was very sure if a new president would be chosen. Paz Zamora's MIR operated as the "king maker," negotiating potential coalition deals first with the right-wing ADN and then with the ruling MNR. Some eighteen MIR congressmen initially refused to vote for a MIR-ADN alliance; but, in the end, the combination of congressional seats of the MIR, ADN, and CONDEPA resulted in a majority of 97 votes out of a total 157 seats for the two houses, the Senate (27) and the Chamber of Deputies (130). The new government of "Patriotic Accord" (Acuerdo Patriótico, AP) or "National Unity" represented an odd pact between yesterday's political enemies—Banzer and Paz Zamora. Under Banzer's military rule in the 1970s the radical leftist MIR was persecuted and its leaders, such as Paz Zamora, were imprisoned. Upon taking office, Paz Zamora explained the strange alliance as the result of a new spirit of national consensus and dialogue. Although the MIR gained the presidency by means of the pact, the price seemed

TABLE 4.2

Voting Results for General Elections, May 7, 1989

Parties	Votes	Percent	Seats
MNR	363,113	23.00	49
ADN	357,298	22.62	46
MIR	309,033	19.60	41
CONDEPA[a]	173,459	11.00	11
IU[b]	113,509	7.20	10
Subtotal	1,316,412	83.42	157
Other Parties	99,457	6.27	0
Valid Votes	1,415,869	89.66	--
Blank Votes	68,621	4.34	--
Nullified Votes	94,558	6.00	--
Totals	1,579,048	100.00	157

[a]Conscience of the Fatherland (Conciencia de la Patria)
[b]United Left (Izquierda Unida)

Source: Informe R (La Paz), Centro de Documentación e Información (CEDOIN), Supplement, X:187 (January 1-11, 1990), p. 3.

high as the ADN controlled the vice-presidency and ten of the eighteen cabinet slots including the critical finance and planning ministries, which determined economic policy. In addition, former General Banzer, who had twice sacrificed the opportunity to regain the presidency, was delegated undefined powers behind the throne as head of a bipartisan council responsible for "political decisions."

Within its first 100 days, the National Unity government found itself in a showdown with some 80,000 disaffected teachers, who launched an impressive national hunger strike to protest low average salaries of $70 per month. Nevertheless, the Paz Zamora–Banzer government refused to deviate from the neoliberal economic model and austerity policies of the MNR's New Economic Policy, despite preelectoral hints by Paz Zamora that he would put a "human face" on economic hardship. Instead, taking a feather from the cap of the previous Paz Estenssoro leadership, the Patriotic Accord imposed a state of ciego on November 15 and, in a predawn sweep, arrested some 850 strikers and activists and sent many to internal exile centers. The Catholic Church, which quickly condemned the repression, found itself once again mediating between government and people. In the end, it seemed that the political styles of the two Paz governments were not very different. Paz Zamora's so-called new-style politics rejected the "easy populism" and "sterile radicalism" of the revolutionary era no less than the politics of his uncle, the old revolutionary patriach Paz Estenssoro, had done. Indeed, political experts had been saying for some time that, in Bolivia, ideology was "out" and pragmatism was "in." Few critics believed that Paz Zamora's "unscrupulous pragmatism" could fulfill campaign promises to "moralize the state," and to "govern for all Bolivians, especially the poor and disinherited who were like foreigners in their own country."[32]

Despite the uncertainties of the future, exercise of the popular vote in May 1989 consolidated the electoral process and civilian rule after long years of repressive military regimes. Since 1982, elections had become politically stabilizing and necessary not only for a climate of renewed economic growth but also for the goodwill of the international financial community. And experts argued that the new-style politics since 1985 represented a renewed drive for national unity as well as the end of a political era begun with the Chaco War in 1932. The political spectrum had narrowed, as once ideologically polarized parties gravitated to the center. Whether this recent tendency represented pragmatism or opportunism, or whether it would soon be challenged by a new populism (perhaps of the right), was unclear. But it was obvious that an entire generation of MNR political warhorses were now too old to monopolize command and that a younger, more pragmatic, realistic, and technocratic generation of politicians was now crowding the wings. But could fragile civilian governments simultaneously preside over political democracy, the just transformation of postrevolutionary society, and the reactivation of the battered economy?

NOTES

1. Christopher Mitchell, *The Legacy of Populism in Bolivia: From the MNR to Military Rule* (New York: Praeger, 1977), p. 19.

2. Ibid., p. 59; Herbert S. Klein, *Bolivia: The Evolution of a Multi-Ethnic Society* (New York: Oxford University Press, 1982), p. 232.

3. Richard S. Thorn, "The Economic Transformation," in James M. Malloy and Richard S. Thorn, eds., *Beyond the Revolution: Bolivia Since 1952* (Pittsburgh: University of Pittsburgh Press, 1971), pp. 168–169.

4. Herbert S. Klein, "Prelude to the Revolution," in Malloy and Thorn, *Beyond the Revolution,* p. 42; and William E. Carter, "Revolution and the Agrarian Sector," in Malloy and Thorn, *Beyond the Revolution,* p. 246.

5. Klein, *Bolivia,* pp. 238–241. In *The Legacy of Populism* (p. 56), Mitchell specifies $200 million in "economic assistance" for 1954–1961.

6. James M. Malloy, *Bolivia: The Uncompleted Revolution* (Pittsburgh: University of Pittsburgh Press, 1970), pp. 182, 184; Mitchell, *The Legacy of Populism,* p. 52.

7. Mitchell, *The Legacy of Populism,* pp. 44–49; Malloy, *Bolivia,* pp. 185–187.

8. Malloy, *Bolivia*, p. 186.

9. Mitchell, *The Legacy of Populism*, pp. 45–48; Malloy, *Bolivia*, pp. 198–215.

10. This conclusion is based on the excellent in-depth study by Mitchell *The Legacy of Populism*, pp. 5–9, 49.

11. Cf. Malloy, *Bolivia*, pp. 216–242.

12. Mitchell, *The Legacy of Populism*, pp. 53–56.

13. Ibid., pp. 67–77.

14. Ibid., pp. 84–88.

15. James M. Malloy, "Revolutionary Politics," in Malloy and Thorn, *Beyond the Revolution*, pp. 144–157.

16. Mitchell, *The Legacy of Populism*, pp. 108, 111–112, 119; Mariano Baptista Gumucio, *Historia contemporánea de Bolivia, 1930–1978*, 2nd ed. (La Paz: Gisbert, 1978), pp. 276, 282–283.

17. Mitchell, *The Legacy of Populism*, pp. 112–113.

18. Ibid., pp. 122–123.

19. Ibid., p. 127; Klein, *Bolivia*, p. 255.

20. Robert J. Alexander, "The Labor Movement During and Since the 1952 Revolution," in Jerry R. Ladman, ed., *Modern-Day Bolivia: Legacy of the Revolution and Prospects for the Future* (Tempe: Center for Latin American Studies, Arizona State University, 1982), pp. 70–73.

21. Both the 1979 and 1980 election results are based on Waltraud Queiser Morales, "Bolivia Moves Toward Democracy," *Current History*, Vol. 78, No. 454 (February 1980), pp. 76–79, 86–88; see also James Dunkerley, *Rebellion in the Veins: Political Struggle in Bolivia, 1952–82* (London: Verso Editions, 1984), pp. 244–48.

22. For slightly different election figures, see Dunkerley, *Rebellion*, p. 260.

23. Jerry R. Ladman, "The Failure to Redemocratize," in Ladman, *Modern-Day Bolivia*, pp. 361–369; James M. Malloy, "Bolivia: The Sad and Corrupt End of the Revolution," *UFSI Reports* (1982/No. 3, South America), pp. 8–9. For actual vote tabulation, see Dunkerley, *Rebellion*, p. 289.

24. *Keesing's Contemporary Archives*, Vol. 24 (February 1983), pp. 31943–31944.

25. Based on Melvin Burke and Waltraud Queiser Morales, "Bolivia," in Jack W. Hopkins, ed., *Latin America and Caribbean Contemporary Record*. Vol. 3, 1983–1984 (New York: Holmes & Meier, 1985), pp. 295–306.

26. Robert J. Alexander, "Bolivia's Democratic Experiment," *Current History*, Vol. 84, No. 499 (February 1985), pp. 73–76, 86–87.

27. This election data is drawn from Waltraud Queiser Morales, "Bolivia," in Abraham F. Lowenthal, ed., *Latin America and Caribbean Contemporary Record*. Vol. 5, 1985–1986 (New York: Holmes & Meier, 1988), pp. B34–B37.

28. *Latin America Weekly Report*, August 9, 1985, p. 1.

29. Joseph B. Treaster, "Ex-Dictator Favored in Bolivia Elections," *New York Times*, May 7, 1989, p. 3.

30. Joseph Treaster, "Bolivians Go to Polls for New President," *New York Times*, May 8, 1989, p. 6.

31. Earlier, the final tally of the electoral court, announced on May 28, 1989, had reversed the positions of Sánchez de Lozada and Banzer. The latter received 26.8 percent of the vote and Sánchez de Lozada, 26.4 percent. In this earlier count, Paz Zamora followed with 22.1 percent.

32. Quoted in *Hoy Internacional* (La Paz), various dates.

5

Postrevolutionary Society

A scholar of revolutionary change once observed: "Not all revolutions end in triumph, however, and not all triumphs are irreversible."[1]
The consequences of the Bolivian Revolution have been debated heatedly,
with mixed conclusions. Popular interpretations suggest that the revolution has been "thwarted," that it remains "unfinished," or that it has
"ended." And in many respects the revolution does appear to have
failed: economic dependency, external political influence, and militarism
persist, and workers and peasants remain dispossessed. Yet postrevolutionary Bolivia is starkly different and more complex; a host of new
actors and social forces now compound the old.

THE STRUGGLE TO CONSOLIDATE
OLD AND NEW SOCIAL GROUPS

Labor has become more powerful, united, and class-conscious,
although the demise of COMIBOL and the influence of the FSTMB after
1985 has altered the balance of proletarian forces and interests. Peasants,
now among the most active and organized of the popular sector, are
especially receptive to the renewed revolutionary alliance of workers
and peasants. Because of economic austerity, the extensive internal
migration of peasants and ex-miners to tropical regions and the growth
of the "informal" cocaine economy are transforming the political, economic, and social face of the nation. Militarism has become more efficiently
corrupt and repressive, and more widely unpopular. A new actor, the
Catholic Church, which had feared to use its social and moral voice in
the past, since 1980 has consistently identified with democracy, non-
payment of the debt, and social justice. In the most basic sense, then,
the revolution succeeded; it disrupted the old order and introduced
fundamental changes that have made the Bolivia of today significantly
different from that of the 1950s. Thus the new social forces and groups
that continue to struggle in the spirit of the 1952 Revolution are the
direct progeny of that historic event.

110

The challenge of Bolivia's postrevolutionary governors—especially the civilian rulers after 1982—has been the question of how to consolidate a traditionally fragmented multiethnic society. The weak Bolivian state, a key factor that, ironically, had contributed to revolutionary success, now complicated the realization of the central goals of the revolution—national unity and socioeconomic development. The revolution mobilized and politicized social interest groups and empowered each to exert uncompromising demands on the government. Extreme political instability and the cyclical shifts between progressive-populist rulers and reactionary-repressive ones have historically represented attempts by the governors to control the changing society. After the revolution, however, this control process has become more difficult: Once the people had experienced the exhilaration of popular rule, only military repression could keep them down. One important social legacy of the revolution has been the empowerment of peasants and the labor unions (especially that of the miners). Whether military or civilian, governments have been able to ignore the popular classes only through all-out repression.

Postrevolutionary social history can be divided into alternating periods of populism and militarism, during which popular social welfare interests were subordinated to dependent economic growth. Periods of popular control include 1952–1957, 1960–1961, 1970–1971, 1978–1980, and 1982–1985. The intervening years were characterized by conservative party or military rule, which was generally antagonistic to peasants and labor. Limited alternatives have trapped both the state and the popular classes in a vicious circle of confrontation that often culminated in military intervention. Bolivian history demonstrates that only one condition has been able to break this cycle of interest group cannibalization of the state: a broad national consensus and multiclass alliance. National solidarity coalesced in 1952, in 1978, and again between 1981 and 1982. The sad irony of Bolivian society is that only severe crisis and adversity create national cohesion, if even then. The unprecedented political and economic crises of the 1980s have encouraged such solidarity between Bolivia's two powerful postrevolutionary social groups—labor and the peasants.

The Peasants

The most important achievement of the revolution for the peasants was the 1953 land reform, largely for social and psychological reasons rather than economic ones. Although the peasants remained impoverished and often powerless, they were now free to live, work, and die wherever they chose. The term *campesino* officially replaced the derogatory *Indio*, in line with the pro-indigenism and populism of the revolution. The

The lowland city of Montero (60 kilometers from Santa Cruz) and the regional headquarters of the National Institute of Colonization (Instituto Nacional de Colonizacion, or INC), once central in the administration of new agricultural settlements in the Oriente. During the harvest season, Montero is a central meeting point for the farmers of the northern Santa Cruz Department; there they shop and frequent the many *chicherias* (bars that serve the fermented maize beer popular in the valleys and lowlands of Bolivia) (photo by Allyn MacLean Stearman).

failure of agriculture to "take off" after the land reform was caused more by inadequate and ineffective state policies than by the supposed shortcomings of the Indians as independent small farmers. Indeed, the Bolivian peasants have been very entrepreneurial, effectively responding to market stimulus and demand. Government threats to their land and economic well-being, such as the planned agricultural taxes in 1963 and 1968 or the recent laws to limit and criminalize coca production, have unleashed massive protests. The entrepreneurial drive and necessity to survive have drawn peasants to the eastern jungles into the agricultural booms in sugar and cotton and, later, into coca cultivation and paste processing.

Although peasants were excluded from political and social power before 1952, independence after the revolution was also elusive. The tutelage of the rural bosses, the bureaucrats, and the military often substituted for the tutelage of the landlords. In 1953, the new National

Confederation of Peasant Workers of Bolivia (CNTCB) struggled to preserve peasant autonomy from other dominant social and political interests. The dilemma was that, although most political groups feared and discouraged independent peasant organization, the peasant sector was too large and important to ignore or repress. The power of the peasant majority could be awesome, and many feared an explosion if it were frustrated. Moreover, because the peasantry represented a potentially significant power base, the government could not permit opposition groups to woo away this sector. As a consequence, co-optation and controlled mobilization became the preferred policies of postrevolutionary governments toward the peasants. Governments manipulated the peasantry through local peasant intermediaries or leaders (*caciques*), who headed rural peasant unions (*sindicatos campesinos*). Generally, national peasant congresses were officially financed and influenced through compliant local caciques, who were paid directly by the government-appointed minister of peasant affairs.

The first MNR-Paz administration both feared and encouraged the mobilization of peasant unions and militias. Before the national army was reconstructed, both Siles (the second MNR president) and, later, Paz Estenssoro were forced to turn to peasant militias against angry miners. In March 1959, for example, some 800 armed peasants converged on Oruro to help the government put down a miners' strike. This policy destroyed the historic miners-peasants-students pact, which was the foundation of revolutionary governments and reforms. After 1956, the MNR routinely exacerbated divisions in the peasant movement and weakened peasant autonomy for partisan political ends. Rival caciques and sindicatos—such as José Rojas in the Cochabamba valley stronghold of Ucureña, Miguel Veizaga of the valley's Cliza peasant syndicates, and the highland unions of Toribio Salas in Achacachi by Lake Titicaca— were pitted against one other by the urban politicians.

After 1964, this pattern continued, but with a fundamental difference. During the violent peasant rivalries of 1957, 1959, and 1960, the military restored order in the countryside, thus supplementing the original control formula of peasants against miners with a variation: the army against the other two. This encounter helped René Barrientos, the so-called peasant president, forge his rural peasant support base to counter the influence of the MNR–middle class–controlled urban centers. The new alliance was formalized by the 1966 Military-Peasant Pact. Hence the only social force potentially powerful enough to challenge the army was neutralized and committed to "support and defend, firmly and loyally, the military institution . . . against the subversive maneuvers of the left."[2] Successive military presidents each assumed the title of "maximum leader" (*jefe máximo* or *líder único*) of the campesinos.

Although President Banzer reinstituted the Military-Peasant Pact, after the Massacre of Tolata in January 1974 it became a fiction perpetuated by peasant leaders on the government payroll. Banzer recessed the national leadership of the peasant union on November 9, 1974, and later appointed an official campesino coordinator, Oscar Céspedes Sotomayor, according to the obligatory civil service law, which had been manufactured for that purpose. Colonel Alberto Natusch Busch, subsequently best remembered for the bloody 1979 coup, became minister of campesino affairs. When General Juan Pereda Asbún, Banzer's hand-picked successor, campaigned for the abortive 1978 elections, he was touted as the peasants' candidate in an attempt to manufacture populist support and stifle widespread urban opposition. As depicted in numerous official photographs, military and political leaders would don the native *gorro* (woolen peasant hat) to symbolize their campesino ties in but one of many government methods of manipulating the nominally independent peasant sector.[3]

By 1978, the revolutionary alignment of miners, peasants, and students had reemerged. The catalyst was uniform opposition to a long line of military strongmen—Banzer, Pereda, Natusch Busch, and García Meza. The violent attack on unions by García Meza created a powerful populist coalition unified by the goal of redemocratization. Because the old CNTCB of some 2 million members in the 1970s had been co-opted by the military, a new peasant union, the Sole Unionist Confederation of Peasant Workers of Bolivia (Confederación Sindical Unica de Trabajadores Campesinos de Bolivia, or CSUTCB), was founded in 1979. Led by Genaro Flores Santos, the CSUTCB commanded the support of 3 million peasants, then about half of the Bolivian population. Active in peasant unions in the 1970s, Flores was exiled between 1971 and 1974 and from 1974 to 1978 ran peasant affairs from his hiding place in Bolivia.

The influence of Flores and the CSUTCB increased after the takeover of the old CNTCB headquarters in downtown La Paz by paramilitary forces during the García Meza coup. Grassroots unionists, in retaking their headquarters, were arrested and killed; among them was the leader of PS-1, Marcelo Quiroga Santa Cruz. Flores escaped and organized union resistance clandestinely. He eluded the security forces but was shot down on July 19, 1981. The security forces confined him to a police clinic without adequate medical care for nearly a month before international pressure by friendly embassies and human rights groups finally secured his release and exile to France. Although the delay left him paralyzed and confined to a wheelchair, Flores, an Aymara Indian and leader of the indigenist party, the Tupac Katari Revolutionary Liberation Movement (Movimiento Revolucionario Tupac Katari de Liberación, or

MRTKL), became a peasant hero by surviving García Meza's paramilitary goons.

As executive secretary of the Peasants Confederation, Flores was one of the top five leaders of the powerful COB. By supporting counterunions, the military governments after García Meza attempted to undermine his dynamism and power, which were perhaps comparable in the peasant sector to the personal popularity of Lechín with the miners. The Torrelio administration sponsored a massive peasant convention in Cochabamba of the "officialist" CNTCB on June 19, 1982, to preempt the upcoming CSUTCB congress on July 5–8 in La Paz. The officialists claimed to be the sole representatives of the peasant syndicates and smeared the CSUTCB as infiltrationists and leftists. Although the official CNTCB renewed the Military-Peasant Pact, the CSUTCB militants revoked it and renewed the solidarity of miners, peasants, and students within the COB. The radical unionists denounced agribusiness and the agrarian "new rich," and drafted a new agrarian reform law that became the basis of COB and peasant demands throughout the 1980s.

Under the populist Siles (1982–1985) peasants variously supported and opposed government policy. Most of the opposition was directed against the IMF austerity program and several U.S.-sponsored anti-drug bills. Reminiscent of the 1979 peasant road blockade (the largest peasant mobilization since the revolution), a major blockade in April 1983 won Siles's signing of an agrarian decree that gave legal status to the peasant-managed development corporation (CORACA). During the Paz administration (1985–1989), peasant agitation increased as coca eradication programs and the New Economic Policy generalized poverty and violence in the countryside. In close solidarity with the COB, peasants launched roadblocks, occupations, and hunger strikes, becoming as radicalized and threatening a social force as the miners had once been. Indeed, one expert concluded that the Bolivian peasant union was perhaps the most activist broad-based peasant movement in Latin America. Peasants fiercely opposed the eradication (Plan Trienal) and criminalization (Ley de Sustancias Controladas) of coca production and forced both Siles and Paz Estenssoro to back down even after the latter went ahead with the unpopular laws in January 1989. Organized demonstrations in La Paz and violent confrontations between the Peasant Coca Growers Unions and the "Leopardos" (UMOPAR, the rural narcotics control force) in the countryside resulted in peasant deaths in mid-1987, 1988, and 1989.

Little basically changed under the Paz Zamora government despite the fanfare of the Cartagena Drug Summit Agreement in February 1990. This agreement apparently accepted the Bolivian narcotics control strategy of "Coca for Development." The peasant unions (as well as the COB, most political parties, and many people in general) feared and opposed the increasing militarization of the Bolivian drug problem under the guise of economic development. During his first year in office, even President Paz Zamora, key proponent of the alternative development strategy, criticized the "drug war" approach of the U.S. Drug Enforcement Agency and the U.S. Embassy in La Paz. Although peasant lobbying was instrumental in the initial passage in July 1987 of the Comprehensive Plan for Development and the Substitution of Coca Cultivation (Plan Integral de Desarrollo y Sustitución, or PIDYS), which recognized the social value of coca and affirmed voluntary eradication contingent on regional development efforts, the nearly $700 million necessary for implementation during 1989–1993 was lacking. The leaders of the CSUTCB opposed the U.S. offer in early 1990 of $41 million in additional military aid if the Bolivian armed forces agreed to formally participate in drug control—that is, in the "Colombianization" of the drug war.

In other areas, overall peasant demands centered on fair farm prices and lower transportation costs, and on agricultural credits for small farmers to redress the traditional urban bias at the expense of the impoverished countryside. Peasants also wanted to revitalize the agrarian reform and expand Indian rights. The CSUTCB congress in Cochabamba from January 16 to 20, 1984, echoed these concerns and formulated a new Fundamental Agrarian Law (Ley Fundamental Agraria) to replace the 1953 reform. Similar CSUTCB goals were adopted during the conference from June 26 to July 5, 1987. At the same time, delegates strongly condemned the Paz Estenssoro "neoliberal economic program," the government's General Law of Agrarian Development, and proposed bills to "privatize" public education and health care—two especially popular social welfare achievements of the revolution. Moreover, a leadership crisis in the CSUTCB was narrowly avoided in 1988–1989.

In a real sense, the partial and mixed achievements of the revolution initially undermined peasant solidarity and encouraged passivity. The agrarian successes of the revolution were real: By 1975, some 80 percent of peasant children were attending school, compared to 15 percent in 1950; 34–45 percent of agricultural families had benefited from land reform; and new educational opportunities had increased social mobility. However, the 1952 reforms also created a middle and rich peasant group that has continued to exploit poorer farmers and the landless rural proletariat. Remnants of the old rural elite, the new rich, and co-opted campesino leaders have used semilegal tactics of bribery and infiltration of peasant unions to undermine and reverse the agrarian reform law in many regions of the country.[4] A 1988 church-sponsored study on land use revealed that only 4 million of the 36 million hectares of cultivatible land (from a total 108 million hectares) covered by the agrarian reform law belonged to campesinos, whereas 32 million hectares were in the

Low-income migrant housing in the city of Santa Cruz funded by Bolivia's Department of Housing and Urban Development (Consejo Nacional de Vivienda, or CONAVI). Because the cost of these homes (well over $10,000) is beyond the reach of the city's poor, mostly middle-income families live here (photo by Allyn MacLean Stearman).

hands of agribusiness, which produced only 20 percent of the nation's food. Reforms have been especially tentative in new areas of migration. Although more than a half million highlanders have settled in the lowlands and have formed new syndicates since the revolution, they have discriminated against the lowland Indians (who remain virtual slaves) and the new wage-earning rural proletariat.

In the future, as peasant unions become more radicalized and influenced by parties of the left (which in the past devoted their energies to the miners and FSTMB) and by growing Indianist (*Katarismo*) movements, fragmentation could increase. Conversely, continued poverty and social instability in the countryside as a result of the debt crisis, as well as present and future neoliberal austerity programs, could also encourage the development of greater unity and political autonomy. The future challenge to peasant leadership is to nurture unity and activism in the once-tame and co-opted peasant sector. As the pace of urbanization, migration, rural development, and economic privatization continues, a revitalized and unified peasant movement remains necessary to preserve the achievements of 1953 and to win more equality and opportunity for the campesino in the 1990s. Miner, peasant, and student solidarity supports that end and strengthens the popular indigenist classes, who in the final analysis still have much to achieve in postrevolutionary society. Although Bolivia currently lacks the powerful guerrilla movements of Peru's Shining Path (Sendero Luminoso) or the Tupac Amaru Revolutionary Movement (MRTA), radical-left peasant groups such as the Zarate Willka Armed Liberation Front do exist and could grow if progress for the campesinos remains stalled indefinitely.

The Miners and Labor

Improvements in the socioeconomic status of the peasantry have clearly been less than successful; and the same is strikingly true of labor, especially the miners. In few Latin American or Third World countries has the labor movement been as powerfully organized and influential in politics as in Bolivia. Until recently, the miners have been the radical elite of the labor movement. Historically, their power was based on the government's fiscal dependence on tin exports. When strikes shut the mines down for any length of time, the state was forced either to compromise or to apply repression. Since 1940, miner-state relations have seemed an endless battle between the state's military arm and the working class.

After the revolution, although armed miners controlled the mine sites, they achieved only partial decisionmaking control at the national level—and then just from 1952 to 1956. The MNR policy of "worker control" (control obrero) meant constructive participation in the reformist, middle-class government, not actual control. During the economic stabilization and implementation of the Triangular Plan between 1956 and 1964, labor was blocked from power; then, from 1964 to 1969, it was subject to total repression. A brief period of labor reorganization and coparticipation in government during 1969–1971 culminated in another period of repression from 1971 to 1978.[5] Brief reorganization and activism in 1978 was quickly followed by another violent period of persecution from 1980 to 1982.

The long struggle by militant miners against brutal working conditions and government repression reinforced the radical consciousness and proletarianization of this social group. Though of Indian and peasant stock, the miners were transformed—in a process of "cholofication" and "depeasantization"—into proletarians and the sons and grandsons of proletarians. Class struggle became deeply ingrained in their social outlook such that they developed very early the class consciousness and solidarity that eluded the peasants until later. Unlike the majority of campesinos, who were relatively powerless, the miner minority developed disproportionate political and economic clout. The miners zealously guarded the autonomy of the Bolivian Mine Workers' Federation (FSTMB) from political manipulation by governments. Before 1985, the FSTMB totaled around 60,000 members (about 1 percent of the total population and 4 percent of the economically active population) and, since its founding, has been dominated by the charismatic Juan Lechín, whose leadership became synonymous with the union to the dismay of younger aspirants and opponents in the Communist Party and other Marxist factions.[6]

Although no Bolivian government could completely co-opt or control the miners, their power was limited and largely negative, given that they had won but meager concessions from the industry and the government for the rank and file—and those at great cost. The miners were especially critical of postrevolutionary gains. The state-owned COMIBOL (often headed by a military administrator) was perceived as the "inheritor of the Rosca," a second superstate whereby the middle class maintained control over economic decisions in the mines, and as a "false nationalization" that had not altered Bolivia's subservience to international capitalism. The miners perceived Bolivian labor as doubly exploited: first by the state and then by foreign imperialism through the state. In their view, the struggle between miners and the state represented an irreconcilable clash between the internal interests of the working class and the external demands of the foreign investors and creditors. At the same time, most Bolivian governments, especially military ones, felt that the FSTMB served as a school for radicalism, socialism, and subversion, and that the real issue was the clash between the limited economic interests of the miners (and labor in general) and the long-term interests of the nation as a whole.

Within the COB, the miners were the spearhead of labor militancy, employing tactics of direct action such as the coercive strike and the hunger strike to pressure governments. As with the miners, however, the power of the COB was limited. Ironically, though a "lord of the country" because of its ability to shut down the economy, labor remained a "slave" to Bolivia's economic underdevelopment. The core of the labor movement comprised more than 300,000 members in 1976 (about 6 percent of the population of 4.6 million, or 20 percent of the 1.5 million economically active Bolivians), and labor families were estimated as high as 1.4 million, or about 30 percent of the population. Organizational membership within the COB numbered some 500,000, about 11 percent of the population.[7] Because the COB was composed of many different unions (factory workers, teachers, peasants, miners), it was never highly disciplined and unified; hence it undercut the power of labor. In some unions, trade unionism, co-optation of leadership, elitism and opportunism were greater problems than in the FSTMB, traditionally the most militant union in the COB. Moreover, labor agitation, especially by the miners, often remained isolated from other social groups. However, between 1978 and 1980, the labor struggle came to spearhead the broad popular dissatisfaction of the people with the militarists and the "narcoterrorists." As worker disruptions provoked increasingly bloody military repression, military rule became completely illegitimate by 1982.

Although the labor movement was a major supporter of Siles's rise to power in 1982, relations became extremely tense soon thereafter. The historical dilemmas between state and labor have remained unresolved and have greatly intensified because of the severe economic crisis in the 1980s. Siles had promised a more progressive distribution of national wealth and labor cogovernment, but the international bankers had other plans. When the miners insisted upon worker management of COMIBOL (temporarily achieved in 1971 under Torres), Siles gave in to an equal-representation plan in 1983; but the miners wanted majority worker control. Overall, labor demanded the democratization of work and profits, and worker control of the entire decisionmaking apparatus of the state. The split between Lechín and Siles personified the stalemate between labor and the state over these goals. On May Day 1984, 60,000 Bolivian workers marched to attain the worker control that had been denied them since the revolution and to move Bolivian society toward socialism. The new middle class and the military were equally intent to prevent either outcome. Indeed, as the economy worsened (wages shrank to $10–$30 monthly) and the 1985 elections neared, the polarization between labor and the rich private sector resembled all-out war between socialist and capitalist economic systems. Worker demonstrations, hunger strikes, and blockades seemed endless. Although labor never realized either of its demands between 1982 and 1985, it did help bring down the UDP government.

Ironically, if labor unrest seemed uncontrolled under Siles, it briefly became less so under Paz Estenssoro, because the MNR-ADN regime resorted to all-out repression. During the latter's tenure there were two states-of-martial law and a stream of antilabor privatizing decrees such as the New Economic Policy (Nueva Política Económica, or NPE). Although the economic austerity pleased Bolivia's international creditors and was welcomed by the Reagan administration, one consequence was the "rationalization" or "relocalization" of labor—that is, mass firings and unemployment. Overall, as many as a half-million jobs could have been lost because of the NPE. By 1986, 10,000 people had been fired in the private sector of the capital and 20,000 in the public sector. The FSTMB and COMIBOL (the latter being the largest employer in the country in 1984, with 28,000 mine workers) were devastated: More than 25,000 miners had been sacked by June 1987. The mine crisis was the culmination of long-term neglect, the siphoning off of profits to fuel the huge state bureaucracy, and the collapse of the Sixth International Tin Agreement (a commodity price-support program of twenty-three tin-producing and -consuming nations). In October 1985, the floor gave way under the international tin market, and uneconomic producers such as Bolivia found themselves still mining but earning less than production costs. Although the international crises of debt and tin were real, the "privatization" policies of the 1980s permanently crippled the once-powerful FSTMB and the COB, and entrenched the power of the new rich.

The New Middle Class and the New Rich

Social revolutions serve to level societies and to redress the more extreme disparities among social classes. In Bolivia, social leveling ended soon after the revolution, and new inequalities and class disparities subsequently developed.[8] From the start, a tension existed between the aspirations of the lower classes and those of the rising middle groups, and soon the major political parties in power (MNR, FSB, and ADN) represented a new social hierarchy. The revolution and succeeding decades of economic expansion and development facilitated the upward mobility of the middle sectors, the rise of the "new rich" (nuevos ricos), and the reemergence of traditional elites. Bolivia's population was constantly changing and becoming more urban: 50 percent were living in towns in 1974, compared to 34 percent in 1950; and literacy had improved from 31 percent to 63 percent. Bolivians were also younger, with more than half under 20 years of age; and they were more homogeneous now that floods of highlanders had migrated to the lowlands by way of roads that had never existed before. Indeed, the widespread economic crises of the 1980s intensified relocations from highland to lowland and from one occupation to another.

Modernization revived and restructured the middle and upper classes and integrated new groups into society. One important group was the urban middle class, which was economically dependent upon state administration and bureaucracy. A consequence of the state capitalist economic program since the revolution has been the steady increase of white-collar public employees from 48,000 in 1967 to 97,000 in 1973, and 217,000 by 1984. The central government payroll increased sixfold between 1970 and 1977. And a new class of developmentalist technocrats and modernizing entrepreneurs developed and became extremely powerful in the 1980s. By the 1970s, a large professional and service community and prosperous sector of commercial importers-exporters was already serving the consumer needs of the well-to-do. And in the same decade, a new commercial agricultural and ranching elite—the lowland rancher bourgeoisie, based in sugar, cotton, livestock, and various agribusiness ventures—developed in Santa Cruz, then Bolivia's second largest city and most thriving center of regional, social, economic, and political power. By the 1980s, much of this monied elite was indirectly or directly influenced by drug power. In the private mining sector during the 1970s and especially in the 1980s, medium and small mining producers prospered while the state-run COMIBOL suffered and will eventually be privatized.

The new middle class, especially the new rich, had a stake in continued growth similar to that of the Banzer years and thus favored a free market or neoliberal model of development. But the demands of the workers and peasants for greater reforms, economic redistribution, and socialism threatened the achievements the last thirty years had brought the *nuevos ricos*. They fiercely opposed Siles's UDP-leftist coalition and the attempt to follow a state socialist model of development. The Bolivian Confederation of Private Entrepreneurs, an elite group of about 100 wealthy entrepreneurs, was especially combative as inflation, debt, and populist economics imposed hardships on its members. Paz Estenssoro's New Economic Policy was more to their liking; in fact, it has actually further enriched many wealthy Bolivians, despite economic hard times. The postrevolutionary middle class and the new rich often favored alliances with the military against the working masses. What has been interpreted by most observers as simple military dictatorship was actually a new oligarchy (*nueva rosca*) of military officers, lowland agribusiness proprietors, and wealthy commercial and industrial entrepreneurs.

The "New" Military

Officially, the postrevolutionary military was reorganized and fashioned into a socially productive and developmental force, the Ejercito Productora. In 1952, the Bolivian army consisted of 18,000 to 20,000 men, with an elite officer corps of 1,200 to 1,300 men and a mass of Indian conscripts who served from ten to twelve months.[9] By 1953, the officer corps probably had been reduced by approximately 300 men and 70 percent of the conscripts had been discharged, leaving a force level of about 5,000. The name of the army had been changed to the Army of the National Revolution, and cadets in the military academy (which was reopened in October 1953) swore a loyalty oath to the MNR. Recruitment theoretically emphasized more lower-class entrants or "sons of the people" (*hijos del pueblo*), but most represented the middle class as before. The high command was restructured, with three new posts responsible only to the president: commander-in-chief, commander of the army, and commander of the air force.

From 1953 to 1963, the army experienced its "dark days" of severe budget cuts and demoralization according to General Alfredo Ovando Candia, who came to symbolize the resurgence and institutional integrity of the "new" army. Prior to 1952, defense drew 20 percent of the federal budget, only 10 percent in 1952, 7 percent in 1957, and 12 percent in 1963. However, the turning point for the army came in 1957, when its political prestige increased as a counterweight to worker-peasant militias. By 1963, important changes marked the reemergence of the army as a political and social power. The force level had been increased to 10,000 in August 1963 and to 15,000 by December. The School of Higher Military Studies was established in 1960 and the Supreme Council for National Defense, in 1961.

U.S. military assistance also contributed to the growth of the military. Average annual military aid, which in 1958–1959 was approximately 0.2 percent of that year's total aid, jumped to more than 2 percent per year in 1962–1963 and reached 3 percent in 1964. Between 1960 and 1965, the United States extended $10.6 million in military assistance. One source cites $59 million in total military assistance to Bolivia from 1950 to 1978, most of it in the form of outright grants, training, and excess defense articles; it also notes that 4,650 students trained during that period.[10] In the 1950s, an average of twenty-five officers graduated from military training in the United States yearly, but by 1964 Bolivian graduates from the U.S. Army Special Warfare School at Fort Bragg exceeded those from any other Latin American country. As demonstrated by Table 5.1, more Bolivian officers graduated from the training program of the Southern Command's (SOUTHCOM) School of the Americas in Panama than did officers from other South American countries. One such officer was Captain Hugo Banzer Suárez, president of Bolivia in the mid-1970s. The introduction of Ernesto "Ché" Guevara's guerrilla foco into Southeastern Bolivia between March 1967 and October 1967 provided the opportunity for massive North American military aid and led to the establishment of a fifty-man U.S. military mission to train the elite Bolivian Ranger Battalion.

By 1969, several dilemmas confronting the military institution had come to a head. Professionalization seems to have encouraged greater politicization of the armed forces, but the diversity of the officer corps, societal polarization, and ideological and generational tensions made it difficult for the military to maintain an institutional and ruling consensus. Officers became fundamentally divided over national development, national security, and the relationship between the two. Moreover, military

TABLE 5.1

South American Graduates of SOUTHCOM in Relation to Total Armed Forces and Population

Country	Armed Forces (thousands)	Graduates	Population (millions)	Armed Forces (per 10,000 population)	Graduates (per 10,000 population)	Ratio of Every Graduate to Number of Armed Forces
Argentina	160	613	27.7	58	0.2	1:290
Bolivia	24	3,573	5.3	45	6.7	1:6.7
Brazil	455	349	122.0	37	0.03	1:1,233
Chile	115	2,130	11.0	105	1.9	1:55
Colombia	65	4,097	24.8	26	1.7	1:15
Ecuador	35	3,124	8.0	44	3.9	1:11
Paraguay	15	1,039	3.2	47	3.3	1:14
Peru	150	3,585	17.6	85	2.0	1:43
Uruguay	29	920	2.9	100	3.2	1:31
Venezuela	58	3,134	17.3	34	1.8	1:19

Sources: World Military Expenditures and Arms Transfers, 1971-1980 (Washington, D.C.: U.S. Arms Control and Disarmament Agency, March 1983); and Christopher Dickey, "'Southcom' Hub of U.S. Latin Role," Washington Post, May 23, 1983, pp. A1, A15.

elites were subject to conflicting pressures from society's reactionaries, from an expanded middle class, from a raging youth and radicalized labor movement, and from U.S. advisers and counterinsurgency experts. Between 1969 and 1979, military interventions repeatedly occurred for a complex of reasons—notably, for the protection and promotion of the military institution, but also because of driving personal ambitions and basic differences regarding the policies and goals of the national future. This turmoil fed coups and countercoups, as well as two opposed military tendencies: the traditionalists versus the populists.[11]

The traditionalist school was represented by officers such as Barrientos, Miranda, and Banzer, and was characterized by a traditional-liberal approach to development, as well as by military professionalism. From this perspective, national development could best be achieved through economic growth without structural revisions or popular mobilization. International communism and its internal subversion represented the primary national security threat. The solution to both implied close ties with the West (especially the United States) and state economic tutelage—the latter specifically in the interests of private domestic enterprise and foreign investment. Military rule was essential to preserve the social order and peace that would permit development.

The populist school attracted officers such as Ovando and Torres, and emphasized a radical-developmentalist approach to Bolivia's problems. Both groups were nationalistic, but the populists were more sensitive to external political and economic control. To their mind, economic imperialism, not communism, was the greatest threat to national sovereignty and security; and the military, from their standpoint, was an institution of national development and modernization, and the agent for structural reforms. In the words of General Ovando in 1969, the armed forces were the "coparticipants and efficient agents of the battle against economic underdevelopment."[12]

By 1980, another major turning point in military-civilian relations had occurred. Within two years, the country had experienced four military coups, each demonstrating the polarization and disintegration within the military, accompanied by growing military contempt for civilians. In the last two coups of Natusch Busch and García Meza some 500 persons were killed. At that time, categorization of the military as traditionalists and populists no longer made much sense; the differences within the military establishment were as simple as the "good" military versus the "bad." Classifications like Barrientistas, Torristas, institutionalists, personalists, Banzeristas, hardliners, softliners, lefists, and rightists became meaningless as the institution confronted the "cocaine military" and its "narcoterrorist" and paramilitary allies trained by Argentinean national security forces and ex-Nazi SS-men. The "cocadollar coup" of García Meza broke the mold for coups; it was unlike any other in a country with the world record for coups and revolutions. In this morass of repression, corruption, and degradation, could any respectable military men be found? And what would happen to the country in the interim?

THE SOCIAL PROBLEM OF NARCOTICS TRAFFICKING

Cocaine and the Paramilitaries

General Luis García Meza may be remembered as "the Melgarejo of the twentieth century." He gathered around him a coterie of military men whom international law-enforcement authorities implicated in the smuggling of cocaine: Interior Minister Luis Arce Gómez; the commanders of major military regiments, Colonel Arturo Doria Medina, Colonel Faustino Rico Toro, and General Hugo Echeverría Tardío; military attaché to Venezuela, Colonel Norberto Salomón; the minister of education, Colonel Ariel Coca; and the air force commander, General Waldo Bernal Pereira. In June 1980, *Presencia*, the Catholic daily in La Paz, published a list by the Bolivian Permanent Assembly of Human Rights (Asamblea

Permanente de Derechos Humanos, or APDH) implicating in contraband and drug traffic some forty persons, more than half of whom were military men from generals to captains, police officials, and civilians. Indirectly involved, according to the public denunciation, were Generals Banzer and Pereda, and two FSB presidential candidates, Carlos Valverde Barbery and Alfonso Dalence. Previously, on February 23, the opposition weekly newspaper, *Aqui*, edited by the Jesuit priest, Father Luis Espinal Camps, published an article entitled "Cocaine and Paramilitary Groups," which charged the complicity of General Banzer and others. On March 22, a month after the article had appeared, Father Espinal was found tortured and assassinated. On the day of the coup the offices of *Presencia* were destroyed and its editor and employees harassed; later, the daily was temporarily closed and censored.

Paramilitary forces, which had existed under previous governments from the MNR on through Banzer, had become a power unto themselves, threatening even to members of the military. Especially since the 1971 Banzer coup, paramilitary organizations, composed of adherents of the different military factions, gunmen for the drug gangs, and neo-Nazi militants—somewhat like the "death squads" in Brazil and later Argentina—terrorized opponents of the military regime.[13] Luis Arce Gómez, former minister of interior under García Meza, recruited members of the Special Security Services (SES), which were being trained by former Nazi officers such as Klaus Altmann Barbie, "the Butcher of Lyon," infamous for the death and torture of thousands of Frenchmen and Jews while he was Gestapo chief in Lyon, France. U.S. intelligence officers helped conceal Barbie from French prosecutors and aided his escape to Bolivia in 1951, where he became a citizen in October 1957. Barbie, friend to many high-ranking Bolivian army officers since 1967, was protected by the drug-connected military hardliners, and was received openly in the presidential palace by the last military president, General Guido Vildoso, as late as July 1982. Extradition attempts by France and Germany, stalled since 1972, finally succeeded when Barbie was expelled by Siles in February 1983.

The drug connection was so blatant that it became a major national embarrassment for the military and Bolivia. Most notorious was Arce Gómez, cousin to Roberto Suárez, "coca baron" of Santa Cruz and estimated to be the biggest supplier of coca paste, averaging more than 1 ton a month in 1981, to U.S. markets. The U.S. Drug Enforcement Agency (DEA) charged that as minister of interior, Arce issued permits to transport coca and levied a $40 tax on each bale of leaves, of which he received a personal cut of $10, contributing nearly $500,000 to his private coffers yearly. When the Carter and Reagan administrations refused to normalize diplomatic relations after the coup, Arce reportedly

The Club de La Paz, a European-style cafe and favorite gathering place for Bolivia's *políticos*. Klaus Altmann (Barbie) was generally known to take his morning cup of coffee and *salteñas* here (photo by author).

threatened to "drown" the United States in cocaine. Arce suggested to U.S. advisers that the best hope to stamp out the trade was for the United States to extend a $3 billion loan to Bolivia as compensation for the loss of the coca plantations. In March 1981, on a "60 Minutes" segment, Arce denied the drug connection and, in response to charges by U.S. Senator Dennis DeConcini (D–Ariz.), implied that the senator was being used by Castro communism.

Wide-scale corruption and political instability went hand in hand with the drug money. The barons of the "cosa nostra"—like the tin barons earlier—financed rightist plots supplying automatic weapons and materiel. Numerous military and governmental scandals were uncovered, some dating to Barrientos and Banzer, but none as spectacular as the "La Gaiba" incident. In a tropical zone near the Brazilian border the military junta had established a front company, "Rumy Limited," to smuggle out of the country $1 million worth of precious gems. Siles's UDP exiles in Lima leaked a written agreement of the deal, which guaranteed 50 percent of the profits to the junta. Bolivian and foreign newspapers—after the fall of García Meza—exposed the evidence to the world, thoroughly discrediting the entire military establishment.

Between 1979 and 1982, the military and paramilitary forces committed atrocities that ranked Bolivia among the major human rights offenders in the hemisphere. During García Meza's rule, according to an official government spokesman, there were at least 2,500 political prisoners; the mines were bombed and 900 people were killed. The paramilitaries, the National Office of Investigations (DIN), and the Special Security Services (SES) were implicated in the 1979 death of Marcelo Quiroga Santa Cruz, the 1980 death of Father Espinal, the 1981 destruction of COB and exile of more than 500 labor leaders, the arrest and torture of priests and religious leaders such as Father Julio Tumiri Javier (former chairman of the Bolivian Human Rights Assembly); the destruction or closure of many religious (and secular) radio stations; and the arrest of scores of journalists. Two political parties, PS-1 and MIR, charged the paramilitaries with the assassination of eight MIR politicians on January 15, 1981. In 1984, the deputies introduced legislation in Congress to extradite García Meza and Arce Gómez from Argentina and try them for these and other crimes of assassination, genocide, and corruption.

Numerous agencies including Amnesty International, the United Nations, the Inter-American Commission for Human Rights of the OAS (Organization of American States), the U.S. Catholic Conference, the World Council of Churches, and the U.S. Senate's Subcommittee for Inter-American Affairs publicized the human rights abuses of the García Meza government. Senator Edward Kennedy had a strong statement of criticism read into the *Congressional Record* of August 1981. Finally, in late 1989, after more than three years of delay, García Meza was finally brought to trial. In what was being hailed as a case "unprecedented in recent Latin American history," more than 1,000 witnesses were to be called, with court procedures not expected to finish before 2089! In addition, Luis Arce Gómez was captured in a surprise raid in December 1989 and turned over to U.S. prosecutors. In March 1991, more than a decade later, Arce was sentenced to the maximum punishment of thirty years' imprisonment on drug trafficking charges.[14] Throughout the difficult decade of the 1980s, the Bolivian Catholic Church, once a traditional "bastion of conservatism," vigorously opposed the evils of "narcoterrorism" and drugs, the continued social and political repression, and the extreme economic injustice of the IMF and NPE austerity policies.

The Church and Human Rights

The Bolivian Church has traditionally been a weak and conservative institution, closely linked to the state, which has often subsidized religious education and the salaries of priests. The mid-1970s represented a turning point in the gradual transformation of the church from an institution

Dating to early colonial rule, Plaza San Francisco is the favorite site for popular demonstrations, especially worker and teacher strikes, because of its centrality. Of the many
churches in La Paz, this best captures the majesty of imperial and Catholic Spain. Although
the separation of church and state was established in 1961, about 90 percent of the
Bolivian population professes the Catholic religion. In the 1980s, the influence of the
church has been used repeatedly on behalf of social peace and human rights (photo by
author).

supportive of the state and the social status quo to one actively committed
to social reforms. As in other Latin American countries, changes were
partially the result of the Vatican Councils, the Latin American Bishops'
Conference meetings in Medellín and Puebla, and the rise of "liberation
theology." The church was also radicalized by the presence of many
foreign priests: Perhaps 75 to 80 percent of its 800 priests are from
Italy, Spain, Germany, and North America. These new currents divided
the church between the more socially conscious clerics and hierarchy,
and the more conservative.

The most important stimulus of change—the increased repres-
siveness of military regimes encouraged by the "doctrine of national
security"—originated in Bolivia itself. In the name of anticommunism,
the state violated human rights and began to interfere in the social
mission of the church. Bolivia's church was not especially radicalized
compared to the church in Central America; liberation theology was not
accepted. But the church came to identify its mission with social

improvement for the people and grassroots organization. The Bolivian Permanent Assembly of Human Rights (APDH) was established in 1976 by Fathers Julio Tumiri and Luis Espinal, specifically to speak out against Banzerist oppression; but eventually more and more of the church hierarchy came to support the Assembly and to see it as the permanent voice for justice and peace. A pastoral letter of the Bolivian Bishops' Conference (Conferencia Episcopal de Bolivia, or CEB) entitled "Peace and Brotherhood," issued in November 1976, argued that the church was not concerned with any specific political model but, rather, was responsible for the ethical and moral character of political systems. This "doctrine of the church on state power," as well as the new reformism and humanism of the church, set it on a collision course with the military and made it the object of systematic repression from 1978 through 1982.

The hunger strike in December 1978 found strong church protection. Archbishop Jorge Manrique, then archbishop of La Paz, supported the demonstration, which began in the cathedral of La Paz with a handful of miners' wives seeking unconditional national amnesty. Before the end of the strike, nearly a thousand people around the nation were demonstrating in churches, because there the military personnel were unlikely to kill them. Archbishop Manrique publicly criticized Banzer's lack of humanism toward the peaceful protest. The church also openly condemned the "Massacre of All Saints" in 1979, when more than 200 people were killed by the authorities.

The García Meza terror triggered another church-military confrontation. On July 18, 1980, Archbishop Manrique issued a mild letter of concern, read in churches and published in *Presencia*. In reaction, the regime launched a campaign to vilify the archbishop as a "supporter of extremism and terrorism" and to divide the Bolivian Church into "foreign extremist and red" clergy versus the native orthodox and nationalist Bolivian clergy. *Presencia* was satirically labeled the "morning daily of the bishops and the 'thirdworldist' priests." The church's position against the human rights violations was formulated in another pastoral letter, entitled "Dignity and Liberty," issued in September 1980.[15] It expressed the view of Archbishop Manrique and other bishops that the church should not interfere in politics or use violence, but also that the state had the duty to respect the rights and dignity of man as well as the religious freedom of the church to fulfill its mission of evangelization. The experience with militarism had clearly shaken a relatively complacent Bolivian Church.

In 1989, Archbishop Luis Sainz of La Paz, deepening the activist tradition of former Archbishop Manrique, harshly criticized Paz Estenssoro's economic austerity policy for leaving 200,000 people unemployed and eroding gains in education and health guaranteed by the revolution. He denounced the "sin" of unjust social structures and often mediated between striking miners and workers and the government. In the 1980s, church organizations, such as the Bolivian Bishops' Conference headed by Bishop Julio Terrazas, regularly issued pastoral letters demanding the peoples' rights and successfully mediated within the political arena to achieve social peace. In the 1990s, the church continues to find itself pitted against the harsh economic policies of Paz Zamora and defending greater economic human rights. Both Archbishop Sainz and Bishop Terrazas have insisted that human dignity, social justice, and national solidarity were damaged by the policies of Paz Zamora. The church's prestige has increased as a result of this consistently progressive stand to the point that it has become the most credible institution in society—an institution that one hopes will be a bulwark against the erosion of basic social and human rights to education and health care, and against a more difficult social crisis, that of "narcotraffic."

Education and Health

Social welfare services, especially in the areas of education and health, have traditionally been considered sacrosanct achievements of the Bolivian National Revolution. Shortly after coming to power, the MNR government enacted the 1953 education reform and the 1955 Education Code, which centralized the entire school system under the control of the Ministry of Education and Culture and guaranteed free, universal public education. Eight years of primary school (five years of basico and three years of intermedio) became mandatory; four years of secondary or medio schools (called colegios for boys and liceos for girls) and four years of postsecondary and university education were voluntary and freely available in urban areas. Despite high attrition rates, student enrollment and literacy grew rapidly during the 1960s and 1970s: The number of peasant children attending school increased from only 15 percent in 1950 to 80 percent in 1975, and in the same period adult literacy doubled from approximately 30 percent to 60 percent. Indeed, for rural Bolivians the most important benefit won by the revolution was a 50 percent expansion of educational opportunities. In education, one study concluded, Indian citizens were "the main beneficiaries of the revolution."[16]

As early as the 1940s, peasant communities had fought for the human right to education, struggling against social oppression, prejudice, and official neglect to establish pilot rural schools. To the rural poor (then and now), education was precious "social capital" through which the next generation could escape inequality and poverty. One outstanding educational experiment was the highland Indian school of Warisata, which the noted Latin Americanist Frank Tannenbaum visited in 1939 and praised as a model for Latin America:

> The president [President German Busch] will effectively realize the enormous task of indigenal education which should not be understood to be incorporation of the Indian into civilization but the adaptation of civilization to the Indian. When this is achieved this nation can begin to move ahead on a great cultural base. I have the hope that this will be so because I have witnessed that in Bolivia there is a greater effort than in all the South American countries to extend nationality to the Indian masses.[17]

Despite administrative reforms and budget cuts by Bolivian governments before 1985, none had dared a frontal attack against the historic and constitutionally guaranteed prerogatives of education and health. However, the New Economic Policy of Paz Estenssoro and Paz Zamora sought to decentralize and "privatize" health and education and thereby to reduce the central government's legal, administrative, and financial responsibility. According to the proposed plan, responsibility for education and health would revert to Bolivia's nine departments and local municipal governments. Despite certain merits of decentralization, critics argued that only three departments had the revenues to finance health and education needs and that the results would be a further erosion of services. A similar 1987 program had already decimated social security benefits, which were guaranteed after the revolution by the 1956 Ley General del Trabajo y de la Seguridad Social (the first Code for Labor and Social Security) and disbursed by the Caja Nacional de Seguridad Social (the National Social Security Fund). In 1983, about 22 percent of the 6 billion national population (some 1.3 billion persons) were insured under the system, which ran its own hospitals and funded the cost of medicine, food, medical equipment, salaries, and loans. Fiscal laws in 1987 and 1990 resulted in a 15 percent cut in the fund's resources and defaults on payments by the state and private employers.

The campaign to privatize education and health was the result of various World Bank and IMF reports (and the accompanying financial pressures by both institutions) that were designed to reduce the central government's fiscal spending so that it could meet its sizable international debt repayments. Ironically, the World Bank's own *World Development Report 1990* made clear that efforts to reduce poverty would not succeed in the long run "unless there is greater investment in the human capital of the poor. Improvements in education, health, and human nutrition directly address the worst consequences of being poor" and some of the most important causes of poverty.[18] Unfortunately for 80 percent of Bolivians, a direct consequence of the mandated economic stabilization

These Kolla men have migrated from economically depressed Altiplano towns to eke out a new life in this migrant barrio in the city of Santa Cruz; most homes are primitive and makeshift, but at least this one has running water provided by the municipality (photo by Allyn MacLean Stearman).

program was a drastic decrease in education and health services and a marked increase in national poverty. The 1990 report by the United Nations Children's Fund (UNICEF) concluded that "the most poor and vulnerable children have already paid the Third World's foreign debt at the cost of their normal development, their health and their access to education."[19]

By 1990, statistics reflected the previous decade's grim deterioration in quality of life and the hard-won gains in education: More than 50 percent of the population was illiterate (compared to 37 percent in 1976 and UNESCO estimates of 26 percent in 1985), and 80 percent of the children living in rural areas did not finish primary school.[20] Government funding for education declined as a percentage of state expenditures by approximately half and by some 25 to 50 of GDP (Gross Deomstic Product) percent from 1985 through 1987. In 1981, education represented 19 percent of the national budget compared to 11 percent for 1986 and 9 percent for 1987; also in 1981, education's share of GDP was 3 percent but only 1.5 percent in 1986 and 2 percent in 1987. Education expenditure per capita (expressed in constant 1980 dollars) averaged $31 for the period 1975–1980, $24 for 1981–1985, only $10 in 1986, and $17 for 1987–1989.[21]

Compounding the disaster in education, months-long nationwide strikes by teachers for higher salaries repeatedly disrupted the school year for 2 million students in 1986 through 1991. Although teachers enjoy certain social status and job security in Bolivia, traditionally wages have barely sufficed for the minimum necessities of life; and since 1985 both wages and job security have seriously declined. Some 80,000 teachers and support workers in the state educational system (40,000 in the Confederation of Urban Teachers and 30,000 in the Confederation of Rural Teachers, mostly composed of women) demanded a monthly salary of $300 rather than the average $30 to $70 per month they were earning in rural and urban schools. Because the strikes were considered illegal by the government, many teachers were summarily fired. Moreover, the political agenda of the government was to continue to erode the power of unionized labor. Inasmuch as the Bolivian Mine Workers' Federation (FSTMB) was decimated through repression and massive firings after 1985, the unions for teachers and peasant workers had become the spearhead of labor militancy. One minister of education complained that, "for years, the teachers' union, controlled by extreme left groups, has carried out prolonged strikes which gravely harm the population. This problem has worsened given the factor of the teachers' low salaries. This indicates the necessity for breaking down the monolithic strength of the union."[22] In November 1989, the Paz Zamora government implemented this philosophy and ended a hunger strike by teachers by imposing martial law and arresting more than 800 strikers.

In 1988 and 1989, the all-out war between teachers and the government intensified because of a bitter dispute over university funding. In Bolivia there are nine low-cost public universities that have traditionally maintained strict university autonomy (somewhat curtailed by 1972 legislation known as the Fundamental Law of the Bolivian University) and have predominantly served students from worker and peasant families; and there are several expensive and elite private universities. A government-sponsored television campaign criticized the low academic standards of public institutions and blamed university professors (60 to 70 percent of whom are men) for having converted the campuses into "trenches in an anti democratic campaign" by "small, marginal political groups." The minister of education and culture Enrique Ipiña Melgar especially criticized the universities' policy of admitting all secondary school graduates as "a populist-political fallacy."[23]

Erosion in health services for Bolivia's population had also occurred. The infant mortality rate was now the highest in all of Latin America,

Sanitation and running water are chronic problems in Bolivia. Despite the chronic water shortage in the department of Cochabamba, for these little Cochabambinas (residents of Cochabamba) it's time for a bath (photo by author).

given the national average of more than 200 per 1,000 live births in 1985 and as many as 650 per 1,000 in some rural areas, compared to 150 per 1,000 in 1975; 50 percent of children between one and six years of age were malnourished; and 60 percent of school-aged children suffered from goiter and 45 percent from anemia as a result of iodine and iron deficiencies, respectively. Major cuts in central government spending for health care (spending had fallen by half in 1986) and deterioration in housing and sanitation directly contributed to the health problem: 65 percent of urban homes lacked even potable water. Studies in 1985 concluded that "all major health indicators have worsened in the past two and a half years as a result of the economic crisis and the government's New Economic Policy."[24]

Although the Bolivian government sometimes disagreed with the recommendations of international health agencies, when the World Health Organization (WHO) in 1987 recommended the decentralization of the health care system in order to ensure greater efficiency and "health for all," the government seized the opportunity to initiate privatization of health and education and eventually save the state the salaries for some 100,000 public workers. At the same time, however, family planning has been an area of sharp dispute between the government and international agencies; indeed, birth control remains a highly controversial issue in Bolivian society. The World Bank has argued that "improved health is intrinsically related to nutrition and to reducing birthrates."[25] As a pro-natalist country, Bolivia has the highest birthrate in Latin America (6.8 live births per mother), a birthrate closely followed by those in Honduras, Ecuador, and Nicaragua. (The 1985 regional average is 4.2.) Bolivia also has one of the lowest rates of birth control use in the region (under 15 percent).[26] However, because Bolivia is largely underpopulated, with the slowest population growth rate in Latin America (a seeming paradox resolved by the fact that the high birthrate is offset by an infant mortality rate of 33 percent), the government prefers to encourage population growth.[27]

Unfortunately, without sufficient health and nutritional programs to "humanize" population growth and to eradicate preventable childhood illnesses (the cause of 50 percent of all infant deaths), this official policy has ensured neither population growth nor development. Moreover, because the majority of Bolivians are self-employed in the precarious "informal economy" and in the "black economy" of the drug trade where health benefits are unheard of, the people's dependence on acutely underfunded state facilities and already overwhelmed private religious and international nongovernmental organizations is greater than ever. As yet, the National Social Security Fund does not cover the 80 percent of the population made up of campesinos and people lacking formal employment. In the countryside, medical service is extremely limited; most peasants (and the urban poor who cannot afford private medical care) rely on natural healers, the *curanderos*. The regional director of UNICEF has summed up the Bolivian social tragedy by stating, "It's absurd to think that the economic dynamics of a country can establish or reestablish itself when the majority of the population can't even meet basic, elemental necessities, like just satisfying hunger."[28] In mid-1990, the alarming statistics forced the Paz Zamora government to recognize the blight in health and education; it announced a $110 million investment for 1990–1992 to the Fund for Social Investment, which had recently been established to deal with Bolivia's alarming problem of "structural poverty."[29]

Bolivia's drug problem also has negative implications for national health and welfare. Despite the billions in drug profits, cities (such as Santa Cruz) that have catered to the illegal trade boast more motels than primary schools. Environmental destruction of soil and rivers as a result of coca eradication with herbicides such as tebuthiuron (Spike) and chemical dumping from clandestine cocaine processing labs presents potential health hazards as well. As a result of economic hardship, the median age for working children has fallen from 10 years to 6 years. And as more children have become involved in drug trafficking and production (stomping leaves or selling cheap forms of the drug), the number of homeless street children has also increased. Statistics indicate that perhaps as many as 90 percent of these waifs take drugs and live a life marginalized away from education, nutrition, health care, and, indeed, society itself.

Dangers of a Drug Culture?

The cocaine problem has worried many Bolivians as more attention has turned of late to the societal dimension of drug addiction. The problem exists and is growing, especially among the well-to-do sons of the establishment and middle class, as the smoking of marijuana and cocaine-laced cigarettes (*pitillos*) spreads among the young. Other societal implications of the drug culture—corruption, violence, political unrest, and social divisions—have worried Bolivians for some time. Differences of attitudes within families in the trade and disruptions in the economy, land prices, and agriculture have been socially divisive. That is, the illegal cocaine "industry" divides families and towns in Bolivia into those "in" the trade and those "out" of it. Entire peasant families have gone over to the traffic, though perhaps only to stomp leaves or grow coca, a long and honorable tradition in Bolivia. An estimated 60,000 families depend on the "industry"—and that may mean as many as 350,000 persons, or 5 percent of the total population and up to 20 percent of the labor force. The traffic has became a livelihood, a way of life, and, especially since the economic decline of the 1980s, a means of survival. Throughout the decade, all attempts by the military and police to wipe out the production of cocaine have been resisted with roadblocks and other direct action by the peasants of the Chapare and coca-growing regions. Indeed, direct anti-government peasant resistance has greatly intensified.

Cocaine dollars have provided the renegade military with both a new economic independence from the United States and a political power base independent of the people and society itself. If the military and drug enforcement forces have been unable to control the peasantry and reduce either coca or cocaine production, is it realistic to expect that civilian governments can succeed, especially in the task of keeping the military and the special narcotics police honest? Agents of the U.S. Drug Enforcement Agency have revealed time after time the corruption of the narcotics police, local judges and authorities, and even national public figures in the Siles, Paz Estenssoro, and Paz Zamora governments. The celebrated seizure of President Siles on June 30, 1984, by rightist military officers and the elite "Leopardos" narcotics squad (a coup attempt that may have been supported by drug money) is a case in point. The frustrated coup demonstrated the deterioration of military discipline and hierarchy as well as the renegade power of both pro- and anti-drug militias. Corruption in the drug traffic, and in the control of that traffic, is so widespread that enforcers are sometimes revealed as the criminals. A U.S. State Department spokesman on the drug trade has been quoted as saying that "there is probably nothing short of communist revolution or nuclear obliteration that will stop it."[30] A critical variable in the persistence of the cocaine "industry" is the devastated Bolivian economy. Starvation and despair for many of Bolivia's peasants, and quick riches for the middle class and political elite, have made the economics of cocaine an issue central to successful control and eradication. Indeed, for the first time in 1990, the economics of coca cultivation was severely tested as the local price of the small green leaf dropped drastically because of stepped-up enforcement and interdiction in Bolivia and far-off Colombia. Unless the Bolivian economy can escape underdevelopment and dependency, however, the drug problem and its societal consequences will ultimately persist.

NOTES

1. Samuel P. Huntington, *Political Order in Changing Societies* (New Haven: Yale University Press, 1968), p. 315.

2. Christopher Mitchell, *The Legacy of Populism in Bolivia: From the MNR to Military Rule* (New York: Praeger, 1977), p. 98.

3. For the official Banzerista account of those years, see Daniel Salamanca Trujillo, *Los campesinos en el proceso político boliviano: documentos de la C.N.T.C.B.* (Oruro: Editora Quelco, 1978).

4. An excellent development of this argument is Kevin Healy's *Caciques y patrones: una experiencia de desarrollo rural en sud de Bolivia* (Cochabamba: Ediciones El Buitre, 1982); see also Healy, "The Rural Development Role of the Bolivian Peasant *Sindicatos* in the New Democratic Order," paper presented at the Twelfth International Conference of the Latin American Studies Association Meeting, April 10, 1985, Albuquerque, New Mexico, p. 37.

5. June Nash, *We Eat the Mines and the Mines Eat Us: Dependency and Exploitation in Bolivian Tin Mines* (New York: Columbia University Press, 1979), pp. 256–292.

6. The membership figures were estimated on the basis of *Bolivia en cifras 1980*, p. 297; Melvin Burke and Eileen Keremitsis, "Bolivia," in Jack W. Hopkins, ed., *Latin America and Caribbean Contemporary Record*. Vol. 1, 1981–1982 (New York: Holmes & Meier, 1983), p. 228; Mitchell, *The Legacy of Populism*, p. 44; and René Zavaleta Mercado, "La acumulación de clase del proletariado minero en Bolivia," mimeograph, (n.d.), p. 10.

7. Ibid.

8. Jonathan Kelley and Herbert S. Klein extensively develop this thesis in *Revolution and the Rebirth of Inequality: A Theory Applied to the National Revolution in Bolivia* (Berkeley: University of California Press, 1981).

9. This section is indebted to the excellent study by Charles D. Corbett, *The Latin American Military as a Socio-Political Force: Case Studies of Bolivia and Argentina* (Coral Gables: Center for Advanced International Studies, University of Miami, 1972), especially pp. 29–35.

10. Lars Schoultz, *Human Rights and United States Policy toward Latin America* (Princeton, N.J.: Princeton University Press, 1981), p. 215.

11. Corbett, *The Latin American Military*, pp. iii–xvi, 13–15, 66.

12. Ibid., p. 57.

13. "Bolivia Prosecutes Paramilitary Criminals," *Latinamerica Press*, Vol. 15, No. 11 (March 31, 1983), pp. 1–2.

14. *New York Times*, January 11, 1991, and March 23, 1991.

15. *Dignidad y libertad*, Carta Pastoral Colectiva de la Conferencia Episcopal de Bolivia (La Paz: Editorial Don Bosco, 1980).

16. Kelley and Klein, *Revolution and the Rebirth of Inequality*, pp. 131–135 (quotation on p. 135). For further general information on education, see also Thomas E. Weil et al., *Area Handbook for Bolivia*, Foreign Area Studies, American University (Washington, D.C.: Government Printing Office, 1974), pp. 137–163.

17. *La Calle* (La Paz), August 16, 1939.

18. *World Development Report 1990*, World Bank (Oxford: Oxford University Press, 1990), p. 74.

19. Susanna Rance, "Economic Hardship Causes Andean Ethnocide," *Latinamerica Press*, Vol. 22, No. 12 (April 5, 1990), p. 8, quoting from *The State of the World's Children 1990*, UNICEF.

20. "LP Interview: Bolivia: Future Somber Despite Vast Resources," *Latinamerica Press*, Vol. 17, No. 23 (June 20, 1985), p. 3. See also Marissa Bisso, "Despite Declining Birth Rates, Countries' Approaches to Population Control Vary," *Latinamerica Press*, Vol. 20, No. 11 (March 31, 1988), p. 3, wherein Bolivia's illiteracy rate, based on 1985 U.N. figures from *Women in the World* (1986), is given as 49 percent for females and 24 percent for males.

21. Oscar Zegada Claure, "La Política Presupuestaria de la Nueva Política Económica," *Busqueda*, Revista Semestral de Ciencias Sociales, Instituto de Estudios Sociales y Economicos (IESE), Universidad Mayor de San Simón, Year 1, No. 1 (March 1989), pp. 177–198; and "Presupuesto 1989: Por el sendero de la recesión," *Informe "R"* (La Paz), Centro de Documentación e Información (CEDOIN), Year IX, No. 166 (February II, 1989), pp. 6–7. See also *Finanzas y administración del sistema educativo* (Washington, D.C.: World Bank, 1986) for

comparative figures regarding Latin America and the Third World; this source estimates Bolivia's educational expenditures as 4 percent of GDP and 31 percent of central government expenditures around 1980. Weil, in *Area Handbook*, p. 141, similarly notes that fiscal outlays for education were 19 percent in 1961 but as high as 30 percent in 1971. Indeed, Bolivia has generally held the record in the region for high educational expenditures.

22. "Food and Agriculture," *Bolivia Bulletin* (La Paz), CEDOIN, Vol. 4, No. 2 (April 1988), p. 4, quoting Minister of Education Enrique Ipiña Melgar.

23. "Bolivia: State Plan to Abandon Schools Causes Public Outcry," *Latinamerica Press*, Vol. 20, No. 14 (April 21, 1988), pp. 1–2 (quotation is on p. 2). In 1987, the universities spent $49 million; the 1988 budget proposed $52 million, but the universities wanted $68 million. University attendance has markedly expanded from approximately 13,000 students in 1961 to 33,000 in 1971 and to 140,000 in 1983, according to figures supplied by the National Institute of Statistics (Instituto Nacional de Estadística, INES).

24. For the quotation, see "Food and Agriculture," *Bolivia Bulletin* (La Paz), April 1988, p. 2. For the statistics, see "News Briefs," *Latinamerica Press*, Vol. 20, No. 19 (May 26, 1988), p. 7; "LP Interview: Bolivia: Future Somber," *Latinamerica Press*, June 20, 1985, p. 3; and "En cifras: Bolivia Hoy," *Informe "R"* (La Paz), CEDOIN, Year VIII, No. 156 (September I, 1988), pp. 2–3.

25. Lupe Cajías, "Bolivia: World Bank Ties New Loans to Lower Birth Rates," *Latinamerica Press*, Vol. 20, No. 19 (May 26, 1988), p. 6. The article further notes that the World Bank made $30 million in loans contingent on a new birth control program.

26. Marissa Bisso, "Despite Declining Birth Rates," *Latinamerica Press*, March 31, 1988, p. 3.

27. Juan León, "Study Finds One of Three Infants Dies in Bolivia," *Latinamerica Press*, Vol. 19, No. 47 (December 24, 1987), p. 8. This article refers to the 1987 study done by the Bolivian economist Rolando Morales under the auspices of the United Nations Children's Fund (UNICEF).

28. *Hoy Internacional* (La Paz), March 4, 1986, p. 8.

29. *Ultima Hora* (La Paz), May 4, 1990, pp. 1, 16.

30. *Denuncia*, Comité Nacional de Defensa de la Democracia en Bolivia (CONADE), No. 16 (April 1, 1981), p. 3.

6
Postrevolutionary Economy

The Bolivian economy provides an example of exploitation and "dependent development" par excellence. From the coming of the Spaniards through the tin barons and the postrevolutionary economic elites of the twentieth century, the majority of Bolivia's people have been "orphaned" of the benefits of the country's natural resources and economic achievements. Indeed, although Bolivia is a nation of rich mineral reserves and natural resources, most Bolivians are impoverished, with a per capita income around $300 annually—one of the lowest in the hemisphere. This exploitative dimension has prompted critics to describe Bolivia as a "kleptocracy" and "a beggar seated upon a throne of gold." Bolivia's economic exploitation is largely the result of mismanagement, underdevelopment, and dependency.

THE STATE AND DEPENDENT DEVELOPMENT

The dependency approach to economic relations has been heavily ideologized by proponents and detractors and, therefore, either single-mindedly accepted or rejected by each camp. In the case of Bolivia, dependency is not a matter of ideology or preference, but a simple yet tragic reality of national life. Bolivia is economically dependent because its economy is fundamentally determined by external economic and political decisions and conditions beyond internal national influence or control. Whatever economic resource or indicator one considers—whether the price of tin or other mineral exports, petroleum or natural gas revenues, reliance on food imports or grants, development financing by the IMF or foreign banks, fiscal or monetary reforms, or the politicization and militarization of drug eradication programs and the illicit trade itself—Bolivia's economy has not belonged to Bolivians. The Bolivian state, like most in the Third World, has rarely decided its economic destiny and has restricted capacity to plan, finance, and direct national development.

141

Although prerevolutionary and postrevolutionary governments alike relentlessly pursued economic development and economic independence, these have remained elusive goals. During the 1950s, after the revolution, the economy averaged a mere 1 percent growth but achieved a respectable average growth rate of more than 5 percent in GDP and GNP during the 1960s and 1970s. By 1984, however, GNP had declined by 20 percent, per capita income by 30 percent, economic production by 25 percent, and GDP by 17 percent; and inflation had reportedly exceeded 25,000 percent. The 1990s, by contrast, proffered seemingly new opportunities. Economic "restructuring" increased exports, reduced inflation to 10 percent, and brought 3 percent real growth in GDP by 1989. As Bolivians emerged from the worst economic crisis in decades, they wondered whether the policy shift from Siles's populist austerity to the neoliberalism of Paz Estenssoro and Paz Zamora represented a real or mythical "economic miracle." Did renewed growth mean real improvements for the man and woman on the street and, at last, authentic national development after centuries of economic dependence and backwardness?

History of Economic Dependence

Early Incan economic structure described a primitive but autonomous "state socialism" whereby land was collectively held (I'm referring to the *ayllu* here) and could not be alienated, and the mines and other natural resources were exploited as imperial monopolies. Though a rigidly structured class system with a compulsory labor draft, the economy successfully provided public works and basic social welfare for perhaps 10 million citizens. However, sixteenth-century Spanish rule had introduced one of the first major shifts in economic organization and an externally induced economic dependence. Along with expansive urbanization, the European conquerors concentrated a captive indigenous labor force and the extraction of newly discovered mineral wealth on the central Altiplano. Unlike the more integrated and diversified Incan system, the colonial economy relied on primary mineral resources such as silver and mercury, and soon established the structural dependency on traditional mineral exports that afflicts the modern economy today. Through the *encomienda* and *mita* systems, unlimited and oppressed Indian labor worked the haciendas and mercantilist mining enterprises while creole aristocrats and European elites appropriated the profits.

Mining, which dominated the colonial economy from the sixteenth to eighteenth centuries, remained the backbone—both blessing and curse—of republican economic relations. In near-mythological dimensions, one of Bolivia's most notorious dictators, Mariano Melgarejo, personified the twin evils of the dependent economy: elite corruption

and foreign rapacity. His alliance with the emergent tin mining oligarchy
and free-trade capitalism forged the economic order that the 1952
Revolution overturned. Indeed, polity, society, and economy from 1880
to 1930 were creatures of the new mining plutocracy as Bolivia became
"a state that tin owned," the private fiefdom of the three tin barons—
Aramayo, Hochschild, and Patiño. Not unlike the shocks (defeat in the
Pacific War, economic recession, and decline in international demand)
that terminated four centuries of export dependence on silver in 1900,
the political and economic shocks of the Chaco defeat and the global
Great Depression in 1929 initiated the end of the great tin boom (1900–
1970). Even in its heyday, the tin economy induced a chronic structural
disease of underdevelopment—declining terms of trade—whereby dependence on less-valued exports of primary raw materials generated
trade earnings insufficient to import expensive manufactures and consumer goods.[1] Traditional economic dependence on tin and other industrial metals accounted for 97 percent of export earnings and 90
percent of fiscal revenues, and most foreign exchange proved an intractable
problem. Well into the 1990s, Bolivia remained a monoproducer virtually
hostage to fluctuating world minerals prices.

Development Models and Dependency

Various pre- and postrevolutionary development models attempted
to reform or end this system of monoproduction and dependency, with
merely mixed success. Except for the military reformist models of Busch
(1936–1939) and Villarroel (1944–1947), which combined state economic
leadership, social welfare, and social responsibility for private property
and revolutionary nationalism, not unlike the early revolutionary economic model of Paz Estenssoro (1952–1956), prerevolutionary govern
ments simply sought to cajole more revenues out of the bulging coffers
of the mining superstate's capitalists. Postrevolutionary development
models, ostensibly in reaction to the historical evils of economic dependency, retraced the pendular trajectory between nationalizing or
privatizing forces and state-directed or laissez-faire solutions. Under
these models, severe imbalances in trade and payments continued both
before and after the revolution (most recently in the late 1970s and mid-
1980s) and contributed to the massive debt crisis and government's
virtual bankruptcy. Ironically, as the 1990s progress, the Bolivian economy
remains heavily mired in the dependency that the revolution had
denounced.

The revolutionary economic heritage established a predominantly
adversarial public-private relationship that blamed the private sector and
socially irresponsible capitalism for economic injustice, underdevelop-

ment, and foreign economic penetration. The image and practice of private capital as exploitative generated postrevolutionary popular support for the extensive nationalizations and activist state development policies implemented between 1952 and 1964. The collective opinion seemed to be that, as an economic system, unrestrained capitalism entailed evils that state supervision could prevent and put right. For more radical supporters of the revolution, however, capitalism itself was the problem and socialism its solution. But this last option was never really tried in Bolivia.

Although there was limited government involvement in the economy before the revolution, from 1952 to 1956 Víctor Paz pursued a "revolutionary nationalist" development model whereby the government organized and managed economic development and owned major enterprises. Between 1956 and 1964, an economic austerity was imposed and revolutionary and populist programs gave way to a model of "reformist pragmatism." What developed under predominantly military rule between 1964 and 1982, except for Torres's aborted nationalist populist experiment in 1971, was a model some (confusingly) termed "state capitalism." In 1982, the democratic civilian government of Siles promised to return to revolutionary and populist policies, including 1971 worker cogovernment, but severe economic and political crises determined otherwise. The economic models pursued since 1985 under two presidents (Paz Estenssoro and Paz Zamora) have been characterized as "neoliberalism." Although traditional economists understand this term to mean the "restructure" or rollback of state economic intervention, the state merely shifted its economic activism to free up private investments, maintain "sound" finances (that is, control inflation and labor demands, and meet debt payments), and extract more resources via vigorous taxation. The real thrust of the so-called free-market or neoliberal model was denationalization or reprivatization of major public corporations, which historically have played a major but disputed role in Bolivian economic development.

The Bolivian Mining Corporation (Corporación Minera de Bolivia, or COMIBOL), which managed the "big mining" sector, generated 70 percent of mining production and employed 33 percent of the labor force in mining. The Bolivian State Petroleum Enterprise (Yacimientos Petrolíferos Fiscales Bolivianos, or YPFB) monopolized petroleum and natural gas development, producing some 85 percent of national output. And until the 1985 economic reforms of the Paz Estenssoro administration, the National Smelting Company (Empresa Nacional de Fundiciones, or ENAF), the Bolivian Iron and Steel Corporation (Siderúrgica Boliviana, S.A., or SIDERSA), and the Mining Bank of Bolivia (Banco Minero de Bolivia, or BAMIN) were also important in the processing, development, and export of mineral and natural resources. The state dominated the industrial sector through the Bolivian Development Corporation (Corporación Boliviana de Fomento, or CBF), which managed some twenty companies involved in the production of milk, sugar, cement, and textiles. Transportation through the state airline and rail system, as well as development banking and credit via regional development corporations were also under state direction.

The public sector grew rapidly between 1971 and 1977 under Banzer, in part because it became a principal source of job patronage. By 1978, according to one count, all the governmental units totaled some 200 institutions: 21 central government agencies, 89 decentralized agencies, 60 public or mixed enterprises, 9 regional corporations, and 9 municipal organizations. These units contributed 33 percent of GDP, 13 percent of employment, 59 percent of exports, and 70 percent of investment in 1976. The public enterprises—about 60 of them—dominated the most productive sectors of the economy and represented 13 percent of GDP, 3 percent of total employment, 40 percent of external public debt, and 37 percent of central government revenues.[2] COMIBOL, ENAF, and YPFB alone accounted for some 75 percent of national exports in the 1980s. By 1984, as public-sector expansion continued, an IMF survey and OAS report counted more than 520 public-sector entities.[3] This large public sector imposed not only high fragmentation and complexity on the economy, but also serious problems of state control and coordination.

The proper mixing of "statizing" and "privatizing" forces in the economy became a chronic dilemma for the different development models being pursued by governments—particularly after 1985, when most of the economy was being rapidly reprivatized as state corporations were "rationalized" or sold off outright to private entrepreneurs. This process of privatization became a central aspect of "economic restructuring" in Bolivia and the rest of Latin America, and must have represented a vindication for Bolivia's entrepreneurs. In 1962, the Bolivian Confederation of Private Entrepreneurs (CEPB) was founded to foster "liberalizing" policies by the government and to improve the image of private business. In 1971, under Banzer's development model of "state capitalism," which encouraged private entrepreneurs within an active public sector, the organization became a significant economic and political pressure group to roll back public monopolies in favor of private ones. In 1982, though committed to reform of the public sector, the socialist and militant labor constituency of the Siles government attempted to refocus state activism toward further nationalizations: public takeover of private medium and small mining companies, and the socialization of the transport sector. Foreign investors, the Reagan administration, the International Monetary Fund, the Inter-American Development Bank, and the consortia of foreign lenders to whom Bolivia was deeply indebted all pressured for the "free-market" strategies of the CEPB instead. Privatization—a direct reversal of the nationalist revolutionary tradition—triumphed with Paz Estenssoro's New Economic Policy (NPE) in August 1985. Thus, the economic crises of the 1980s provoked a showdown between radical and traditional development models.

The "state capitalist" model of 1964–1982 achieved high rates of economic growth, averaging 6 percent between 1964 and 1969, about 5 percent during the 1970s, and 6 percent for 1972–1976, but at the expense of economic independence and social equity. The state's activist development role of capturing resources from the economy to provide services and stimulate investments was used to transfer large revenues (through favorable taxation and credit arrangements) to the private sector and the upper and upper-middle classes to the disadvantage of workers, peasants, and the public sector. The results were huge public-sector deficits, undercapitalization, and inefficiency (especially in COMIBOL and YPFB) as well as significant income transfers upward, favoring the rich and contributing to greater socioeconomic inequalities. The private sector, instead of reinvesting added resources into productive economic activity, used the gains to import luxury consumer goods. Moreover, some funds were diverted to the private accounts of military men and to illegal activities in contraband and drug smuggling.

As a consequence, the brief economic "boom" or "miracle" between 1972 and 1976 was transitory, artificial, and not self-sustaining. It left behind a weakened and distorted economy that was overly dependent on foreign financing, skewed toward eastern agribusiness, compromised by ill-conceived industrial projects and infrastructure expansion, and hampered by serious balance-of-payments and fiscal problems. Gambling on a continued oil bonanza, high export prices, and optimistic estimates of petroleum reserves, the model favored a high capital-intense industrial expansion, which neglected agriculture and the traditional economic base in the mines as well as needed investments and exploration in the hydrocarbon sector. Agriculture generated about 10 percent of total exports, contributed 16 percent of the GDP, and employed 45 percent of the labor force, but received only 7 percent of investments allocated in this period. Mining, a major source of the country's foreign exchange and 15 percent of government tax revenues, averaged only an 11 percent investment rate.

Petroleum and tin earnings, plowed back into an import-dependent industrialization, were employed to subsidize the rest of the public sector. As fewer profits were diverted to petroleum exploration and revitalization of the mines, which were allowed to stagnate with a growth rate below 2 percent during 1972–1978, production fell. Traditional exports gradually declined while import pressure increased, establishing a serious trade imbalance. Both COMIBOL and YPFB were financed chiefly by expensive and disadvantageous foreign loans, which contributed heavily to the foreign debt, most of which was incurred between 1971 and 1981. When interest rates skyrocketed, exports declined; moreover, as foreign assistance and borrowing dried up by 1980 because of political and economic pressures, government investment was cut to control the growing public deficit and international debt. The economy entered a deep depression and generalized collapse.

The "state capitalist" model of Banzer was especially hard on the Bolivian people. Figures compiled by an OAS economic report suggested that the "economic miracle" of the 1970s had left the peasants and workers relatively worse off. The wage-freeze policies of the government favored the employers, and political measures such as repression of strikes neutralized the bargaining power of the unions. The situation was particularly acute in mining, where workers received a declining share of industry earnings. Despite labor gains in the services sector, if the increase in wage earners were considered overall, "income distribution moved against labor" in the period 1971–1979, and real wages, though not representative of the entire period, declined by more than 50 percent between September 1981 and September 1982.[4]

Faced with drastic evidence of the failure of the development model pursued by military governments since 1964, the Siles administration promised a more populist development strategy that labor hoped to radicalize toward "state socialism." Both the capitalist and socialist tendencies of Bolivian elites relied heavily on the state to orient and propel development. The capitalist model, as implemented from 1964 to 1982, favored the private sector, the upper-middle and upper classes, the services and import sectors, industrialization over traditional highland agriculture, and the regional interests of agribusiness and petroleum in Santa Cruz. By contrast, the populist model in 1982 attempted to reintroduce many of the social priorities of the revolution—greater economic self-reliance, income distribution favorable to labor, and worker participation in economic management. Although the development plan assumed a mixed economy, public ownership was expected to dominate the essential productive areas to ensure that economic surplus served social ends. This principle of the social responsibility of property was also fundamental to the experiments in "national revolutionary socialism" initiated by the military reformers, Toro, Busch, and Villarroel, and later by Ovando and Torres. The Siles populist model prioritized investment and development in agriculture, mining, oil and gas, and construction. It planned to reduce foreign dependence by encouraging agricultural expansion and self-sufficiency in basic foods as well as industrialization less dependent on imported goods. The new economic direction proposed more regional integration in marketing and infrastructure, and a credit program sensitive to smaller producers. However, deterioration in the external economic sector after 1979 and an unprecedented debt crisis in the 1980s threatened the very future of development.

THE DEPENDENT EXTERNAL SECTOR

Despite significant diversification in trade patterns and export commodities, Bolivia remained a monoproducer of primary mineral exports and an importer of foodstuffs and manufactures. Dependence on wildly fluctuating world mineral prices conditioned the economy to the needs of Bolivia's more industrialized trading partners. In the 1970s, minerals fell to some 60 percent of exports and hydrocarbons increased to 25 percent; and the great tin crash of 1985 caused tin, constituting half the country's exports in the early 1970s, to plummet below 25 percent by the 1990s.[5] However, as traditional export sectors shrank, decreased dependence on minerals and nonrenewable resources proved a double-edged sword as long as Bolivian development preferred predominantly export-led growth over a more autonomous domestic and agrarian-based model able to generate inward development.[6] The "openness" of the Bolivian economy to external trade and investments, and the heavy dependence on external assistance since 1952, further complicated the development process.

Major Exports

Petroleum and gas exports, nontraditional agricultural products (sugar, cotton, coffee, and wood), and manufactures or semimanufactures in the 1970s and 1980s partly diversified the economy. Furthermore, in the traditional mining sector, more tin exports were being processed or smelted after 1971, and by 1974 metallic tin exports represented 9 percent of the value of all exports and nearly 30 percent of all tin production. In 1979, tin metal exports accounted for about 58 percent of tin production and 26 percent of the value of all exports. And between 1980 and 1983, these exports increased in volume and value over ore exports, representing 85 percent of the volume of tin exports and about 26 percent of the value of all exports. Until 1985, therefore, both the hydrocarbon and mining sectors were the most important export earners, and they were expected to remain so for the rest of the decade. But oil prices then fell as the industry entered into glut. Natural gas exports, earning about half of Bolivia's foreign exchange in the 1980s, were also in trouble. Both the production and price of tin bottomed out as the International Tin Council collapsed in 1985.[7]

Tin and other minerals (zinc, antimony, tungsten, lead, and silver) had remained the mainstay and Achilles' heel of the Bolivian economy; by 1985, however, the tin era was effectively over. Tin, which had provided half the country's exports in 1970, had fallen to one-quarter in the 1980s. Bolivia's global share of production had likewise shrunk from the highs of 25–30 percent in the first half of this century to only 10 percent in the 1980s.[8] Bolivia was no longer the world's second largest producer, averaging since the revolution only about 15–17 percent of world supply, and for several years running had been overtaken by Brazil. Mineral production in the public mining sector and the private medium and small mines now accounted for only 40 percent of exports, compared to the high of 97 percent in 1952 and the low of 45 percent in 1984. During the 1970s, mineral prices remained relatively high, peaking in 1974, declining, and then jumping to an unprecedented high in 1979. That year, tin represented 67 percent of mineral export earnings and 46 percent of total export earnings.[9] By the 1980s, however, both price and production bottomed out. In 1979 the price of tin was a high $8.20 per fine pound, but by the second half of 1980 it failed to meet the costs of production after dropping from $5.60 a pound to $2.38 in 1986. Tin production in 1970 was 29,000 metric tons, 34,000 in 1977, and 27,000 in 1982, but it reached record lows of 9,000 in 1985 and 8,000 in 1987.[10] Between 1980 and 1981, mining sustained a mere 1 percent growth rate, which deteriorated to a −12.2 percent negative growth rate for 1981–1982, and to −19.4 in 1986. But by 1988–1989, the sector had rallied, growing by some 25 percent in 1989.[11] COMIBOL, which represented fourteen large state mines, had been operating at a deficit for so long that it was slated for privatization. Losses in 1981 were between $30 and $60 million; and in 1982, the state mines lost about $55,000 daily. COMIBOL needed some $700 million in investments to rehabilitate the mines, which once contributed some 70 percent of mineral exports and 33–40 percent of employment, or around 24,000 workers. After 1985, as a result of mine closings and the NPE policies, 20,000 miners were dismissed.

Petroleum, first exported in 1966, averaged 11 percent of exports for the rest of that decade. By 1974, petroleum exports doubled to 25 percent of total exports, averaging 16 percent for 1970–1976 and representing an average annual growth rate of 33 percent. By 1980, however, production had fallen to 22,000 barrels daily, or half of 1976 production (largely because of limited exploration), and exports had stopped. As domestic consumption continued to increase, Bolivia was forced to import oil. In 1988, production remained at about 20,000 barrels daily. Despite previously rosy predictions, if new reserves were not discovered, Bolivia would continue to be a net oil importer for the rest of the century. The decrease in petroleum reserves and the crisis in YPFB aggravated tensions between the government and two foreign oil companies, Occidental Boliviana and Tesoro Bolivian Petroleum. A dozen foreign firms, mostly U.S. companies, had invested in Bolivian fields since the favorable General Hydrocarbons Law of March 28, 1972, but only two remained. Under the new law, foreign investors were granted liberal tax concessions (50 percent of production was tax-free for thirty years) and a 40–60 percent share of production on discoveries. Occidental signed its first contract in 1973 for a concession of 2.5 million acres (1 million hectares) augmented by an additional 1.5 million acres (600,000 hectares) in 1977 in the departments of Santa Cruz, Chuquisaca, and Tarija. The "Tita" field was one of its most productive. Tesoro entered in 1974 with more than 2.25 million acres (900,000 hectares), and 225,000 (90,000) more in Tarija and the Gran Chaco were added in 1977. Tesoro's "La Vertiente" field contributed about 30 percent of Bolivia's total hydrocarbon production (oil and natural gas) in 1983.

In 1983, the state YPFB produced more than 8 million barrels of oil, and Tesoro and Occidental produced 2.8 million barrels, of which 40 percent constituted the government's share. The remaining 60 percent was sold back to YPFB at world market prices. The government, in turn, sold this production to the consumer at subsidized prices of one-third the cost—a loss to YPFB of around $100 million annually and perhaps some $1 billion between 1974 and 1985. Critics of the government's energy program charged that the two foreign companies had failed to pay full taxes to the government (some $200 million), thus encouraging widespread agitation for further nationalization of the hydrocarbon sector. Víctor Paz cut short this rancorous debate when YPFB's activities were privatized and handed over to the foreign companies.

Sales of natural gas incurred similar deficits because of higher domestic consumption and subsidization, but the future of this resource was no brighter because of problems with payment terms involving Argentina and Brazil. The former already owed Bolivia some $300 million for natural gas sales and was not likely to pay anytime soon. Natural gas was not exported until 1972, when it represented a mere 4 percent of exports; it doubled to 8 percent by 1975, and rose to 37 percent and 27 percent in 1988 and 1989, respectively. In the 1980s, gas reserves were estimated at 5 trillion cubic feet (142 billion cubic meters), and exports became an important source of foreign exchange earnings. Gas sales to Argentina since 1972 have helped the export picture, although after 1983 disputes have occurred every year over pricing and contract renewal. Sales to Argentina had generated an annual income of around $330–370 million, with a daily flow at one time of 215 million cubic feet (6.1 million cubic meters). By 1988, these sales were earning only

$240 million, compared to $400 million in 1985, because of the drop in price by nearly half. In 1989, Argentina owed Bolivia some $309 million for natural gas exports; but with the economic crisis in Argentina, collection proved difficult. Nevertheless, there was an outcry in late December when Paz Zamora swapped a portion of this potential hard currency for a reduction in the Bolivian debt ($795 million) to Argentina as well as for assured sales to that country until 1992.

Trade and Aid

Other economic goals of the revolution were a favorable trade balance, diversification of Bolivia's trade partners, and a decreased reliance on external economic assistance. Throughout the mid- to late 1980s, Bolivia's balance of trade generally remained positive, in part because the depression and the extreme scarcity of foreign reserves stifled economic activity, and in part because government controls kept imports down. Despite a steady decline in exports throughout the decade, imports remained even lower, except for the years 1985 through 1987, when imports exceeded exports. According to figures released by the Central Bank in 1990, the balance of trade turned unfavorable in 1985 and reached its lowest point with a negative $197 million in 1987. The commercial balance became a positive $10 million in 1988 and ended the decade with a $200 million surplus of exports over imports.[12]

Bolivia succeeded in diversifying its trading partners during the 1970s, no longer relying exclusively on the United States, Canada, and Western Europe, which together had represented around 90 percent of Bolivian exports and 70 percent of Bolivian imports in the 1965–1970 period. By 1975, exports to Europe and the United States were down to around 50 percent, (33 percent to the United States alone), and imports had declined to 45–50 percent. In 1980, Bolivia's exports to the United States were 29 percent but only 17 percent in 1987, and imports fell from 25 to 16 percent. There was an increase in trade with Asia, especially Japan, but most diversification occurred with the Latin American trade partners, especially Argentina and Brazil. Thus Bolivian exports to Argentina rose from 24 percent in 1980 to 45 percent in 1987, and imports from Brazil increased from 11 to 19 percent in the same period.

Trade in 1989 continued to expand commercial relations, especially with European and Latin American partners. Argentina and the European Community accounted for 58 percent of Bolivia's total exports of $821 million (or 28 percent and 30 percent, respectively); but exports to the United States were down to 13 percent. Imports from Brazil and the United States were 19 percent and 21 percent of Bolivia's total imports of $622 million. Similarly, imports from Argentina and Asia (primarily

Japan) represented 30 percent of imports, or 15 percent share for each country.[13]

Between 1965 and 1976, exports to the Latin American Free Trade Association (LAFTA) countries and the Andean Pact members expanded from a low 3 percent in 1965 to a high of 36 percent in 1975. Similarly, imports from LAFTA countries expanded from 10 percent in 1965 to 34 percent in 1975 and 36 percent in 1976. LAFTA, created in 1960 by the Treaty of Montevideo, organized a Latin American free-trade zone. Bolivia joined in 1966 and was given special tariff preferences as a less developed country. Trade with LAFTA, especially imports, expanded rapidly. The Andean Pact, established by the Cartagena Agreement on May 26, 1969, had aspired to a fully developed Andean common market by 1988. Chile, Colombia, Ecuador, Peru, and Bolivia were original charter members, and Venezuela joined in 1973. Chile decided to withdraw in 1976. For its part, Bolivia threatened to withdraw from the Andean Pact several times. Many Bolivian entrepreneurs feared that projected final elimination of all tariff barriers among the members (once realized) would penalize Bolivian trade outside the Pact and impede industrialization. The trend of the integration scheme has been for the more industrially developed members to reap more advantages in increased exports and overall economic growth. Bolivian analysts feared that the common external tariff would cause Bolivian imports from the group to expand greatly, but at higher costs to the Bolivian market. Since establishment of the Pact, both imports and exports with member countries have remained relatively low, around 5–6 percent and 7–9 percent respectively.

A controversial issue in Bolivia was the Andean Pact's Decision 24, which established uniform policies toward external foreign investments in member-countries. Chile used this agreement as a pretext to withdraw from the Pact; and Bolivian entrepreneurs pressured for a similar decision, believing that Decision 24's restrictive rules would discourage investments in the less developed member-countries such as Bolivia. At the same time, however, the Pact's structure controlled many negative practices of foreign capital and discouraged intra-member competition for scarce foreign investments. The provisions of Decision 24 limited the repatriation of profits by foreign firms to 20 percent and protected domestic enterprises from inordinate foreign ownership and control through loans, royalties, and technology transfer. Both the mining and petroleum industries were exempted from these regulations. The withdrawal of Chile, political instability in the region, strains between Colombia and Venezuela, and the economic downturn and debt crisis in the 1980s disrupted Andean Pact trade and weakened these experiments in regional development and integration. The Paz Estenssoro and Paz Zamora governments suspended Decision 24 in order to open the Bolivian economy to foreign investors and implement Decree Law 21660, the second, economic-reactivation stage of the NPE (also known as Decree Law 21060).

On the vital subject of foreign aid, Bolivia achieved limited success by diversifying its sources of foreign assistance by 1990. Since 1942, U.S. aid to Bolivia has represented a formidable instrument of external leverage over internal political and economic decisionmaking. Specifically, the United States contributed $1.4 million in total assistance from 1942 through 1947 when the MNR–military reformers ruled, but more than $19 million from 1948 through 1951 during the oligarchic restoration. Then, aid jumped to $310 million from 1952 through 1964 and to $341 million from 1965 through 1976 as the United States attempted to control the postrevolutionary events.[14] In 1948, North American assistance ($6.4 million) represented a significant 34 percent of Bolivia's central government expenditures. Notably, average U.S. aid ($18 million) grew to more than 200 percent of central government expenditures for 1954 through 1956, totaling about 8 percent of Bolivia's GDP ($355 million) by 1956. Although the average U.S. contribution (about $30 million) decreased during the 1960s to 58 percent of Bolivian government expenditures and 5 percent of its GDP, in 1964 (the year of the military coup against the MNR) overall aid ($62 million) peaked at 128 percent of central government expenditures, or nearly 12 percent of GDP. By 1976, U.S. assistance ($37.5 million) had fallen to 9 percent of government expenditures and 1 percent of GDP. Despite an increase in actual dollars from $245 million to $341 million, U.S. assistance for 1965–1976 was half the U.S. share of the central government's budget (falling from 23 percent to 12 percent) during the critical postrevolutionary years of 1957–1964.[15] In short, a clear pattern emerged: During periods of U.S. foreign policy crisis, overall aid to "unfriendly" regimes markedly declined; but it rose significantly when "friendly" administrations regained power. Similarly, Bolivian military expenditures as a percentage of U.S. assistance and the central government's budget notably jumped upward in direct relation to such political shifts.

Although U.S. aid strongly influenced Bolivian economic and political policy between 1953 and 1964 as MNR leaders struggled to consolidate the revolution and realize its economic goals, by the mid-1970s private investments and loans as well as newfound oil revenues made the economy less dependent on U.S. funding. When the United States suspended $22 million in economic assistance after the military takeover in 1979, the internal pressure was less than that in the early 1960s. Bolivia also received more assistance from the Soviet Union: $70 million for a volatization plant and $500 million in credits for metallurgical development in COMIBOL.

Natural disasters in 1983 and the debt crisis again temporarily increased the influence of U.S. aid on the Bolivian economy. During

TABLE 6.1

U.S. Aid to Bolivia (in millions of dollars)

	FY 1988	FY 1989 (estimated)	FY 1990 (revised 9/5/89)
Economic aid[a]	64.8	48.4	55.8
Economic Support Fund	7.8	25.5	30.0
International narcotics control[b]	15.0	10.0	9.2
Military aid[c]	0.4	5.8	53.5
Totals	88.0	89.7	148.5

[a] Includes development aid, food aid, Peace Corps, and Inter-American Foundation.
[b] Does not include funds for DEA and regional anti-narcotics programs.
[c] Includes military grants, military market and concessional loans, and military training (International Military Education and Training or IMET).

SOURCE: Larry Nowels, Congressional Research Service, as cited in Latin America Update, Washington Office on Latin America (WOLA), Vol. 14, No. 5 (September-October 1989), p. 6.

García Meza's rule, this pressure was apparent: Not even $200 million in Argentine emergency loans sufficiently mitigated the cutoff of U.S. aid. After the return to democracy in October 1982, the United States programmed a total of $225 million in assistance through 1983, of which $7 million was military aid and $5 million related to drug enforcement. In 1983, some $50 million (largely food commodities and Food for Peace aid) were earmarked for disaster relief. West German, Canadian, Swiss, and Swedish disaster relief for 1983 and 1984, in addition to assistance from public international agencies, somewhat relieved Bolivian dependence on the U.S. treasury. Nevertheless, U.S. aid constituted the bulk of Bolivia's assistance.

In the 1980s, U.S. aid to Bolivia pursued three important goals: the reduction of cocaine traffic, "free-market" economic stabilization, and support of Bolivian democracy. Aid for 1984 included $13 million in development assistance, with a modest military component of $5 million for a 300-member paramilitary drug control force and some $30 million in USAID agricultural programs. In 1985, the United States released $8 million in aid to Bolivia. And by January 1986, overall U.S. aid totaled $65 million. Indeed, during the 1989 elections, the U.S. ambassador emphasized that U.S. assistance to Bolivia, at $100 million per year, was the highest in South America and the third highest in Latin America (see Table 6.1 and Tables 7.1 and 7.2). This level of foreign assistance was maintained in 1990. Indeed, under the "Andean

Initiative," the centerpiece of the Bush administration's drug policy toward the Andes, Bolivia remained the major recipient of economic aid for the region. For fiscal year 1991, Bolivia's economic assistance again totaled $100 million (43 percent of economic aid for all four Andean recipients: Colombia, Ecuador, and Peru, as well as Bolivia). Moreover, the Bush administration promised Bolivia $148 million in economic assistance for fiscal year 1992.[16] Despite pledges by the Bush administration for the continued economic support of Bolivian democracy, the United States confronted the dilemma of conflicting goals. U.S. policy appeared to be more concerned with drug enforcement and IMF stabilization than with renewed democracy and development. Ironically, the hardships imposed by economic stabilization compromised the success of coca-eradication programs, and the tactless pursuit of both policies threatened the survival of Bolivia's delicate democracy.

"RESTRUCTURING" STATE AND ECONOMY: THE DEBT CRISIS

The economic crises of the 1980s forced a reconsideration of the traditional development role of the Bolivian state and, indeed, a "restructuring" or rollback of the public sector. None of the economic development models attempted or implemented since 1952 had been able to resolve Bolivia's fundamentally structural dilemma of traditional dependence on primary mineral exports. When even this floundering export sector finally collapsed, Bolivia was unable to meet its excessive debt liability, and soon a critical foreign exchange deficit ensued. The state, which had always seemed so powerful in jobs, patronage, and repression, now seemed powerless (or unwilling) to tap private interests, which were already too panicked by political and economic instability to maintain investments and full production. Massive budget deficits led to chronic inflation, which spiraled into hyperinflation as hundreds of labor strikes forced repeated wage concessions. These, in turn, only further fueled price rises and inflation. Bitter class conflict broke out as the costs of depression, debt, and austerity exacted a brutal and unequal toll on society.

One response to this economic catastrophe was the imposition of "new" economic policies, first under Paz Estenssoro and then under Paz Zamora. These policies sought to "depoliticize" the economy and to cause a shift from "Popular Revolution" to "Liberal Revolution." They were not authentically new but, rather, were relics from postrevolutionary stabilization programs of the 1950s, 1960s, and 1970s, and perhaps even from the era of the tin magnates during which private capital ran both state and economy. What emerged was a hybrid "Andean Thatcherism" that rapidly dismantled the myth and mystique of the social welfare model of development promised—but incompletely delivered—by the revolution. In its place was erected a conservative liberal or "neoliberal" program that aggressively proceeded to attack the disease virtually without heed for the social consequences of the cure.

The Debt Crisis

The economic depression and staggering external public debt of $5.8 billion contracted by 1988 were rooted in three causes: the structural crisis of the Bolivian economy, the rapid increase in interest rates in the industrialized nations, and the global economic recession. During the Banzer era, the structure of Bolivia's development financing altered radically. With the petrodollar glut in 1974, the international bankers invested heavily in Third World countries such as Bolivia, which seemed to have a bright future in estimated petroleum reserves and mineral exports. Because of this unsubstantiated hope, credit expanded and external borrowing easily tripled between 1971 and 1978. More than 20 percent of new development loans were contracted with commercial banks under stringent terms of prevailing interest rates, short-term repayment periods, and special refinancing arrangements. By 1978, the proportion of the debt with multilateral organizations had decreased from 70 percent to 54 percent, and the portion of the debt with interest rates above 9 percent had increased from less than 1 percent to 34 percent.[17] These "hard" loans, in contrast to "soft" development loans from governments and multilateral organizations, fell due after 1979, when global interest rates were high and the Bolivian economy was in severe decline.

More than 80 percent of the external debt was contracted by governments preceding those of Siles and Paz Estenssoro—some 60 percent by Banzer's government alone. For example, it took almost seventy years to accumulate an indebtedness of $782 million through 1970 and only seven years to incur a debt of $2.3 billion by 1979. An additional $738 million in loans was assumed during 1979–1981. In 1984, the government would have needed 75–120 percent of its export earnings and virtually all new borrowing to refinance and meet the interest payments on the accumulated public debt estimated at $4.9 billion. By 1987, debt service on the nearly $5.8 billion debt reportedly fluctuated between 45 and 50 percent of GDP. Nearly 20 percent of this debt, amounting to more than $1 billion in 1987, was owed to private banks.[18] The typical pattern in the 1980s was a failure to meet even interest payments. In June 1984, for example, Siles was unable to pay the $22.5 million in interest due on some $720 million, because the

Bolivian treasury was out of foreign reserves. To keep Bolivia solvent, then, the 128 commercial banks insisted on an IMF stabilization plan, a stipulation of an April 1981 agreement between the García Meza government and the banks.

An IMF stabilization program, however, posed fundamental political and economic dilemmas. A new standby loan would have to meet several key "conditions": a reduction in the fiscal deficit; devaluation of the peso and a single, free-market exchange rate; an end to all food and fuel subsidies; and a freeze in wages. Politically, the Siles government was heavily dependent on labor and the COB, which categorically opposed IMF conditions that severely penalized the workers. Between October 1982 and August 1984, labor paralyzed the economy with five general strikes, the last in protest of partial stabilization measures. The four-day COB strike in July 1984 cost the economy $17 million in daily losses. The working and peasant classes were already facing starvation wages (a worker's salary averaged around $50–$35 a month between 1985 and 1989), aggravated by rampant inflation (which has been cited as anywhere from 4,000 to 25,000 percent in 1985). The economic crisis was intensified by major droughts and floods during which more than $900 million in agricultural products were lost, at a time when 80 percent of the population was already desperately deprived, earning an income unable to meet more than 70 percent of basic necessities. According to a 1981 census, Bolivians consumed only 60 percent of nutritional requirements and 47 percent of children under 5 years of age suffered nutritional deficiency. Given this plight, one can understand why most Bolivians, not just labor militants, perceived IMF austerity as the long arm of neo-imperialism. Indeed, both the hesitant and partial application of IMF measures by Siles and the decisive and complete implementation by Paz Estenssoro meant massive social unrest.

Economically, IMF "conditionality" provoked a bitter controversy. Economists argued that Bolivia's problems were structural—problems that the IMF stabilization would aggravate in the long term.[19] IMF programs had an established history in Bolivia: a plan in 1958, eleven standby agreements between 1959 and 1969, and one such agreement in 1973. These programs, critics held, had solved neither the causes of inflation nor the imbalances in production and trade, and had favored the privileged. In April 1984, the Siles government implemented a partial adjustment that devalued the Bolivian peso for the third time since Siles had come to office; and although the government controlled foreign exchange and enforced an obligatory remission of all foreign exchange earnings to the Central Bank at the official rate, both the black market and the speculation in dollars thrived, eroding both salaries and foreign reserves. The COB temporarily broke with the government over the stabilization package, but the private sector complained that the stabilization measures were insufficient. Currency controls prevented the private sector from securing the credit and foreign exchange necessary to import and produce, and subsidies fueled inflation. Thus the private entrepreneurs anxiously pressured the government to meet IMF conditionality, while labor demanded default on the debt.

Initially, Siles promised to hold debt payments to 25 percent of total export earnings, because the first priority was to fulfill the basic needs of the population. In 1984, debt service payments alone totaled $970 million, whereas export earnings amounted to only $600 million. On June 15, however, the government officially announced a "temporary postponement" of debt payments to its international banking creditors, without the accrual of additional interest, until the debt was renegotiated. This unilateral moratorium represented a historic precedent. (Bolivia had suspended debt payment in 1931, but only as a result of a negotiated moratorium.) The "defaults" by Latin American countries such as Mexico and Argentina, and Bolivia under García Meza in 1981, were de facto, reflecting the inability to pay rather than an official policy decision. But in 1984, Bolivia in effect formally announced that it would not pay until it was able to do so without risking social disaster. This action, though a calculated risk, put pressure on the private banks to influence a less "hardline" IMF program. In the final analysis, Bolivia was merely borrowing to pay the borrowers, who had as much or greater interest in seeing that the debts were renegotiated.

The default decision was met with varied international and domestic reactions. The private sector predicted an economic boycott and the denial of all future credit. The COB applauded the action as the first victory since the nationalization of the tin mines. International opinion ranged from negative to the positive hope that the Bolivian action would pressure the international financial community to seek real solutions to the global debt crisis. The Siles government sought the collective bargaining of all debtor nations (that is, a multilateralization of the Bolivian debt within the Latin and Third World debt) and a shared responsibility among the debtors, foreign creditors, and the industrialized nations. At the June 1984 Cartagena meeting of the Latin debtor nations, Bolivia proposed a reduction in interest and a fixed rate. The plan found support inasmuch as a 1.5 percent increase in interest rate enlarged the Latin American debt by more than $5 billion. Bolivia argued that without global structural reforms, no sacrifice could solve the mammoth debt. However, the New Economic Policy of Víctor Paz (and its continuation by Paz Zamora) quickly ended aggressive regional and multilateral lobbying and recommitted Bolivia to timely payment of the debt no matter what it took.

The New Economic Policy

Announced on August 29, 1985, the New Economic Policy was hailed as another Bolivian "economic miracle" when Paz Estenssoro left office in 1989 because of the apparent success (and even popularity) of the draconian austerity. Indeed, during the May 1989 elections, the London *Financial Times* headlined: "Bolivia shows how austerity wins votes." The country "is the first Latin American democracy to demonstrate that tough economic austerity measures can, when well executed, win votes, despite severity."[20] Thus Bolivia was represented as a model to the rest of Latin America indicating how democracy, austerity, and prosperity were not incompatible. But was this the true lesson of the NPE? Summarized, its program sought to control labor, liberalize foreign investments, decentralize and reprivatize public entities, and impose classic IMF austerity measures (freezing wages, laying off workers, cutting subsidies, lifting price controls, devaluing the currency to stimulate exports, reducing the government deficit, and reforming taxes to create more revenue).

But the fundamental problem with the NPE was its staggering and unequal social costs. Although some experts doubted the overall and long-term health of the Bolivian economy in the wake of the NPE—whether structural inflation was cured or real growth in GDP was achieved, or even whether investments would steadily improve—few disputed that the social impact had been brutal. The austerity was imposed with blitzkrieg, military precision involving martial law and political repression, especially of labor. A whole class and generation of miners and their once militant labor unions were decimated by mass layoffs in what was called the "white massacre." At one point, worker purchasing power had declined by 70 percent and the minimum salary fell to $6 per month. Even the middle class, including many office workers in the public sector, experienced relative impoverishment. An Inter-American Development Bank study revealed that the per capita annual income of $1,178 in 1980 had fallen to $789 in 1987 and was actually five times less than the national average, $140, for campesinos.[21] The price of food staples increased at more than three times the rate of salaries, and the minimum wage fell by 50 percent. The peso was devalued some 95 percent, and an unrelenting credit squeeze affected commerce and further intensified the decline of agriculture and the indebtedness of small farmers. Thousands of destitute campesinos and unemployed miners migrated to coca-growing regions and organized militant unions to defend their crops. Some 20–25 percent of the economically active population (200,000–400,000 people) were unemployed, and nearly all of the social welfare benefits, which had provided some security for the impoverished, were swept away by the NPE.

Yet there were impressive positive economic statistics as well: annual inflation between only 10 and 15 percent, real growth of 2–3 percent in GDP, more foreign currency reserves, investments up 8 percent, an improved trade balance, and a stable peso. Moreover, according to one finance minister, major rescheduling and buy-backs of the debt had reduced what had been an estimated $5.8 billion in 1988 to $4 billion in 1989.[22] In addition, the interest-to-export ratio had improved and was now down to 45 percent of export earnings. New credits, foreign loans, IMF stand-by assistance, and U.S. aid were coming into the treasury. Indeed, Paz Zamora's faithful adherence to the NPE, despite preelectoral promises to "humanize austerity," resulted in a renewed IMF agreement through 1991, which promised to secure some $475 million in renewed external credits from major multilateral lenders.

In short, the NPE had saved the economy for the international bankers and unregulated foreign investments that began to displace public and local ownership in "joint venture" schemes. Although the NPE had espoused the "free market," "liberalism," and "sustained growth," the realities were private monopolies, state repression, and greater dependency. Impressive macroeconomic statistics notwithstanding, one could question whether the NPE was actually working in Bolivia, much less whether the Bolivian model could be copied in Peru, Argentina, or Brazil. As one peasant union leader complained, "The government's statistics don't reflect the growing number of families forced to live in tents; the thousands of malnourished kids who get only a piece of bread and a cup of tea a day; the hundreds of campesinos who have come to the capital in search of work and end up begging on the streets."[23] In the final analysis, the NPE encouraged many Bolivians to seek a "kinder" economy elsewhere—in the informal drug sector.

THE STATE AND COCAINE

Bolivia possessed the potential to become a relatively prosperous country if resources had been exploited wisely, yet less than 3 percent of its 350,000 square miles (900,000 square kilometers) of arable land is under cultivation, and only 10 percent of its territory has been explored systematically. The absence of development planning before 1962, and misconceived economic programs thereafter, compromised desperately needed improvements. The windfall opportunities created by the oil boom in 1974, and the boom and bust in cotton, which placed 124,000 acres (50,000 hectares) in production in 1975—four times the amount worked in 1970 and 1981—left massive agricultural debts assumed by the state and thousands of unemployed workers. More than 10 percent of the population had migrated to the lowlands over the years, only to be left destitute by a failed economic system. Oil profits—some 11 percent for Santa Cruz department—were not used to generate self-sustaining regional development but, rather, were squandered on massive public works and services for the departmental capital. When the agricultural slump hit in the late 1970s, it coincided with the increased popularity of cocaine usage in the United States. Both conditions stimulated a meteoric rise in cocaine traffic. Floods in 1983, which damaged 100,000 acres (40,000 hectares) of prime agricultural land and disrupted sugar, rice, and soybean harvests, as well as the social suffering and economic dislocation caused by the NPE, further aggravated already intractable problems.

The economic linkage among the drug traffic, economic crisis, and distorted development is apparent. The Bolivian state failed both to tap the nation's resources and to provide a living for its citizens. Debt, natural disasters, the collapse of the tin market, and the NPE austerity exacerbated social misery. The country's governors profited from the drug trade during the 1980s, and naturally the desperate people followed suit. Like contraband, traditionally a vital source of underground employment and informal revenue, cocaine was another logical method of economic survival. Bolivian coca producers were responding to foreign market demands much like rational economic actors had responded throughout the country's economic history. The drug traffic was but a recent consequence of Bolivia's perverse and dependent economic system, and a newer form of economic exploitation. However, the insiduous trade not only damaged the legal Bolivian economy but also became a growing danger to the United States, the major market for illegal cocaine.

Cocaine and the Economy

Estimates of the value of cocaine earnings fluctuate widely from $1 to $8 billion annually. However, less and less of this money, perhaps only $300 to $600 million (as much as Bolivia's legal exports)—remain in the country. Initially, drug profits fueled a general economic boom as money poured into local construction, conspicuous-consumption imports, and contraband investments. Even profits on a minimum trade of $1 billion left a small percentage to "trickle down" and generate work for the army of unemployed or underemployed in the tropical lowlands. As a director of the National Commission Against the Narcotics Traffic tersely pointed out, "dollars go a long way in a poor country."[24] By the mid-1980s, local economies were saturated with coca dollars and excess cocaine profits flooded Swiss bank accounts or Miami real estate brokerage houses, thus depriving the Bolivian treasury and formal economy of all but spin-off benefits while saddling the country with a difficult inflation and parallel market for U.S. dollars. One Bolivian government study concluded that if the 160,000 metric tons of coca leaf grown in 1985 could be produced and sold as cocaine in Miami, the resulting $3.3 billion profits would cancel most of the country's foreign debt.[25]

Some economic effects of the coca trade benefited the poorer classes, who were heavily drawn into growing coca as a rational survival decision. One campesino revealed the typical motivation of small producers: "We've always produced coca, and we don't see why we can't anymore now. They tell us to destroy the coca crops in exchange for roads; we can only answer that we may be ignorant but we are not stupid, because the sale of coca to accumulation centers feeds our families."[26] For the small peasant producer, coca production and sale—even to official government collection centers at half or one-third the drug trade price—have made economic sense. In 1980 prices, a hectare of coca generated an income of 15,000 Bolivian pesos, compared to 600 pesos for bananas, which still had to be shipped to market via inadequate roads and were subject to rapid spoilage. In the mid-1980s, a hectare (2.5 acres) of coca crop sold for US$5,000, compared to a coffee yield of US$500; moreover, coca plants could be harvested as many as three or four times a year. A destitute campesino family, if they chose traditional agricultural work, would be paid only one-fifth or one-fourth of the wages to be had in the coca plantations (cocales). There were even spin-off benefits for the middle class: administrative sinecures. The narcotics control process generated its own vast bureaucracy, with vested interests in prolonging the struggle against the traffic indefinitely.

In 1978, the production of coca was estimated at 27,500 U.S. tons (25,000 metric tons), twice as much as Bolivians needed for licit uses, according to a study commissioned by the United States; and in 1990 production was estimated at 88,000 U.S. tons (80,000 metric tons).[27] For centuries, coca production had been an integral part of the economy; the leaves could be grown, harvested, and distributed legally. Traditionally, coca and food subsidies from the highland mining center stores (pulperías), were an integral part of a mine worker's wages. The diversion of leaves into paste production created massive scarcities in the mine centers and actually cost COMIBOL significant revenues. Indeed, COMIBOL was compelled to maintain a steady coca supply rather than suffer lower productivity and miner unrest. By 1983, Bolivia was producing four times its domestic needs, and 50–60 percent of the coca leaves were being used in the processing of cocaine (some 80 metric tons annually), at one time rivaling Peruvian coca production levels. The Chapare or the Yungas (lush inter-Andean valleys) of Cochabamba department produced 80 percent of Bolivian coca leaves, and the La Paz

The May 1990 Festival of the Chica in Socaba, a small town several kilometers from the city of Cochabamba. The peasants of this region have been among the more militant in protecting the traditional cultivation of coca leaf (photo by author).

Yungas produced 20 percent (the latter largely used for internal consumption). In the 1980s, some 60 percent of Chapare production was used in the narcotics traffic and only 40 percent was sold to government collection centers, according to the Directory of Coca Control and Commercialization. Cultivators received twice as much for a coca crop from the traffickers as from the government, and numerous peasants complained that corrupt authorities actually resold the crops to the drug traffickers, thereby cheating the poor producers of the extra profits.

In 1982, then U.S. Ambassador Edwin Corr commented that "the only way to have control in Bolivia and Peru now is to involve the farmers themselves."[28] For the Bolivian peasant, however, control made little economic or cultural sense. Culturally, coca was perceived as "the sacred leaf of the Incas," as "an innocent and miraculous little leaf" that was suddenly to be controlled and largely wiped out. Economically, it was perceived by the peasant as one more official scam or exploitative game, whereby the "little men" lost and the government officials, military, rich elites, and foreigners won at their expense. Peasants agreed with Anthony Henman, author of *Mama coca*, that in South America any industry with the economic importance of cocaine would inevitably be controlled by the same political and social elites who control all the other important resources of the continent. Indeed, Henman coined the term "informal narcocracy" to describe the continent-wide displacement of Latin American economies, such as Bolivia's, by the drug trade.[29]

Proof was easily found at every level of corruption and misapplication of justice. Only little producers were caught and sentenced to as much as five to ten years of imprisonment for minor involvement in the trade such as small-scale growing or transport by foot. Ignorant Indians, women, and children as young as ten years, used in the "antlike contraband" business, were abused by authorities in their attempt to mitigate the traffic, while big dealers eluded the law. As foreigners helped burn cocales and defoliate crops with herbicides, in what appeared to be an all-out war, peasants in the Chapare banded together to resist the intrusion of the police and the military into their meager economic livelihood. The ultimate political scandal occurred during the García Meza government, when the president reportedly reaped $5 million monthly from cocaine. Even after the return to democracy, scandals involving high officials in the cabinets of Siles and Víctor Paz, in the judiciary, and in parliament itself continued to reveal the complicity of political and economic elites. Moreover, during the 1989 elections, both leading candidates, Banzer and Jaime Paz, were plagued with drug smear campaigns, and a "narcovideo" of ADN politicians and drug czar, Roberto Suárez, fueled the popular rumor that Banzer's campaign was financed by drug profits.

The negative consequences of the cocaine traffic for Bolivia were overwhelming and nationwide, outweighing the small-scale, largely private benefits. The trade threatened the entire national economy, the viability of the state itself, and the basic cohesiveness of society. As a result, Bolivia's economy experienced greater distortions: inflation, money market speculation, decline in investments and foreign aid, and, especially, the disruption of lowland agriculture. Bolivia had made significant agricultural advances in food production during the 1970s; now these achievements were undermined by the "cash" coca crop, which aggravated already substandard alimentation and nutrition. Indeed, over the last twenty years, more than a half-million Bolivians became reliant on food donations just to eat. Moreover, land prices in the coca growing regions soared, making it nearly impossible for the landless to turn to normal agricultural activity. Agribusinesses in sugar, rice, cotton, and coffee were all crippled by the competitive and lucrative cocaine economy.

Cocaine production itself became more modernized and mechanized, moving from labor-intensive to capital-intensive modes employing fewer and fewer workers. Government crackdown in one region of the country only caused drug-related cottage industries and paste production plants to relocate further into inaccessible jungle, resulting in labor instability and forcing constant population migrations. Rural peasant unions, representing some 60,000 coca growers, militantly opposed eradication programs in the absence of equally lucrative substitutes. And a peasant backlash in the form of widespread rural revolution, especially a *Katarista* Indian one, remained a constant possibility.[30] Growers and the peasantry were more persuaded by the exigencies of survival and the immediate economic benefits of the drug traffic than by the hypothetical long-range detriments to themselves or the national economy. Thus the logic of immediacy and desperation undermined a key premise of any effective coca control program—that there was a shared interest in the demise of the trade. At the same time, the traditional dilemmas of underdevelopment and short-sighted U.S. policies impeded successful resolution of the drug traffic problem.

Cocaine and Development

Before the revolution, and since ancient Aymara and Incan times, coca was grown in the lush La Paz Yungas, where the soil was less acidic and the quality of the coca leaf was the best for mastication. Coca was central to the culture, religion, and physical needs of the highland Indians. It served a sacred, healing role in folk medicine and as an offering to the ancient gods, and it was found to alleviate altitude sickness, suppress hunger, and nutritionally supplement the diet. Prescribed ritual and social uses, the geographical growing constraints, and official regulation and taxation naturally limited the coca crop. After the 1953 Agrarian Reform, national governments opened up settlement of the lowlands and diverted revenues to develop the rich, untapped eastern tropics. Expansion of coca growing was directly related to the development of the eastern lowlands, and to the failures of that development.

With the completion of the road from Cochabamba to Santa Cruz in 1954 and construction of later roads from the Altiplano and into the isolated Chapare, the planting of coca expanded as internal, and subsequently external, demand increased. Major demographic changes in agricultural migration and settlement into the lowlands speeded the process. After 1969, a wave of migrants from the valleys of Cochabamba and the Altiplano were drawn to the agricultural bonanza of Santa Cruz. At first, the sugar-cane harvests attracted largely seasonal and male migrants as cane cutters—some 12,000 yearly—during the 1960s. The magnet in the 1970s was the rise of cotton and its insatiable demand for labor of all kinds, including women and children. Cotton employed 34,000 pickers in 1974, many of them whole families, half of whom settled permanently. In fact, a 1979 survey of the city of Santa Cruz found that 44 percent of the city's residents were migrants; and a 1980 census estimated that some 22,000 migrants from the valleys and Altiplano settled yearly in the city of Santa Cruz. At the time, the department of Santa Cruz boasted the highest per capita income in the country.[31]

Underdevelopment, uneven development, and dependent development were fundamental causes of the cocaine traffic problem. As one journalist observed, "all of the country's endemic disadvantages—its landlocked borders, inaccessible interior, wretched rural poverty, political instability, ingrained government corruption, and long-standing tradition of contraband—emerged as pillars of strength for the cocaine industry."[32] Uneven economic development provided the transportation infrastructure, the agrarian settlement, and migration important to coca cultivation; but the unprecedented, but artificial, economic growth in the Oriente under the state capitalist model, and the impressive, but temporary, profits in sugar, cotton, and rice during the 1970s, delayed the coca growing explosion. However, by 1978, when thousands of peasants were left unemployed in the wake of the agrarian slump, coca production seemed both the logical and only alternative for survival. For those accustomed to the "boom town" lifestyle, it also provided an attractive option.

The obvious, but complex, relationship between the coca trade and rural development left North American officials ambivalent about further agricultural and infrastructural expansion, as such expansion appeared to facilitate further coca growing. One U.S. ambassador was quoted in the press as saying that electrification would permit the narcotics traffickers to work through the night, and more roads would merely aid the exit of the coca from the country. The problem appeared to be circular.[33] The failure to support development would only increase economic pressures to turn to the trade, whereas short-run development could actually assist the cocaine traffic. Because of this dilemma, the United States sought to combine development efforts with eradication and enforcement measures. Unfortunately, the emphasis was on enforcement.

The U.S. approach to the cocaine problem was fundamentally negative and self-defeating. Rather than assume some responsibility for the problem, given that as many as 15 million Americans might be users of the drug, the United States shifted the onus onto the producing country,

A Yapacaní colonist and her child standing outside their homestead. The Yapacaní settlement, near the Yapacaní River, has been an area of colonization since the 1960s. Many of the early settlers were ex-miners trucked in by the Bolivian Development Corporation (photo by Allyn MacLean Stearman).

as part of the campaign against the "Four C's": communism, cocaine, contraband, and corruption. U.S. policy expected a country such as Bolivia, whose very underdevelopment left it prey to the illegal traffic, to overcome that underdevelopment, almost single-handedly, and to control the problem with extremely limited assistance—when the United States, with its massive economic resources, sophisticated enforcement machinery, and political power was unable to do so at home. Bolivian enforcement officials estimated that $1 billion were necessary to control the traffic, whereas the United States tentatively offered $57 million over five years. The Bush administration, despite its heightened rhetoric and diplomatic activism in the "war on drugs," proposed $2.2 billion in military and economic aid for 1990–1994 to the three Andean producers, Colombia, Peru, and Bolivia, of which the proportion for economic development was considered inadequate. Bolivia's share in economic and military assistance, allocated for fiscal year 1992, exceeded $200 million.[34] Although the Bush policy (known as the so-called Bennett Plan in Bolivia) was more sensitive to the demand-side argument and deemphasized eradication measures, the thrust remained enforcement and interdiction, especially by military means.[35] The limited U.S. economic commitment, particularly to the areas most in need of assistance, belied a real desire to solve the drug problem. Americans basically mistrusted the Bolivians and were unwilling to pour massive funds down what was perceived to be a bottomless well. Former Ambassador Corr revealed the private U.S. view: "This is a social problem that will probably never be solved. Our goal is to make it manageable."[36]

Manageability encouraged the emphasis on eradication and enforcement, but U.S. officials have themselves argued that "enforcement itself is not a solution. Farmers have to realize that they can have a better way of life."[37] Nevertheless, eradication and enforcement were not only more easily implemented and monitored but also less expensive than extensive development assistance. However, enforcement made peasants bear the brunt of coca eradication as coca crops were burned or defoliated with controversial herbicides. Often, compensation for the destruction or the promised crop substitution, road development, and welfare improvements were delayed or mismanaged, or fell short of expectations. For example, the Law for the Control of Coca and Dangerous Substances of July 1988 sought to regulate production in three geographical zones: the Yungas, a traditional and legal growing sector; Cochabamba Department, divided into traditional, transitional, and illegal areas; and the tropical Yapacaní, an illegal zone. Peasants were to be paid $2,000 per hectare to eradicate more than 33,000 hectares over five years. But most of this crop-substitution money was rarely forthcoming from the national government. Moreover, although the law had projected an eradication goal of 5,000 hectares for 1989, only 1,100 hectares had been eradicated by June and who knows how many more start-ups had occurred elsewhere. Of course, this eradication shortfall resulted in a temporary "glitch" in economic aid receipts. By the end of 1989, only some 2,400 hectares (6,000 acres) had been eradicated. With more repressive measures, authorities achieved the 7,500-hectare eradication quota mandated by law for 1990. But the dangers in these methods were the anti-Americanism engendered among a population that had traditionally been very pro-American and the loss of peasant faith in the government—both of which had a very destabilizing effect on the fragile return to civilian democracy.

U.S. anti-narcotics policy ignored fundamental political obstacles. Just as the central foreign (and domestic) policy goal of the United States was to reduce the cocaine traffic to manageable proportions, the key political objective of the Siles, Víctor Paz, and Paz Zamora governments was to remain in power. The two priorities often conflicted. Moreover, the elite anti-narcotics police—trained by the United States and supported by U.S. funds—were perceived by the people as "the other Mafia" and as a cabal of paramilitary coup-plotters against democracy. Another dilemma was the direct and indirect infringement on Bolivia's sovereignty entailed by the U.S. drug control policy. Especially in 1990, campaigns for the defense of national sovereignty, spearheaded by numerous popular peasant, labor, political, and religious groups, rallied to the cry of "no to militarization, yes to development." Desperately needed economic assistance was tied to progress in drug enforcement and eradication, generally measured in terms of the number of seizures. Numerous high-ranking and working-level U.S. officials of both the Reagan and Bush administrations held remarkably similar positions: No measurable progress on drug control, no foreign assistance. By 1990, U.S. aid was further conditioned on the military's entry into the drug war. For most Bolivians, including the majority opposed to and embarrassed by the drug connection, these policies were reminiscent of the nearly four decades of servility to U.S. foreign policy interests at the expense of Bolivia's legitimate quest for full national sovereignty. The anti-narcotics program, therefore, clashed with a fundamental goal of the Bolivian revolution—independent foreign, as well as domestic, policy.

NOTES

1. This thesis was popularized in Bolivia by various economists, including Víctor Paz Estenssoro, "Bolivia," *Pensamiento económico latinoamericano* (Mexico City: Fondo de Cultura Económica, 1945).

2. L. Enrique García-Rodríguez, "Structural Change and Development Policy in Bolivia," in Ladman, *Modern-Day Bolivia*, p. 176.

3. *Short-Term Economic Reports, Vol. IX, Bolivia. Magnitude and Origin of the Economic Crisis of 1982 and the Economic Policies of the Constitutional Government*, SG/Ser.G.41.14 (Washington, D.C.: Department of Economic Affairs, General Secretariat, Organization of American States, 1984), pp. 26–27.

4. Ibid., pp. 13, 19–20.

5. John Crabtree et al., *The Great Tin Crash: Bolivia and the World Tin Market* (London: Latin American Bureau, 1987).

6. Jerry R. Ladman, "Prospects for the Future," in Ladman, ed., *Modern-Day Bolivia: Legacy of the Revolution and Prospects for the Future* (Tempe: Center for Latin American Studies, Arizona State University, 1982), pp. 371–381.

7. The International Tin Council (ITC) was a twenty-two-nation body of consumers and producers of tin that administered the International Tin Agreement (ITA) and sought to manage production and keep the price of tin stable. In times of glut, the ITC would buy up excess tin supplies and stockpile these in order to shore up the price, thus regulating and adjusting the tin industry to prevent a major market collapse.

8. Crabtree, *The Great Tin Crash*, pp. 61, 69, 83.

9. "Bolivian Economic Report, 1979–1980," U.S. Embassy, La Paz, July 1980 (mimeograph).

10. *Short-Term Economic Reports*, p. 51; *Evaluación económica 1989*, Informe Confidencial (La Paz: Müller & Asociados, January 1990), pp. 6–7, 181.

11. *Short-Term Economic Reports*, p. 9.

12. "Balanza comercial boliviana fue positiva el pasado año," *Opinión* (Cochabamba), March 26, 1990, p. 2. For differing figures on the balance of trade, see *Evaluacíon económica 1989*, p. 16; Samuel Doria Medina, *Estabilización y crecimiento, reto del mañana: balance y perspectivas de la economía boliviana* (La Paz: Editorial Offset Boliviana [EDOBOL], 1988), pp. 12, 52; and Samuel Doria Medina, *1987 la quimera de la reactivación, balance y perspectivas de la economía boliviana* (La Paz: Editorial Offset Boliviana [EDOBOL], 1987), pp. 15, 84.

13. Based on figures from a 1990 report by the Central Bank of Bolivia, and presented in "Balanza comercial boliviana fue positiva el pasado año," March 26, 1990, p. 2.

14. James W. Wilkie, "U.S. Foreign Policy and Economic Assistance in Bolivia, 1948–1976," in Ladman, *Modern-Day Bolivia*, pp. 83–85.

15. Ibid., pp. 90–91, 103.

16. "Andean Initiative, Legislative Update," Washington Office on Latin America (WOLA), March 1991, p. 7.

17. *Short-Term Economic Reports*, pp. 22, 25–26, 75–77.

18. For a similar interpretation of how Bolivian governments contracted nearly $6 billion in external debt between 1952 and 1987, see "Deuda externa (I): como y quienes nos endeudaron," *Informe "R"* (La Paz), Centro de Documentación e Información (CEDOIN), Año III, No. 161 (November II, 1988), pp. 6–7.

19. Melvin Burke, "The Stabilization Programs of the International Monetary Fund: The Case of Bolivia," *Marxist Perspectives*, Vol. 6 (Summer 1979), pp. 118-133.

20. Robert Graham, "Bolivia Shows How Austerity Wins Votes," *Financial Times* (London), May 18, 1989.

21. Erick Foronda, "Bolivia: Paz Has Trouble Selling 'Economic Miracle,'" *Latinamerica Press*, Vol. 21, No. 5 (February 16, 1989), p. 7.

22. Finance Minister Ramiro Cabezas, quoted in *Latin American Weekly Report*, August 10, 1989, p. 7.

23. Foronda, "Bolivia: Paz Has Trouble Selling 'Economic Miracle,'" p. 7.

24. Jackson Diehl, "U.S. Drug Crackdown Stalls in Bolivia," *Washington Post*, January 23, 1984, pp. A1, A20.

25. *Latin American Weekly Report*, January 3, 1986, p. 11; and October 25, 1985, p. 6.

26. *Presencia* (La Paz), July 23, 1982.

27. Coca Production figures, like most statistics in Bolivia, vary widely. The statistics provided here are based on a composite of sources, of which the following are a representative sample: *Presencia* (La Paz), July 25, 1982; *El Mundo* (Santa Cruz), July 26, 1982; William E. Carter and Mauricio Mamani P., *Coca en Bolivia* (La Paz: Editorial Juventud, 1986), pp. 110–112; Ray Henkel, "The Bolivian Cocaine Industry" (pp. 60–64), and Harry Sanabria, "Coca, Migration and Social Differentiation in the Bolivian Lowlands" (pp. 90–96), in *Drugs in Latin America: Studies in Third World Societies*, No. 37 (Williamsburg, Va.: Department of Anthropology, College of William and Mary, 1986); *Los Tiempos* (Cochabamba), May 4, 1982; *Latin America Weekly Report*, September 13, 1984, p. 9; David Kline, "How to Lose the Coke War," *Atlantic*, Vol. 259, No. 5 (May 1987), p. 22; "Andean Chiefs and Bush in Drug Accord," *New York Times*, February 16, 1990, pp. A1, A9; and "World Drug Crop Up Sharply in 1989 Despite U.S. Effort," *New York Times*, March 2, 1990, pp. A1–A2.

28. Jackson Diehl, "Anti-Cocaine Agents Head for Fields," *Washington Post*, November 12, 1982, p. A19.

29. Anthony Henman, *Mama coca* (Colombia: El Anacora Editores, 1981); and Anthony Henman, Roger Lewis, and Tim Malyon, *Big Deal: The Politics of the Illicit Drug Business* (London: Pluto Press, 1985).

30. *Katarismo* has been expressed in the form of legal political parties and peasant organizations as well as clandestine guerrilla forces such as the Katarist Liberation Front (Frente de Liberación Katarista, FULKA). The movement takes its name from Tupac Katari, a famous eighteenth century Indian rebel leader whose real name was Julian Apaza. Tupac Katari fought against the Spanish and died attempting to regain the freedom and land of the Aymara Indians.

31. Allyn MacLean Stearman, *Camba and Kolla: Migration and Development in Santa Cruz, Bolivia*, (Gainesville: University Presses of Florida, 1985).

32. Jonathan Kandell, "The Great Bolivian Cocaine Scam," *Penthouse* (August 1982), p. 164.

33. Alfredo Medrano, "Chapare: agroindustria a cambio de erradicar cultivas de coca," *Los Tiempos* (Cochabamba), July 25, 1982, p. 4.

34. Andean Initiative, Legislative Update," Washington Office on Latin America (WOLA), March 1991, p. 7.

35. Waltraud Queiser Morales, "The War on Drugs: A New U.S. National Security Doctrine?" *Third World Quarterly*, Vol. 11, No. 3 (July 1989), pp. 147–169.

36. Jackson Diehl, "Economy Booms in Cocaine Country," *Washington Post*, November 11, 1982, pp. A1, A29–A30.

37. Ibid., November 12, 1982, p. A19.

7

Bolivia's Foreign Policy

Bolivia's external relations have been influenced by three important conditions: geopolitics, economic and political dependency, and persistent domestic instability. Despite numerous internal governmental shifts, the persistence of these conditions throughout Bolivia's history as an independent nation has endowed its foreign policy with a basic continuity that has had both positive and negative consequences. Persistence in achieving certain goals—particularly a Pacific seacoast—has combined with limited successes to create a mood of frustration and desperation which characterizes the external relations of many a Third World country with greater assets than Bolivia.

DETERMINANTS OF FOREIGN POLICY

The fundamental determinants of Bolivia's foreign relations are intertwined and have demanded almost simultaneous attention for foreign policy success. Singly or in combination, they have complicated the realization of core foreign policy objectives such as sovereign access to the sea and a more visible and nonaligned political posture regionally and globally. Overcoming the tenacious constraints of geopolitics, dependency, and internal instability, as well as the sense of impotence imposed by these constraints, remains the major challenge confronting the foreign policy agenda of present and future Bolivian governments.

Geopolitics

Defined as "geopolicy, or the dynamic aspects of those combined geographic and political factors that influence the options and strategies of a nation's foreign policy," geopolitics has been an important dimension in the Bolivian struggle for political and economic sovereignty.[1] Traditionally, Bolivia has been perceived by its neighbors as a geographical anomaly, as an unnatural state unable to harness its extreme regionalism and its racial and cultural diversity into a unified, strong, and centralized

173

nation. Geopolitical factors have also rendered Bolivian foreign policy a reactive and defensive response to the persistent expansionism of its neighbors. As the strategic "heartland" and geopolitical center of South America, dividing north and south, east and west, and endowed with valuable and extensive natural resources coveted by its neighbors, Bolivia historically has been a zone of intense intraregional rivalry and conflict.

In major wars and confrontations with Peru, Chile, Argentina, Brazil, and Paraguay, Bolivian territory was reduced by half, whereas its geopolitical vulnerability, isolation, and economic impoverishment were increased. Geopolitical forces were at work when Bolivian independence from Spain was delayed until the liberations of Lima and Buenos Aires; when in 1839 the Peru-Bolivian Confederation was undermined by Peru, Chile, and Argentina; when Bolivia lost its seacoast in 1879 to Chile and Peru; when Brazil seized the Amazonian territory in 1903; and in 1935, when Bolivia lost much of the Chaco to Paraguay.

Bolivia's neighbors have defined their geopolitical interests as the preservation of a weakened and divided Bolivian buffer state—an unwilling pawn in the "balance of power" jockeying by the more powerful Southern Cone actors. From the Brazilian perspective, expansion into Bolivia would increase Brazilian influence in the Andean region and fulfill a "manifest destiny" toward the Pacific; it would expand vital economic and mineral assets of iron ore, oil, and natural gas necessary for Brazilian development and great-power stature. Similarly, in Argentinean foreign policy, Bolivia has been an object of northward expansion and considered a possible, though long-range, route to the Pacific (versus the Beagle Islands route). Bolivia has served as a balancer in Argentina's long-standing rivalry with Brazil and Chile. Economic and geopolitical tensions between Peru and Chile have impinged directly on Bolivia's strategy to regain coastal lands. And the "ABC" powers of Argentina, Brazil, and Chile have repeatedly intervened—directly or indirectly—in Bolivian internal affairs, supporting incumbents or opposition movements and manipulating interest groups for their own foreign policy ends. These geopolitical constraints have been integrally related to the problem of dependency and its impact on foreign policy.

Dependency

Many Latin American countries grapple with economic and political dependency, so the problem is not unique to Bolivia; but its dependency may be more pronounced because geopolitics and domestic instability have made it difficult for Bolivia to offset detrimental consequences unilaterally through its foreign policy. Bolivia is a large and potentially wealthy nation able to influence external factors only very minimally, because dependency has rendered it a "penetrated" and "semisovereign" system, controlled by internal social and economic elites as well as by powerful external economic and political interests. Whether in the form of Spanish colonial monopolies, twentieth-century tin barons, or Wall Street bankers—or of the United States or the IMF today—powerful external economic interests have circumscribed the options for a truly independent foreign policy. A dependent foreign policy for Bolivia has meant external relations conditioned by the ideological, class, and economic interests of other countries—that is, by its neighbors and by the United States.

A dependent foreign policy was traditionally imposed upon Bolivia by the United States by means of three weapons: tin quotas and prices, aid and loans, and the manipulation of diplomatic relations and recognition. Although Bolivian dependence on tin for national and governmental revenues declined after 1970, the United States remained the largest consumer (around 50 percent) and stockpiler of Bolivian tin. General Services Administration (GSA) sales continued to be used to pressure conformity with U.S. interests in foreign, as well as domestic, areas. The decision to sell 20,000 tons of tin in December 1981 provoked sharp Bolivian protests and Bolivia's temporary withdrawal from the International Tin Council on June 26, 1982. Of course, when the Bolivian tin era came to a precipitous end in 1985, this weapon was no longer very useful. Nevertheless, the announcement of GSA sales from the tin stockpile in 1991 evoked cries of protest.

In the early 1940s, an aid and loan policy was developed that provided a fine-tuned instrument whereby the United States could ensure favorable domestic governments and supportive foreign policies, such as support of the Allied war effort and a declaration of war against the Axis. Shortly after the revolution, this pattern continued as the Eder Mission and the Agency for International Development (AID) established administrative checks and controls over Bolivian development policy through the power of the purse. Radical economic-development policies and distributive programs were systematically weakened by North American experts in favor of capitalist development schemes, which helped undermine important socioeconomic goals of the revolution. U.S. aid and military assistance to Bolivia were the highest per capita in Latin America between 1960 and 1964. Under "friendly" military governments such as Banzer's, loans and grants increased; for example, they tripled in the one year between 1973 and 1974. But under the "unfriendly" García Meza regime, U.S. aid was abruptly curtailed, successfully undermining that unsavory government. In the 1980s, aid was used to pressure the successive military as well as civilian governments (those of Torrelio, Vildoso, Siles Zuazo, Paz Estenssoro, and Paz Zamora). Times were especially difficult for President Siles (1982–1985) because the severe Bolivian economic crisis, compounded by major natural disasters, increased the government's vulnerability to U.S. pressure. Moreover, Siles's reformist populism was not popular with North American foreign policy managers. Delays and cuts in U.S. aid in early 1983, for example, served to moderate the influence of communist ministers in the cabinet of the newly elected Siles Zuazo. But external pressures seemed to have little effect on the Siles government's independent, Third World foreign policy. Such independence was not the case with the foreign policies of the Paz Estenssoro and Paz Zamora governments, which followed the lead of the White House.

Domestic Instability

During a round of negotiations to regain territorial access to the sea, a Chilean diplomat observed that Bolivia's greatest liability was its lack of national stability and unity: Ineffective internal control has translated into ineffective foreign policy. Ironically and tragically, Bolivians have sought the use of external relations to manipulate domestic dissent and impose from without the stability and unity that could not be generated from within. Historically, the seacoast issue has served to generate an artificial national consensus that has generally been detrimental to resolution of the maritime problem. The Siles Zuazo government's representative to the Organization of American States (OAS) stated in a speech "that the external policy could be the major factor of national unity to save the country."[2] This fallacious strategy doomed the foreign policies of both the military and the civilian regimes, hindering the effectiveness of Bolivia's diplomats and the country's credibility abroad. Nevertheless, no Bolivian government has been able to escape the unfortunate linkage between domestic instability and external affairs. The problems of rampant partisanship, ideological polarization, and the chronic threat of military intervention have impinged upon the foreign policies of the recent civilian governments. Especially under Siles, cabinet instability about every three to five months resulted in three different foreign ministers in 1983 alone; and by late 1984, there had been six cabinet changes in two years of rule. The greater cabinet stability under Paz Estenssoro, however, did not result in a more successful foreign policy. Clearly other factors were at work as well. The new seacoast initiatives of the Paz Zamora government assumed that the international and inter-American climate, and the internal political conditions within the countries of Chile and Peru, were also critical. Bolivian domestic instability, although it often hampered success in foreign affairs, generally did not disrupt the relative constancy of Bolivia's overall foreign policy objectives.

OBJECTIVES OF FOREIGN POLICY

Historically, internal regime changes have produced two distinctive foreign policy positions: a United States–centric orientation and a Third Worldist stance. In the 1980s, the Siles Zuazo administration alone opted for a nonaligned, Third World strategy, for several reasons. Empathy with the Third World and its struggle for socioeconomic equality and development was a natural extension of a reformist and populist domestic program. A nonaligned approach was perceived as a truly independent foreign policy position, equidistant from the cold war entanglements of both the United States and the Soviet Union. And, finally, the Siles government believed that a "globally involved" policy would maximize the attainment of traditional foreign policy objectives, especially the resolution of Bolivia's landlocked isolation. The Paz Estenssoro and Paz Zamora governments, largely because of their more pragmatic and conservative orientation, reversed much of this logic; but the results for the seacoast question were similarly unsuccessful.

The Seacoast

A constant Bolivian foreign policy goal has been the recovery of some portion of the seacoast lost in the Pacific War. In 1974, an important initiative was taken in the Ayacucho Declaration with Chile, which recognized the importance of a sea outlet for Bolivia. In December 1975, a Chilean proposal provided a Bolivian outlet to the sea north of Arica in exchange for Bolivian territory equal to the area ceded in the corridor and the land equivalence of the 200-mile extension of territorial waters. The convergence of regional and domestic forces made possible this historic breakthrough in negotiations.

At that juncture, President Salvador Allende had already been overthrown by the violent military government of Augusto Pinochet in Chile. Diplomatically isolated because of its human rights violations, Chile was receptive to Bolivia's foreign policy initiatives. Similarly, the military governments of Ernesto Geisel in Brazil and Francisco Morales Bermúdez in Peru encouraged the rapprochement between Pinochet and Bolivian General Hugo Banzer. After Chile received recognition from the international community and aid was restored, the initiative was lost. Peru's counterproposal was rejected by the Chileans, and key political groups in Bolivia opposed the Banzer negotiations. The Bolivians rejected territorial compensation in principle, whereas the Chileans demanded territorial exchange.

Banzer's diplomatic efforts over three years earned little domestic support; rather, the constant criticism revealed domestic divisions that undermined his foreign policy and ultimately backfired against him. Instead of legitimizing his rule, foreign policy was used by the opposition to destabilize him. The failed initiative demonstrated the fundamental differences that separated the Bolivian, Chilean, and Peruvian governments on the maritime question, despite the like-minded domestic policies of the three military regimes. Military governments appeared no more able to surmount diplomatic obstacles than were socialist or civilian governments. By 1977, the diplomatic opening had come to an abrupt end. Bolivia severed diplomatic relations with Chile in 1978, and maintained only consular relations, thus reverting to the situation between 1962 and 1975.

The Siles government continued this nonrecognition policy and exchanged only consular representatives with Chile, arguing that when Chile reopened the seacoast question, Bolivia would reinstitute full exchange of ambassadors. Given Chilean domestic unrest and the ascendance of democratic governments in the Southern Cone, Bolivia's strategy of pressure and diplomatic isolation of Chile was more successful than similar policies in the past. Despite Bolivian domestic problems, the Siles Zuazo government handled the seacoast issue more adeptly than Banzer's had. Avoiding an all-or-nothing bilateral approach, Bolivia, in conjunction with the "Ninth Attempt to Dialogue With Chile," pursued the seacoast question decisively in every conceivable foreign policy forum. In the spring of 1983, Chile had intimated that some kind of dialogue with La Paz was possible. Latin American watchers interpreted this as the first major overture since 1978.[3] At the Santo Domingo meeting of Latin American parliaments in February 1984, Bolivia supported a resolution not to extend recognition to dictatorships, thus indirectly applying pressure on Chile.

During the Falklands War, Bolivia favored Argentinean claims to the Malvinas, generating support for its own territorial hopes. Bolivia took its case to the Andean bloc, the La Plata grouping of countries, the OAS, the United Nations, and the Nonaligned Movement. The seacoast issue was included in the Regular Sessions of the OAS from 1979 to 1983. Bolivia's plight was the special concern of the "Small Island and Land-Locked Developing States" resolution adopted in the OAS and elaborated in the "Report on the Maritime Problem of Bolivia" on November 20, 1982. Late in December 1982, at the Thirteenth Foreign Ministers Meeting of the La Plata Basin nations in Brasilia, the seacoast campaign continued. It figured prominently at the Andean Pact parliament in March 1983 and at the Caracas bicentennial celebration of Bolívar's birth in May. Early the same year, Siles had discussed the topic at the United Nations during his visit to New York. Several Third World forums in 1983, the Coordinating Committee meeting in Managua, the Seventh

Summit of the Nonaligned Movement in New Delhi, and the Fifth Meeting of the "Group of 77" in Buenos Aires provided further opportunities to gather support for Bolivia's territorial aims. Numerous bilateral talks with Argentina, Brazil, France, Spain, Panama, and Yugoslavia—to mention a few—enlisted additional supporters. Although there were no tangible results to these comprehensive and aggressive overtures, an international climate sympathetic to Bolivia's position appeared to be forming.

The Paz Estenssoro administration initially continued the multilateral strategy in the OAS and in the Andean parliament into December 1985, emphasizing that the seacost was an issue of permanent hemispheric interest. However, a significant shift then occurred in the United Nations after Bolivia failed to censure the Chilean human rights record, and in January the foreign ministry was reorganized and Chilean-Bolivian diplomatic relations upgraded. Thus a new bilateral strategy emerged under the direction of Bolivia's recently appointed consul general to Chile, Ambassador Jorge Siles Salinas, brother-in-law of the Chilean foreign minister. During the "Día del Mar" celebrations in March 1986, Víctor Paz formally announced the decision to take a new course and pursue a "new pragmatic imperative." Of course, critics argued that this "Chileanization" of Bolivian foreign policy would not work because Pinochet was a weakened and bankrupt dictator. And they seemed to be correct. After the official Bolivian proposal was presented in the 1986 Montevideo meeting, there was an ominous silence from Chile. The Bolivians proposed to buy outright a ten-mile strip north of Arica along the Peruvian border. In July 1987, Admiral Merino, president of the Chilean military junta, responded: "To Bolivia, nothing, ever!"

Nevertheless, the diplomatic offensive to secure a sovereign seacoast continued indefatigably under Jaime Paz Zamora, who emphasized in his August 1989 inaugural address that only a coastline could mitigate the tremendous geographical and economic obstacles to national development and the constrictive geopolitical encirclement of Bolivia by its powerful neighbors. His call for a "new twenty-first century mentality" on the maritime question combined elements of all foregoing policies— multilateral, inter-American, and bilateral. President Paz Zamora appealed for a common Latin American spirit of well-being and launched a series of meetings with Latin American presidents (from Argentina, Brazil, Venezuela, and Peru) to gain their diplomatic support on the seacoast question. At the United Nations General Assembly in September, he expressed hope for a democratic change of government in Chile as a way to open dialogue. In 1990, an extensive diplomatic offensive in Europe began to familiarize that community with Bolivia's aims. Practicing a style of personal shuttle diplomacy (the *diplomacia de contacto personal*),

Paz Zamora visited major European capitals that spring and fall (those of Spain, Italy, Belgium, Sweden, and the Federal Republic of Germany); and he consulted with the Vatican and the European parliament. Indeed, his many travels were the object of much domestic criticism by the political opposition.

Closer to home, in New York, Paz Zamora reaffirmed the Bolivian position before the UN General Assembly in March 1990: "Bolivia will never renounce its basic thesis: to recover its condition as a maritime nation with which it was born as a sovereign and independent nation."[4] And in Latin America, when he attended the inauguration of newly elected Chilean President Patricio Aylwin, the seacoast question was raised. The Bolivian foreign chancellery believed that a long-standing obstacle to movement on the maritime issue had been the authoritarian military government of Pinochet—in part because Bolivia had severed ambassadorial-level relations with Pinochet in 1978 and had made maritime talks a necessary precondition to the restoration of full diplomatic relations. A central strategy in Paz Zamora's seacoast diplomacy was to appeal to the democratizing sentiments in the region, and Aylwin was the first democratic president elected in Chile since 1973. However, when the two met in March, Alywin reversed the position of La Paz and insisted that Bolivia should reestablish diplomatic relations with Chile as a precondition of a new dialogue on the seacoast; once relations exist, argued Aylwin, anything can be discussed.[5] Paz Zamora then turned to the Latin American parliament (composed of parliamentarians of the region), meeting in its Fifth Extraordinary Session in La Paz. Summoned at Bolivia's initiative to consider the U.S. military intervention in Panama, the Latin American parliament strongly endorsed La Paz's seacoast aspirations (affirming the 1979 OAS resolution). Parliamentary leaders from fourteen countries of the region urged Chile and Bolivia to capitalize on the "democratic opening" in the region and to hold popular plebiscites on the seacoast problem. Finally, during a three-day visit to Washington in May, Paz Zamora reportedly urged President Bush's support of Bolivia's maritime status.[6] Nevertheless, at the end of this hectic round of diplomacy, Paz Zamora announced that "relations with the democratic Chilean government are good but unchanged."[7]

As the dilemma of Bolivia's landlocked status continued into the 1990s, the problem seemed intractable—perhaps as the Berlin Wall and the question of the two Germanies must have once seemed in Central Europe. But there were words of wisdom. After the shock of the historic failure at Charaña, then Bolivian chancellor, Eduardo Arze Quiroga, concluded:

> It will be impossible to speak of an effective solution to Bolivia's landlocked status, without first achieving a sufficient increase in power and influence

which will permit us to negotiate with Chile under conditions of equality. A truly fundamental solution will only be achieved when the cultural and economic growth of Bolivia provides a sufficiently adequate capacity to negotiate."[8]

Unfortunately, the United States, overly influential in many other Bolivian affairs, did not champion this particular Bolivian cause, thereby ignoring one powerful, potential avenue to promote pro-American sentiment with little cost to itself. Instead, U.S. relations with Bolivia tended to ignore basic Bolivian national interests. Historically, major bilateral problems focused on tin prices and stockpiles, a stable political climate, and a subservient foreign policy. More recently, the explosion in coca leaf production and processing into cocaine paste, and the "war on drugs" itself, virtually dominated diplomatic relations.

Relations with the United States

The strategic importance of Bolivian tin for U.S. industrialization and defense, as well as the inordinate poverty and weakness of Bolivia, became the basis for a long-standing dominance by the United States. By the end of World War I, U.S. influence in Bolivia had no rival. The major tin company, Patiño Mines, was incorporated in Delaware in 1924, and the second largest, Caracoles Tin Company, was established in 1922 by the Guggenheim family. Given its geopolitical conditions and its economic dependence on the United States, Bolivia was unable to pursue a neutralist foreign policy in World War II and during the cold war era. Increasingly, its foreign policy was determined by the United States.

After briefly flirting with the Axis cause in 1943, diplomatic and economic pressure by the United States encouraged Bolivia to declare war on the Axis. A policy of nonrecognition, which the other Latin republics (with the exception of Argentina) also imposed at U.S. insistence, altered the political coalition government formed by the December 1943 Villarroel coup and led to the ouster of the MNR members opposed by the State Department. Bolivia was also encouraged to break diplomatic relations with Peronist Argentina, which had challenged U.S. hegemony in the Western Hemisphere by its Nazi sympathies. Only in June 1944, after Axis businesses were confiscated and agents expelled, did the United States and the other Latin foreign offices recognize the Villarroel government. A similar policy met with less immediate success in the case of Argentina. By 1944, the United States was no longer in need of Bolivian tin, leaving the Bolivian regime extremely vulnerable to diplomatic and economic pressure. The State Department report on the "Fascist Connections of the New Bolivian Regime," despite sparse evidence, proved successful. Argentina, however, was larger, more powerful, and had greater economic independence with which "to build a strong independent political position on the war."[9]

The economic carrot-and-stick policy was instrumental in influencing the domestic and external policies of Bolivian governments before and after the 1952 Revolution. In late 1941, economic and military aid encouraged the Peñaranda government to settle with Standard Oil, whose properties had been confiscated in 1937. The Bolivian foreign minister agreed to a $1.7 million indemnification in 1942, after which some $25 million in U.S. economic aid poured into the country. Until 1968, U.S. aid to Bolivia was the highest per capita in the world. Ironically, this support in the 1960s helped promote military regimes that, in the 1970s and 1980s, sought to reject U.S. influence, although military aid between 1972 and 1976 alone totaled $47 million—enough to outfit five army regiments.

During the military governments of Barrientos (1964–1969) and Banzer (1971–1978), relations with the United States were more cordial, especially after the strain of the MNR years and during the last years of the Paz Estenssoro government (1960–1964). In 1960, when the Eisenhower administration refused economic assistance to state enterprises, Bolivia threatened to apply to the Soviet Union. Before his election in 1960, Paz had visited Moscow and opened a legation in Prague. He now hoped to trade off normalized diplomatic exchange with the Soviets in return for development aid. Nikita Khrushchev initially offered some $150 million to assist the state-owned tin mines and oil industry. The leftists in the MNR, the Bolivian Communist Party, and the Bolivian House of Deputies favored the Soviet offer over that of the United States. Fearing an opening to the Soviets, the United States soon extended credit to Bolivia's Petroleum Company, and in 1961 Bolivia adopted the pro-Western Triangular Plan of development coordinated by the United States and West Germany. By 1964, when Bolivia again sought assistance for COMIBOL, the Soviets did not respond, and Bolivia found itself completely dependent on U.S. aid.[10]

Given its own revolutionary heritage, the Paz Estenssoro government identified with the Cuban Revolution and decided in January 1961 not to break off diplomatic relations with Cuba. Although Bolivian-Cuban relations were not cordial, Bolivia was among four Latin nations that did not support the diplomatic isolation of Cuba and its expulsion from the OAS. However, U.S. pressure and the majority resolution in the OAS favoring expulsion caused the government to reverse its position in July 1964. During the 1962 Cuban Missile Crisis, Bolivia opposed military sanctions against Cuba and abstained from portions of the resolution passed in the OAS. In 1963, Yugoslavia's President Josip Broz Tito visited Bolivia. As Tito was the founder of the Nonaligned Movement, his visit symbolized Bolivia's desire for an independent foreign policy equidistant from the two superpowers. Then Foreign Minister José Fellmann Velarde explained that "we must maintain the respect of our people, and this we cannot do if there is any suspicion that the United States has a hand in our foreign policy."[11]

As early as 1968, Bolivian–U.S. relations began to shift. The Barrientos government had cooperated closely with the United States in the counterinsurgency war against Ché Guevara's guerrilla foco in 1967. As a result, U.S. military and intelligence forces achieved a high visibility in Bolivia's internal affairs, disturbing the more nationalistic military officers. Mysteriously, a copy of Ché Guevara's diary found its way into the hands of Fidel Castro, generating a scandal that culminated in 1984, when the original copy disappeared and resurfaced in Sotheby's in London. In January 1968, Barrientos, despite his close ties with the United States, invited the Soviet Union to open trade with Bolivia; and in February 1969, he sought Soviet technical assistance for the state oil company. His government also supported the reaccreditation of Cuba in the OAS, against U.S. opposition. The attempt to distance Bolivia's foreign policy from North American influence under Barrientos was continued by the populist-reformist governments of Generals Ovando and Torres.

Influenced by Peru's nationalization of the International Petroleum Corporation in 1968, Ovando nationalized Bolivian Gulf in November 1969, a month after coming into power. In January 1970, Bolivia sent an ambassador to Moscow, marking the first official diplomatic exchange since recognition of the Soviet Union in 1945. The Bolivian ambassador described the upgraded relations as a "victory of the independent foreign policy of President Ovando Candia" and praised the role of the Soviet Union as a "counter-weight to imperialism." Ovando succeeded in attracting a $27.5 million loan from the Soviets that August, and there were plans for extensive Soviet technical assistance for oil and iron ore extraction.[12] In September, General Torres attended the Nonaligned Nations Conference in Lusaka as an observer. Bolivia also upgraded its diplomatic relations with Eastern European governments such as Poland and Hungary. Bolivia's bid for foreign policy independence, occurring at the time of revolutionary military rule in Peru and the Marxist government of Allende in Chile, strained relations with the United States. In response to the nationalization, the new Nixon administration withheld support for loans in multilateral development banks and did not initiate new bilateral economic aid. Treasury Secretary John B. Connally was quoted as observing at the time that "you don't negotiate just with American business enterprise. You negotiate with the U.S. government."[13] Domestic instability and external problems eventually brought the governments of Generals Ovando and Torres down and initiated another swing in foreign policy, symbolized by the $78 million compensation to Gulf Oil.

By August 1971, a policy of "independent neutralism" was reversed by the new head of state, General Banzer. Then, in March 1972, some 100 Soviet diplomats were expelled from the country, and the government restored friendly relations with the United States. This reversal was a clear success for North American policymakers, who had feared the "creation of an international front of left and left-inclined governments stretching from Chile via Bolivia to Peru and Ecuador."[14] Again domestic unrest, as military and civilian governments changed hands in rapid succession between July 1978 and July 1980, left Bolivian foreign policy to continue in the Banzer tradition. With the installation of General García Meza on July 17, Bolivian foreign policy faced a major challenge: how to legitimize a government ostracized by the United States and the Latin community for its cocaine involvement and human rights violations.

The results were less than exemplary and led to several uncoordinated diplomatic overtures. Bolivia's representative to the Nonaligned meeting in New Delhi supported the Cuban claim to Guantanamo, an act that the chancellery in La Paz immediately disavowed. Other informal and unofficial attempts to alter U.S. policy toward Bolivia proved so embarrassing that critics called it Bolivia's "unedited diplomacy." Bolivia's ambassador to the OAS, Alberto Quiroga, had reportedly attempted to buttonhole then Secretary of State Alexander Haig in the halls of the OAS, promising immediate progress in narcotics control if the United States would normalize relations with García Meza. Ex–Interior Minister Arce Gómez initiated his own "personal" diplomacy, hoping to wear down U.S. intransigence. Informally, the Bolivian government tried to alter Colombia's decision not to invite Bolivia's President García Meza to a meeting of Bolivarian countries in Santa Marta, but to no avail.

Given the government's disrepute, the North American policy of isolation and economic squeeze was successful. García Meza was forced to rely largely on economic assistance and diplomatic support from Argentina, which had assisted his coup with money and logistics. President Carter did not reappoint a U.S. ambassador to La Paz, and the "nonrecognition" policy was continued under what was believed would be a more sympathetic Reagan administration. Instead, the U.S. veto in the Inter-American Development Bank held up sorely needed development funds. The United States, which had attempted to influence its allies not to normalize relations with the García Meza regime, was displeased that Japan and Israel renewed diplomatic ties. This diplomatic and economic pressure, including the termination of the drug assistance program, secured the removal of the disreputable interior minister, Arce Gómez, from the cabinet in February 1981. By August, a "recognition by attrition" had set in with the ouster of García Meza. However, Edwin G. Corr was not appointed the new U.S. ambassador until November, when General Celso Torrelio was clearly in power.

For sixteen months U.S.-Bolivian relations had been chilly and severely restricted, but by December the United States sought "normalization" and progress on drug control. The United States lent support to a $220 million IMF loan to Bolivia, and in March 1982 Ambassador Corr praised the improvements in human rights under the Torrelio government and promised the prompt restoration of U.S. aid. Ambassador Corr, former assistant secretary of international narcotics affairs and experienced in drug control programs in Colombia and Peru, was an ideal choice for the new policy line. However, both Torrelio and Vildoso were too politically vulnerable and dependent on the military to cooperate more than half-heartedly with the narcotics campaign. The successor Siles Zuazo government was more willing but saddled by the worst economic crisis in recent history, an unstable coalition, and an innovative foreign policy objectionable to Washington.

The foreign policy of Siles Zuazo confronted the United States with a dilemma. Though his was a democratic civilian government that promised a vigorous antidrug program, it also pursued the kind of independent and neutralist foreign policies that the United States had opposed in the past under the MNR, Barrientos, Ovando, and Torres. Instead of the very conservative and pro-U.S. policy of García Meza, in Central America the new government sought closer relations with Nicaragua and Cuba and favored the Contadora process in El Salvador. Yet the government also arrested and prosecuted high officials implicated in drugs in previous regimes and conducted extensive sweeps into the Chapare coca region. In October 1984, Siles sought to negotiate with major drug figures, despite internal opposition, in an attempt to solve the critical cocaine problem. Nevertheless, U.S. pressure on his administration continued. The United States clearly found Bolivia's Third World foreign policy posture unacceptable.

Bolivia described its new foreign policy direction as "closer relations with all the countries of the world, respecting ideological pluralism . . . and affirming the principles of self-determination and non-intervention."[15] And Vice-President Jaime Paz Zamora stated that "our non-alignment is an affirmation of an autonomous policy in relation to the face-off between the two superpowers. A policy of nonalignment does not mean that we will not have friendly and fruitful relations with the United States, but it also does not signify conformity with North American policies."[16] In practice, the policy sought balanced relations with the global powers and as many countries as possible, as a means of minimizing external dependency and securing development assistance and broad international support for the reformist government. Bolivia renewed diplomatic relations with Cuba in January 1983 and recognized liberation movements such as the Polisario Liberation Front, the Palestine Liberation Organization, and the Salvadoran revolutionary struggle. It established ties with revolutionary Nicaragua and forged closer relations with the Soviet Union and Eastern bloc nations. And the new foreign policy attracted $70 million in Soviet assistance for a volatilization plant and tractor assembly plant in cooperative agreements signed in the fall of 1983.

Bolivia also cultivated friendly relations with Western nations such as Belgium, Spain, Switzerland, France, and Germany, all of which extended extensive economic assistance. Germany resumed the $50 million in aid suspended in 1980, whereas France extended a $14 million credit to finish the Military Hospital in La Paz and planned several binational development projects. Both countries were pleased with the 1983 deportation of Klaus Barbie (Altmann)—an action that had been blocked several times by Banzer in 1972 and 1974 and by recent military regimes. French Foreign Minister Claude Cheysson publicly praised the action of the Siles government and its democratization efforts. Although the Reagan administration had extended generous assistance—some $216 million in aid since 1982, a figure that AID officials expected to reach $300 million through 1987—the United States employed economic assistance to moderate Bolivia's foreign policy. Praise about the new democracy and the strong record on human rights was scarce; most economic assistance was politically tied or favored the private sector. Nor did the administration intercede on Bolivia's behalf with the World Bank and IMF.

In short, relations with Bolivia, while proper, were not especially warm. Accustomed to greater influence over Bolivia's internal and external affairs, Washington interpreted the new independent posture negatively. The radical rhetoric of the Siles coalition stimulated fears of socialism and communism, and its Third World friends were proof of Bolivia's defection from the U.S. camp. Moreover, Washington tried to interfere in the composition of Siles's UDP coalition, which had the only two communist ministers in key cabinet posts in South America. Despite a statement by a high Bolivian official that "the U.S. policy has been excellent in trying to support our democratic institutions," other sources conveyed the rumor that Ambassador Corr would provide immediate economic assistance if the communists were dropped from the cabinet. On one occasion Corr reportedly expressed the opinion that his government would support Bolivian democracy and constitutional government, but within the context of a pluralist society and as democracy is understood in the West.[17] The Reagan administration appeared to be trapped in its own ideological dilemma. On the one hand, the administration was pursuing an all-out drug control program, but with assistance only about 1 percent of U.S. military aid to El Salvador in 1983. On the other, the United States opposed most domestic and foreign policies of the new democracy, thereby weakening the very government that the U.S. policymakers expected to stamp out the cocaine mafia.

The return of Paz Estenssoro was welcomed by Washington for, indeed, he shifted emphasis from nonalignment and diplomatic relations with Marxist regimes to warmer U.S. ties. However, as with Siles, the debt (or economic stabilization) and the drug war were sensitive points of U.S. pressure. The Reagan administration linked improved bilateral relations to progress in drug control, and Paz was willing to demonstrate his compliance by joint military maneuvers (Operation Blast Furnace 1986 and United Forces 1987, 1988, and 1989) and the passage of the controversial Antidrug Abuse Act of 1988 (or Law of Controlled Substances). In November 1985, the United States released $8 million in economic assistance (which had been withheld from Siles) when Paz Estenssoro ordered the narcotics control forces, the "Leopardos" or UMOPAR (Rural Mobile Patrol Unit), into the Chapare on a major eradication campaign that began in December. Nevertheless, various North American delegations, one sent by the Senate Foreign Relations Committee in January 1986 and brief visits by U.S. Attorney General Richard Thornburgh and Secretary of State George Shultz in 1988, never seemed completely pleased. As a result of increased sweeps from 1986 to 1989, numerous violent confrontations erupted among the peasant coca growers, Bolivian narcotics forces, and U.S. drug control agents. Briefly, in March 1989, after another "fact-finding" tour by Thornburgh, the Paz Estenssoro government shifted direction from armed enforcement measures to voluntary crop substitution and announced a global initiative to seek some $600 million in aid from wealthy nations for economic development in the coca regions.

The U.S. response was the declaration of an all-out war on drugs and further militarization involving eradication and interdiction. U.S. economic and anti-drug aid to Bolivia, already $59 million in 1988, was further increased. In 1989, U.S. assistance to Bolivia, according to U.S. Ambassador Robert Gelbard, was the continent's largest, about $100 million; and more than half of this was indirectly related to the drug war. Opponents of the North American drug war charged that the new fear of drugs as a major national security threat was being manipulated by the United States to justify massive U.S. military intervention in the Andean region under the new unconventional war doctrine of low intensity conflict (LIC). Indeed, various U.S. military officials conceived of an Andean strategy wherein Bolivia would become the first country in South America with a formal U.S. military presence.[18] There were heated charges by U.S. Ambassador Gelbard in July 1989 that much of tropical Bolivia represented "free territories" completely in the control of the drug lords. In early 1990, he argued that involvement of the armed forces in the drug war was essential because Bolivian drug traffickers threatened democracy and stability. Although Bolivia did not have an insurgency problem (as did Peru), analysts feared that continued militarization would lead to the "Honduranization" of the country, which could provoke local unrest.

Whether Paz Estenssoro's 1989 tactical shift was merely a preelectoral maneuver was unclear, but given Washington's interests and influence in fighting the drug war, it was no surprise that the new Paz Zamora government promised strict enforcement measures and permitted a larger, often unwelcome, U.S. presence. For example, the temporary stationing of some 350 U.S. troops in Potosí in 1989 and 1990, to extend the airport landing strip, provoked fears of future U.S. intervention. Similar military civic action programs in 1990 not only failed to popularize the image of both Bolivian and U.S. military elements but also spawned popular political campaigns (and unidentified militant insurgent groups) to save Bolivian national sovereignty from further U.S. encroachments.

Paz Zamora's enforcement pledges were met in Washington that September with the Bush administration's 1989 National Drug Control Strategy Report. Part of the program's economic package was increased anti-narcotics assistance ($262 million for Bolivia, Colombia, and Peru combined in fiscal year 1990, and $2 billion for the three countries over the next five years), greater hemispheric coordination, and an enhanced role for U.S. military personnel. Diplomatically, the efforts culminated in the Andean Summit of "four presidents" in Cartagena, Colombia, in February 1990. During this meeting, the Bush administration remained focused on policing and interdiction—or, in the words of the final document, narcotics control "is essentially a law-enforcement matter."[19] In an interview with the press after the summit, President Bush described the meeting between consumers and producers as the "first anti-drug cartel." The three Andean presidents (from Bolivia, Colombia, and Peru) emphasized economic aid and growth as well as more demand-side solutions. Interestingly, the U.S. aid package to the three Andean nations represented only 4 percent of the total $10 billion U.S. drug enforcement budget; and of the updated 1990 aid disbursement figure for Bolivia (about $98 million), 70 percent was intended for "policing" related activities and only 30 percent for alternative development programs.[20] (See Table 7.1.)

TABLE 7.1

U.S. Narcotics-Related Assistance to Bolivia: Fiscal Year 1991 Allocations and Fiscal Year 1992
Requests (in millions of U.S. dollars)

	Military				Economic				
	FMF	IMET	EDA	Subtotal	ESF	DA	INC	Subtotal	Totals
FY 1991 Allocated	35.0	0.9	--	35.9	77.0	22.5	15.7	115.2	151.1
FY 1992 Requested	40.0	0.9	--	40.9	125.0	22.5	15.7	163.2	204.1
Account Totals* FY 1991	96.0	5.1	3.0	104.1	187.0	46.2	56.2	289.4	393.5
FY 1992	142.0	4.9	--	146.9	275.0	53.2	57.7	385.9	532.8

* Total sums of assistance for the Andean Region, which includes Bolivia, Colombia, Ecuador, and Peru.
Some minor accounts have been omitted here.

- Foreign Military Financing (FMF): primary account of military aid, for military and police units
- International Military Education and Training (IMET): training for military and police units
- Excess Defense Articles (EDA): aid and training for military and police units
- Economic Support Fund (ESF): defined as security assistance and primarily used for balance of
  payments support
- Development Assistance (DA): support for specific development, health, and education projects
- International Narcotics Control Assistance (INC): police aid and training

Source: "Andean Initiative, Legislative Update," March 1991, Washington Office on Latin America
(WOLA), p. 7.

  In 1990 and 1991, common Bolivian fears, expressed on the street
and in the press, were the "Colombianization" and "narcotization" of
bilateral U.S.-Bolivian relations—in other words, that diplomacy between
the two governments was being reduced to narcotics control and a fully
militarized war on drugs (as was the case with U.S.-Colombian relations).
And foreign policy was becoming "colonized" as the exclusive province
of several dozen narcotics control agencies, the Pentagon, and perhaps
even the U.S. Central Intelligence Agency (CIA). Several U.S. objectives
fanned such fears. One was the ratification by the Bolivian Congress of
a bilateral extradition treaty with the United States (similar to a treaty
between the United States and Colombia). The convention would facilitate
U.S. prosecution of notorious drug criminals, such as Luis Arce Gómez.
The "expulsion" of Arce Gómez (official Bolivian authorities insist it
was *not* an extradition) from the country in December 1989 was widely
criticized within Bolivia by human rights groups, the Supreme Court,
and opposition political parties as a violation of the constitution and

TABLE 7.2

U.S. Narcotics-Related Assistance to the Andean Region and Estimated Coca Leaf Production by Major Producers (assistance in millions of U.S. dollars and production in metric tons)

	FY1988	FY1989[a]	FY1990[b]	FY1991[c]	FY1992[d]
Economic[e]	136	118	133	233	328
Military[f]	37	110	206	160	205
Total	173	228	339	393	533

	Eco	Mil	Eco	Mil	Eco	Mil	Eco	Mil	Eco	Mil
Bolivia	72	15	74	16	86	63	100	52	148	57
Colombia	1	14	5	82	-	86	50	53	50	80
Peru	63	8	39	12	47	57	70	54	116	59
Total	136	37	118	110	133	206	220	159	314	196

	Production	
Bolivia	68,000	66,000
Colombia	22,000	33,000
Peru	111,000	124,000

[a]Estimated levels
[b]Revised 9/5/89
[c]Allocated; annual totals include military and economic funding for Ecuador.
[d]Requested; annual totals include military and economic funding for Ecuador.
[e]Economic assistance for FY 1988-1990 includes economic aid, or development aid, food aid, Peace Corps, and the Inter-American Foundation; for FY 1991-1992, includes Economic Support Fund (ESF), defined as security assistance and primarily destined for balance of payments support, and Development Assistance (DA), or support for specific development, health, and education projects.
[f]Military assistance for FY 1988-1990 includes: traditional military grants, loans and military training (International Military Education Training, IMET) as well as International Narcotics Control Assistance (INC), or police aid and training, but not funds for the Drug Enforcement Administration and regional antinarcotics programs. Military assistance for FY 1991-1992 military aid includes: Foreign Military Financing (FMF), or the primary account of military aid for military and police units; IMET, or military loans, grants and training; Excess Defense Articles (EDA), or aid and training for military and police units; and INC, or police aid and training in international narcotics control.

Sources: Calculated and recompiled from data based on figures from the State Department, Bureau of International Narcotics Affairs; New York Times, March 2, 1990, p. A2; Larry Nowels, Congressional Research Service, as cited in Latin America Update, Washington Office on Latin America (WOLA), Vol. 14, No. 5 (September-October 1989), p. 6; and "Andean Initiative, Legislative Update," March 1991, Washington Office on Latin America (WOLA), p. 7.

national sovereignty. A new extradition treaty (only a general turn-of-the-century document existed) would legalize the removal and prosecution in the United States of drug kingpins such as Robert Suárez Gómez (who had been serving a fifteen-year sentence in a La Paz prison since 1988) and ex-General Luis García Meza (on trial in Bolivia). In 1991, the Bush administration withheld some $88 million in Economic Support Funds until the treaty was ratified. (See Table 7.2.)

Another objective of U.S. policy was to convince public opinion in Bolivia (and abroad) that the drug problem represented a major national security threat for Bolivia and, hence, that military operations by national and U.S. forces were essential. Reports that foreign drug elements (largely Colombian) had violated Bolivia's national borders and were processing as much as a third of Bolivian coca leaf into cocaine, and that guerrilla groups (most likely aided by the Peruvian Tupac Amaru Revolutionary Movement) were increasingly active, were evidence of a threat. Ultimately, Paz Zamora's administration, despite the rhetoric of "Coca for Development," acquiesced in more and more militarization of the drug problem. The reward was powerful U.S. influence with multilateral lenders and with private commercial banks on Bolivia's behalf; these eventually extended "special" economic treatment to Bolivia. U.S. Ambassador Gelbard frankly admitted in 1990 that "Bolivia has actually received privileged treatment due to our help and presentation, precisely because of the Bolivian actions in the area of drug control."[21]

The all-out "war" on drugs was all the more urgent, according to Bolivian economic adviser Samuel Doria Medina (testifying before the U.S. Congress in March 1990), because in only one year the price for 100 pounds of coca leaf had fallen from $60 to $10. Now "is the best opportunity that we have had in 10 years," argued Doria Medina. "This is the moment to initiate programs of alternative development or the peasants will be forced to continue cultivating coca leaf at very reduced prices, and as a result the streets of the United States will be flooded with cheap cocaine."[22] U.S. policymakers, pleased with the successful eradication in 1990, took note. It seemed that U.S.-Bolivian relations had achieved a high. Paz Zamora was the first democratic president of Bolivia to visit the White House in thirty years (the last was his uncle, Víctor Paz, invited by U.S. President John F. Kennedy). And, according to Ambassador Gelbard, U.S. aid to Bolivia was ninth in the world; the "dimensions of bilateral relations between the two countries are positive and ample."[23]

Inter-American Relations

Given Bolivia's current problems, its foreign policy has been dynamic and relatively successful in sustaining a programmatic continuity belied by political instability and frequent personnel changes. Some of this success was especially evident in relations with the inter-American community. To offset geopolitical liabilities and economic dependency, Bolivia (particularly under Siles) sought to strengthen bilateral and multilateral relations with its Latin American neighbors. Traditional rivalries between Latin nations and shifting military and ideological blocs made this a complicated process. Although the basic principles of Bolivian foreign policy altered little, regional political alignments shaped the ways in which Bolivia could pursue its goals historically. From the independence era until 1969, Bolivia's inter-American relations gravitated toward Argentina. Extremely close relations resulted in 1943, when Argentina assisted the Villarroel coup and attempted to incorporate Bolivia and Uruguay into a pro-Axis bloc.

By 1969, Bolivian policy had begun to tilt toward opening to Brazil. Banzer achieved power through Brazilian assistance in 1971, and extensive Brazilian political, military, and economic penetration occurred until 1978, when foreign policy was realigned with Argentina. The Mutún iron ore and gas exploitation projects so favored Brazilian economic interests that the issue generated a heated internal political debate. Banzer met Brazilian President General Emilio Medici in 1972, and cooperative financial and technical assistance agreements were formalized. Brazilian influence was assisted by the persistence of radical governments in Chile and Argentina, with which the Bolivian government, now ideologically conservative, had little in common. Through Brazil, which had warm relations with the United States in these years, U.S. direction over Bolivia found additional expression. When General Augusto Pinochet assumed control in 1973, Chile temporarily fell into this conservative Brazilian orbit as well.

The Siles Zuazo government developed close ties with Argentina in the aftermath of the Malvinas War and the inauguration of civilian President Raúl Alfonsín. When Siles attended the ceremonies in Buenos Aires, Argentina extended disaster aid, refinanced the $660 million debt Bolivia owed, and expressed warm solidarity with the process of democratization. At Bolivia's request, the new Argentine government also accelerated the extradition of military leaders implicated in drugs and human rights abuses. However, Siles's policy further attempted to balance relations with both of the giants on its borders, Brazil and Argentina, without favoring either. The heart of his strategy was expressed in the mottos that "good regionalism" is "good neighborliness" and that both characterize "good" inter-American relations.

The strategy appeared to be effective. New cooperative accords were signed with Brazil in October 1983, and in February 1984 Siles Zuazo and Brazilian President João Figueiredo met in Santa Cruz to formalize ten economic cooperation accords, including an agreement of understanding to double the amount of natural gas sold to Brazil through 1988. Brazil offered a credit line of $105 million and assistance in steel and energy development. Bolivia in turn favored the election of the Brazilian candidate as the new secretary general of the OAS. At the La Plata Basin group meeting in December 1982 (held in Brasilia), Argentina,

Paraguay, and Uruguay favored Bolivia's democratization and seacoast policy. In late 1983, when the group met in Asunción, the members approved extensive economic disaster and development aid. At the meeting, Bolivia's foreign minister expressed the future aspirations of the Siles policy: "We believe that, one day not far distant, my country will be able to serve as the conduit between the Atlantic and Pacific Oceans."[24] Within Bolivia's broad regional strategy, the Southern Cone nations were to be the fulcrum for democratization and integration of the continent, and Bolivia hoped to be the centerpiece of this system.

Cooperative regionalism was the theme pursued in other inter-American forums as well. In the meeting of Bolivarian countries (Bolivia, Colombia, Ecuador, Panama, Peru, and Venezuela), held in Caracas on May 25, 1983, to celebrate the bicentennial of Bolívar's birth, Bolivia expressed its policy of Latin unity and solidarity as a springboard for its economic development and successful resolution of the landlocked status. Among the Amazon Pact nations, Bolivia assumed a central role as the new seat of the Council of Amazonian Cooperation for 1984.[25] And within the Andean Pact, Bolivia further generated broad support and special consideration during key meetings in May, July, and December 1983. The Andean Development Corporation granted Bolivia a $10 million loan. Also highly supportive were bilateral relations with Ecuador, Panama, and Colombia, which offered to host future Bolivian-Chilean meetings on the maritime problem in 1984.

The Siles government favored the Contadora process in Central America and quickly established relations with Sandinist Nicaragua in October 1982. The action was motivated by several foreign policy principles enshrined in the OAS charter, such as belief in the ideological pluralism of the hemisphere, self-determination, national sovereignty, nonintervention, and an inter-American community of all nations. But the Siles government also owed the Sandinistas a debt of gratitude. In 1980 and 1981, a Bolivian exile delegation representing Siles was permitted an opportunity to be seated with the Nicaraguan delegation and, through them, to voice public opposition to the García Meza regime. The Siles government formally thanked the Nicaraguan foreign minister, Miguel D'Escoto, for the assistance of the Nicaraguan delegation in those critical years of protest. Bolivia's own revolutionary tradition and experience with external influence led the Siles government to oppose any "destabilization" of the Nicaraguan regime by the United States and to favor multilateral mediation efforts in the volatile region. It was also for this reason that Bolivia was critical of the U.S. intervention in Grenada in meetings of both the OAS and the United Nations.

The success of Siles Zuazo's inter-American relations was remarkable in contrast to the record of the preceding military governments. For nearly three years—from September 1979 to August 1982—no Bolivian president had been invited to inaugural ceremonies in any Latin American nation, and the Andean Pact countries decided not to invite García Meza to the Santa Marta summit meeting. Colombia's foreign minister observed that "Bolivia can have whatever government it wishes but one is able to choose who to invite to a meeting in one's own home."[26] Bolivia nearly left the Pact, especially when Ecuador, Colombia, and Venezuela sharply criticized its record on human rights. In the OAS, where once the Inter-American Commission on Human Rights singled out Bolivia for censure and more than two-thirds of the OAS members voted to condemn Bolivia's government, the Siles policy also made gains. Bolivia attempted to revitalize the OAS system by arguing for the readmission of Cuba, in order that the institution would be a truly American system of all the countries of the Americas. Yet Bolivia also proposed a new inter-American system that would exclude the United States and pursue uniquely Latin problems more effectively.

Bolivia's especially acute debt crisis became regionalized as a Latin American crisis in the OAS and special inter-American meetings. The special contribution of the Siles government, and an important inter-American policy initiative, was the linking of the political stability of the hemisphere to the region's political economy. Bolivia emphasized the "close relationship between the degree of economic success and the viability of political democracy" in Latin America.[27] The government argued that the current economic crisis could not be left to private bilateral dialogues between individual governments and banks, but that a comprehensive and regional (indeed, global and multilateral) solution was essential. In the Andean Pact, the Siles government supported a common front on the debt question and encouraged formation of a debtors' group. In fact, a Bolivian contingent of seventy-five persons, including Siles's planning minister and several presidential candidates, attended the meeting on Latin American debt hosted by Fidel Castro in Havana in July 1985. The crisis in international political economy also became the fulcrum for Siles's activism among the Third World bloc of nations, as well as a central vehicle for the broader multilateralization of foreign policy goals. Although the international relations of the Paz Estenssoro and Paz Zamora governments shied away from an aggressive Third World emphasis, both pursued active inter-American relations. Paz Zamora, especially, conceived of Bolivia's foreign policy in the 1990s as concerted cooperation with the big three "ABC" powers of the continent—Argentina, Brazil, and Chile—and sought to "Latin-americanize" Bolivia's economic dependency by developing better inter-American ties, particularly in commercial areas.

Third World Relations

Under Siles, Bolivia's alignment with the Third World countries and the Nonaligned Movement reflected a natural sympathy with shared problems and orientations, such as the quest for an independent foreign policy, economic development assistance, and international economic reform. The Third World approach was launched in Managua at the meeting of the Coordinating Committee of the Nonaligned Movement in January 1983. The Nonaligned nations acknowledged Bolivia's new solidarity with the movement by endorsing the internal democratization of the country and its multilateral foreign policy campaign to regain the lost maritime ports. Foreign Minister Fellmann Velarde's statement that "one day the cause of Bolivia's seacoast would be a global cause" expressed the optimistic mood behind the Siles policy initiative. In short, the Nonaligned Movement provided an ideal forum whereby Bolivia could expand support for key foreign policy objectives and project its policy globally—an ability usually relegated to powerful countries.

The Nonaligned Movement further served as an effective springboard for criticism of the regional Latin American system, especially the archaic machinery of the OAS. With other Latin countries, Bolivia had become disillusioned with the conservatism of the OAS, its dominance by the United States, the continued exclusion of Cuba, and the organization's relative neglect of pressing economic development problems. Accordingly, Bolivia interjected Third World developmentalist and anti-imperialist perspectives into the staid, traditional forum and challenged the region to design a new system more in tune with Latin American needs and more intimately interlinked with the powerful Third World coalition of nations. Bolivia's opening to the Third World and membership in the Nonaligned Movement seemed to represent a growing Latin American trend to form extrahemispheric solidarities and to moderate U.S. influence over national policies. By 1984, some ten Latin American countries had formally joined the movement and others had become closely associated as observers. As one of the vice-presidents of the movement, La Paz interpreted Bolivia's election as a vindication of its new foreign policy direction and activism, and as proof of newfound international prestige after the dark days of oprobrium under García Meza.

The Third World alliance provided Bolivia a congenial circle of operation in the United Nations as well. In contrast to the embarrassing vote of censure by the Thirty-fifth General Assembly in December 1980 (77 countries approved, 49 abstained, and 8 opposed), Bolivia reestablished its credibility as a responsible government. At the Sixth United Nations Conference on Trade and Development (UNCTAD) in June–July

1983 (held in Belgrade, Yugoslavia), Bolivia secured special international financial assistance to improve transportation facilities under the Special Fund for Land-locked Developing Countries. In the spring of 1984, the government also called for broad, multilateral agreements among both the coca and cocaine-producing and -consuming countries to manage the difficult narcotics problem. Bolivia's voting pattern in the United Nations demonstrated the basically neutralist alignment of its foreign policy. Despite the internal agitation and opposition of the Bolivian Communist Party, the Siles government voted with the majority of Third World nations on various United Nations resolutions in January and November 1983 condemning the Soviet invasion of Afghanistan. Also, in November 1983, the government even-handedly opposed the occupation of Grenada in the General Assembly resolution sponsored by Nicaragua wherein 108 countries deplored the U.S. intervention.

Siles's world view recognized the rising Third World bloc as a major lobbying coalition for the restructuring of the global financial and economic system. The bitter history of dependency and chronic difficulties with the IMF and World Bank were experiences that the Third World shared with Bolivia. The Siles administration interpreted the Bolivian economic plight as an external structural crisis that could be solved only by means of a unified Third World coalition of the weak. Pursuing global solutions to the debt crisis, the Siles government anticipated greater leverage not merely for Bolivia but also for other Latin American and Third World nations mired in the debt trap as well.

Under the Paz Estenssoro administration, Third Worldist positions on the debt crisis were surrendered to the Alan García government in Peru. Both Paz Estenssoro and Paz Zamora preferred a conservative and bilateral approach to debt diplomacy, which entailed wooing the U.S. bankers, the IMF, and the Paris Club with their strict austerity and free-market programs. Thus both appointed distinguished private-sector entrepreneurs to diplomatic posts in Washington and Europe. Relations with the United States improved significantly in 1985 after the passage of Paz's New Economic Policy and the nomination of Fernando Illanes, former president of the Confederation of Private Entrepreneurs, to Washington. Overall, unlike Siles, both Paz Estenssoro and Paz Zamora elicited sympathetic responses from major international players to their more traditional debt diplomacy.

FOREIGN POLICY AND THE FUTURE

External relations under Bolivia's three civilian administrations have varied significantly. Siles sought to forge national strength and maneuverability through broad solidarities with Latin American neighbors,

Third World developing countries, and the global community. Such multilateralization served to moderate the constraints of dependency and powerlessness, and to further emancipate both Bolivia and Latin America from the fruitless division of the world into hegemonic blocs. By contrast, Paz Estenssoro and Paz Zamora, although they did not ignore these other areas, emphasized more conventional diplomacy, especially greater cooperation with the centers of international finance capital and the United States. All three civilian governments discovered that intractable domestic and international problems interfered with the aspirations of Bolivian foreign policy: development of natural resources in a manner consonant with major social and environmental responsibilities and vital national sovereignty, control of the powerful international cocaine traffic; and acquisition of a sovereign Pacific seacoast.

Because of the unprecedented economic crisis and the strains imposed by the recent return to civilian democracy, the challenges to Bolivia's foreign policy were indeed awesome in the 1980s. However, the problems of the 1990s could prove to be even greater. Will Bolivia be better able to "come to terms with both the liabilities and the assets of its location" in the new decade and the new century?[28] And will Bolivian policymakers become more effective in containing the traditional influence of the United States in their country's internal and external affairs? Finally, will meaningful democracy, social justice, and economic development prove less elusive in the future than they had in the past? Affirmative answers to these questions assume unprecedented and long-term domestic tranquility—a quality in very short supply but clearly central to successful foreign policy. The key challenge for Bolivia remains unaltered: how to protect delicate national sovereignty by means of an effective foreign policy strategy and structure. In the past, chronic failures of diplomacy had traumatized national unity and morale. Modern Bolivian governments—military and civilian alike—had never quite unraveled the dogged dilemma inherent in the forging of true national unity and consensus, a process essential to overcoming historical powerlessness and dependency. In the final analysis, Bolivians will have to conquer Bolivia from within if they are to truly safeguard their country from further external conquests.

NOTES

1. Riordan Roett, "The Changing Nature of Latin American International Relations: Geopolitical Realities," in *Commission on United States–Latin American Relations: The Americas in a Changing World* (New York: Quadrangle Books, 1975), p. 95.

2. *Boletín Informativo Semanal* (La Paz), Dirección de Prensa e Informaciones del Servicio Exterior, Ministerio de Relaciones Exteriores y Culto, No. 147 (June 30, 1983), p. 9.

3. *Latin American Weekly Report*, March 15, 1983, p. 1.

4. *Presencia* (La Paz), March 24, 1990, p. 7.

5. *Los Tiempos* (Cochabamba), March 7, 1990, p. 1.

6. *Los Tiempos* (Cochabamba), March 20, 1990, pp. A1, B1.

7. *Ultima Hora* (La Paz), May 12, 1990, p. 24; and *Los Tiempos* (Cochabamba), May 7, 1990, p. 1.

8. *Hoy Internacional* (La Paz), December 25, 1983, p. 15.

9. David Green, *The Containment of Latin America: A History of the Myths and Realities of the Good Neighbor Policy* (Chicago: Quadrangle Books, 1971), p. 153. See also pp. 147–161.

10. F. Parkinson, *Latin America, the Cold War, and the World Powers, 1945–1973* (Beverly Hills, Calif.: Sage, 1974), pp. 114–115.

11. Ibid., p. 180. See also pp. 161–179.

12. Ibid., pp. 235–237.

13. Yale H. Ferguson, "Trends in Inter-American Relations, 1972–Mid-1974," in Ronald G. Hellman and H. Jon Rosenbaum, eds., *Latin America: The Search for a New International Role* (New York: John Wiley and Sons, 1975), p. 10.

14. Parkinson, *Latin America*, p. 237.

15. *Boletín Informativo Semanal* (La Paz), No. 144 (May 18, 1983), p. 9.

16. *Washington Report on the Hemisphere*, Council on the Hemisphere (COHA), Vol. 4, No. 4 (November 16, 1983), p. 2.

17. Everett G. Martin, "Democracy Spreads in South America," *Wall Street Journal*, March 16, 1989, p. 30; and "Democracy at the Crossroads," *Latin Perspective* (Montreal), Vol. 1 (November 15, 1983), p. 3.

18. Jo Ann Kawell, "Under the Flag of Law Enforcement," *NACLA Report on the Americas*, Vol. 22, No. 6 (March 1989), pp. 25–30; and Waltraud Queiser Morales, "The War on Drugs: A New U.S. National Security Doctrine?" *Third World Quarterly*, Vol. 11, No. 3 (July 1989).

19. "Andean Chiefs and Bush in Drug Accord," *New York Times*, February 16, 1990, p. A9.

20. See "Andean Initiative, Legislative Update," Washington Office on Latin America (WOLA), March 1991, p. 2. The WOLA document makes clear that although the trend for FY 1991 and FY 1992 is for Economic Support Fund (ESF) aid to increase, the Andean Initiative continues to favor military and law-enforcement aid over alternative development assistance. ESF is defined as a form of security assistance and is generally used by the recipient government for that purpose and not for alternative development programs. In addition, more than $62 million of ESF money may be converted to Foreign Military Financing (FMF), which is the primary account for military and police. In early 1991, Bolivia's ESF aid had been increased to $88 million and the economic aid remained $35.9 million. However, disbursement of the ESF funds was tied to the Paz Zamora government's approval of a new extradition treaty. See

"Washington in Focus," *Latin America Update*, Washington Office on Latin America (WOLA), Vol. 16, No. 1 (January–April 1991), p. 3.

21. *Los Tiempos* (Cochabamba), March 17, 1990, p. B3.

22. *Presencia* (La Paz), March 28, 1990, p. 1.

23. *Opinión* (Cochabamba), April 21, 1990, p. 1.

24. *Presencia*, December 10, 1983, p. 1.

25. *Boletín Informativo Semanal*, No. 148 (July 29, 1983), pp. 8–16, 45–46.

26. *Denuncia*, Comité Nacional de Defensa de la Democracia en Bolivia (CONADE), No. 9 (November 30, 1980), p. 3.

27. *Boletín Informativo Semanal*, No. 150 (August 26, 1983), p. 32.

28. J. Valerie Fifer, *Bolivia: Land, Location, and Politics Since 1825* (Cambridge: Cambridge University Press, 1972), p. 263.

Conclusions

The bread of the people is justice.
Sometimes it is abundant, sometimes it is scarce.
Sometimes it tastes pleasing, sometimes it tastes bad.
When the bread is scarce, hunger prevails.
When the bread is bad, it is discontent that reigns.
                                        —Bertolt Brecht
                                "The Bread of the People"

Bolivia is a nation with a reputation. The country's woes—both chronic and interconnected—have provided material for fantastic historical anecdotes and sensationalist news pieces, contributing to the confusion and disagreement over the most popularly touted facts. Variously, the printed record has noted the country's 150, 170, or 200 coups in more than 160 years of independent history; its inflation in 1985 (reportedly the world's highest) of anywhere from 9,000 to 50,000 percent; and a national debt ranging from $3 to $6 billion. Bolivia has regaled the world with revolutions, coups, floods, droughts, depressions, mega-inflation, cocaine kingpins, "narcoterrorism," and presidents who were mad, lynched, or kidnapped. Few countries have boasted a similar record of labor unruliness, abysmal poverty, and infant mortality. Perhaps Bolivia, and not Gabriel García Márquez's Colombia, is the more appropriate model for Latin America's celebrated fantastic realism. Indeed, in Bolivia truth is often stranger than fiction. Burdened by its exotic reputation, the country's past and present have been stereotyped, oversimplified, or shrouded in complexity. Moreover, its problems seem intractable. Consider the endemic problem of change, for example. Bolivia appears to be in constant turmoil, on the one hand; on the other hand, its recent history suggests that "the more things change, the more they seem the same."

Three themes have remained constant in all this confusion: revolution, political instability, and economic underdevelopment. Within these broad areas, specific and immediate problems have emerged: foreign

200

debt, military dictatorship, precarious democracy, social turmoil, and drug wars. At their root, these current problems are symptoms of the country's underlying and intrinsic structural and cultural crises. Democratization, for example, served as the generic remedy for all the country's political, social, and economic ills after the military withdrew from power in 1982. Thus one news analyst observed:

> Dictatorship or democracy: the apparent polarity of these alternatives, very much in the centre of attention regarding Latin America at the present moment, tends to disguise a deeper contradiction, which is that between on the one hand the forces that are seeking to maintain the present basic social and economic structure, with or without reforms, and on the other hand the forces that are seeking fundamental transformation of society in the interests, and with the full participation of the majority.
>
> The return to formal democracy generally corresponds to an attempt to ensure the continuity of the social order once direct military rule is too corroded to do so, and social pressures are mounting. In situations of economic and social crisis, this process tends to be accelerated by the need to obtain some form of social consensus. The elected government in such cases is subjected to the unfolding of the power struggle existing between these social forces, but in no way implies the resolution of this struggle.[1]

Revealed here are key elements of the struggle for Bolivia's future that transcend the traditional dictatorship-versus-democracy conflict: victory for majority or minority interests, continued radical transformation or perpetuation of the established social order, and the establishment of social consensus. Scourges of cocaine mafias, narcoterrorism, and the narcostate are mere symptoms, not causes, of the Bolivian malaise.

The paradox of poverty also haunts the stoic (yet rebellious) nation. Why has Bolivian society—despite revolution, economic assistance, and technocratic models of growth and development—actually failed to develop? Why have Andean rulers, even the more populist among them, neglected to address awesome deprivation? Has human suffering become ordinary? "The more suffering people there are, the more natural their suffering appears to be. Who will prevent the fish in the sea from becoming wet?"[2] Does the Bolivian case indicate that the success of a development revolution in countries below a certain level of development is extremely tenuous, a "revolution at starvation level" that merely socializes poverty?[3] Indeed, classical Marxism condemns Third World nations like Bolivia to the backwaters of history, waiting upon revolution in industrialized capitalist countries. Third World revolutions in backward, precapitalist agrarian societies become economic impossibilities. Although available material conditions and resources are critical to revolutionary and developmental success, the Bolivian dilemma is not simply being too poor to escape poverty. Rather, the inherent Bolivian economic condition is exploitation and dependency—the absence of both political and economic independence, and the vicious circle wherein the one necessitates the other. In short, Bolivian underdevelopment is a structure of powerlessness.

Thus a critical problem is the model or strategy pursued to achieve social and economic development. Bolivia is hardly unique in its exposure of false development myths—that economic growth in GNP necessarily creates *real* development, or that greater self-sacrifice and belt tightening will do the trick. Accustomed to centuries of bleak poverty, Bolivians have always been austere and frugal. Between 1950 and 1980, the Bolivian economy steadily grew but failed to truly develop (as measured by greater economic self-sufficiency and higher standards of living for the majority). Moreover, Bolivia is only "relatively" poor; the country possesses tremendous potential and vast untapped riches—indeed, more resources than can be used by its limited population (7 million inhabitants to more than 1 million square kilometers). Instead, Bolivia is a textbook case of dependent development, with all its attendant maldistribution and misadministration. For decades the Andean nation has sought a new political-economic model to provide a *salida* (literally, an exit) from the cycle of underdevelopment and economic marginalization that traps most of the Third World in the grip of geopolitical determinism and paternalistic and racist exploitation by the powerful.

The crux of a Bolivian solution is the recognition that everything depends on everything else. The failure to achieve social justice prevents the realization of social consensus, which is a precondition of political peace and order. These, in turn, are part of a greater whole whereby foreign control and intervention continue to fragment the essence of nationhood and lead to extensive social, cultural, and moral disintegration:

> This fragmentation takes place at the administrative levels, in the press, and in cultural activities; it is visible at the highest levels of population where little groups dispute the privilege of being friends of the foreigner; it descends to the people when the desperation of poverty causes one to consent to achieving an advantage by the sacrifice of dignity. . . . Extreme poverty facilitates colonization; men in Bolivia have a lower price. There is a certain level at which poverty destroys dignity; the North Americans have discovered this level and work on it: in their eyes and for their pocketbook, a Bolivian costs less than an Argentine or a Chilean.[4]

Bolivian independence and renewal thus entail the recapturing of cultural wholeness and cohesiveness. Neither the defeated and decadent heritage of Spanish colonialism nor the declining, materialist imprint of North American imperialism can serve as the basis of moral renewal. The heritage that survives undefeated, whole, and vibrant is the Indian one. Within the Aymara culture, strength is the realization that everything is intrinsically related, interconnected (and nothing isolated or separated)—in a word, holistic. Unlike the Western system of wealth accumulation to the detriment of others, economic equality is integral to the indigenous vision of justice. The Aymara believe in *Kuskachana* or *Pampachana*, meaning the leveling or reestablishment of a balance. In the Aymara world view, uncontrolled growth as development is suicide, not progress; and development without respect for the earth negates the sense of themselves, their personal and cultural identity.[5] The message from ancient voices is one not of greed or private property but of community and "peoplehood."

Bolivians must recapture a sense of themselves and of their cultural identity. And the process can only start with compassion and justice for all, because only by respecting the other can one respect oneself. Centuries of oppression and exploitation have left Bolivians gravely ill with alienation; the country has been taught to betray itself, to deny its identity.[6] The disaster of the Chaco War a half-century ago profoundly shook from deep sleep the social conscience of Bolivia's majority and culminated in revolution. And it was Bolívar who warned more than a century ago that "I will be reborn every hundred years, each time that the people awaken." Is a great historic disaster necessary to awaken Bolivia's social conscience now? Are the human statistics of this Andean nation of nearly 7 million not calamity enough? Bolivia has the highest infant mortality rate in all of Latin America (213 per 1,000) and the lowest life expectancy (47 years); half the nation is undernourished, with 70 percent of the children dying before the age of 15 of treatable diseases of poverty; more than 50 percent of the population is illiterate; and the country has one of the worst distributions of wealth in the Americas (the wealthiest 5 percent control 39 percent of the national income and the poorest 20 percent, only 2 percent).[7]

The Catholic Church in Bolivia, which is gradually becoming the *Bolivian* Church now that more native priests are achieving positions of prominence at the national and community levels, has emerged as the dynamic voice and institution of justice and renewal—both by necessity and by default, as political parties, the fragmented left, a weakened labor movement, and the military have all been discredited or become ineffectual. Moreover, the chronic lack of official policies favoring the people has weakened the legitimacy and authority of the state, which is unable to control independent grassroots organizations. Unfortunately, their militancy has not been channelled in ways that can unify the country's dispossessed.[8] Years of repression and political anarchy have created a vacuum; Bolivia needs a vigorous social organization to restructure and reanimate society, and perhaps the Catholic Church can be that moral and institutional catalyst.

At the root of Bolivia's instability, poverty, and cultural decline are extreme inequality and injustice. However, unlike some societies, Bolivians have historically tolerated oppression and repression most unwillingly. They have struggled and rebelled, attaining the dubious reputation of "unstable," as if stability and order were the true measures of social progress and development. As one astute Bolivia watcher observed, "if disorder is so prevalent might it not be order itself?"[9] Truly, Bolivia as a land of struggle may rightly celebrate its militant radicalism because, to paraphrase a North American aphorism, "rebellion in the name of justice is no vice." According to Bolívar, the country named after him represents an "irrepressible love of liberty." As long as the people's spirit of struggle survives, the spirit of Bolivian revolution cannot die, despite the reactionary policies of fleeting regimes. The revolution that "failed" and was "thwarted" or "betrayed" was the MNR Revolution; the people's revolution lives.

NOTES

1. "Democracy at the Crossroads," *Latin Perspective* (Montreal), Agencia Latinoamerica de Información (ALAI), Vol. 1, No. 9 (November 15, 1983), p. 3.

2. Bertolt Brecht, *Gesamellte Werke*, IV, Gedichte (Frankfurt am Main: Suhrkamp Verlag, 1967), p. 738.

3. James M. Malloy, *Bolivia: The Uncompleted Revolution* (Pittsburgh: University of Pittsburgh Press, 1970), pp. 340–341.

4. Sergio Almaraz Paz, *Requiem para una república*, 2nd ed. (La Paz: Ediciones Los Amigos del Libro, 1980), p. 27.

5. "LP Document: Aymaras Challenge Church on Role of Religion in Native Cultures," *Latinamerica Press*, Vol. 18, No. 40 (October 30, 1986), p. 3, taken from *Fe y pueblo*, "Religión Aymara y Cristianismo" (La Paz: Center for Popular Theology, August 1986).

6. "LP Interview: Galeano: 'Listen for Latin America's Strangled Voices,'" *Latinamerica Press*, Vol. 19, No. 6 (February 19, 1987), pp. 3–4.

7. "LP Interview: Bolivia: Future Somber Despite Vast Resources," *Latinamerica Press*, Vol. 17, No. 23 (June 20, 1985), p. 3. These statistics were compiled in the recently published study by Father Gregorio Iriarte, *Esquemas para la interpretación de la realidad* (La Paz: Secretariado Nacional de Pastoral Social, Conferencia Episcopal de Bolivia, 1985).

8. Sofía Vega, "Paz Estenssoro Inherits Fragile Bolivian Democracy," *Latinamerica Press*, Vol. 17, No. 30 (August 22, 1985), pp. 1–2.

9. James Dunkerley, *Rebellion in the Veins: Political Struggle in Bolivia, 1952–82* (London: Verso Editions, 1984), p. xi.

Selected Bibliography

Books

Alexander, Robert J. *Bolivia: Past, Present, and Future of Its Politics.* New York: Praeger, 1982.

––––––. *The Bolivian National Revolution.* New Brunswick, N.J.: Rutgers University Press, 1958.

Andrade, Víctor. *My Missions for Revolutionary Bolivia.* Pittsburgh, Pa.: University of Pittsburgh Press, 1976.

––––––. *La revolución boliviana y los Estados Unidos, 1944–1962.* Second Edition Augmented. La Paz: Gisbert, 1979.

Arnade, Charles. *The Emergence of the Republic of Bolivia.* Gainesville: University of Florida Press, 1957.

Los bancos transnacionales: el estado y el endeudamiento externo en Bolivia. Estudios e Informes de la CEPAL, No. 26 (E/CEPAL/G.1251, June 1983). Santiago de Chile: Comisión Económica para América Latina (CEPAL), 1983.

Barrios de Chungara, Domitila. *Let Me Speak! Testimony of Domitila, a Woman of the Bolivian Mines.* New York: Monthly Review Press, 1978.

Barrios Morón, Raúl. *Bolivia y Estados Unidos: democracia, derechos humanos y narcotráfico (1980–1982).* Instituto de Historia Social Boliviana (HISBOL), and Facultad Latinoamericana de Ciencias Sociales (FLACSO), Universidad Mayor de San Andrés. La Paz: HISBOL/FLACSO, 1989.

Bascopé Aspiazu, René. *La veta blanca: coca y cocaína en Bolivia.* La Paz: Ediciones Aquí, 1982.

Bedregal Gutiérrez, Guillermo. *Bolivia: estrategia de la nueva política económica.* La Paz: Banco Boliviano Americano, Industrias Gráficas, 1989.

Bedregal Gutiérrez, Guillermo, and Ruddy Viscarra Pando. *La lucha boliviana contra la agresión del narcotráfico.* La Paz: Editorial Los Amigos del Libro, 1989.

Bolivia en cifras 1985. La Paz: Instituto Nacional de Estadística (INES), 1986.

Bolivia hacia el 2000: desafíos y opciones, edited by Carlos F. Toranzo et al. Caracas: Editorial Nueva Sociedad and UNITAR/PROFAL, 1989.

Bolivia: neoliberalismo y derechos humanos. Serie: Informes sobre Derechos Humanos, 1. Lima: Comisión Andina de Juristas, 1988.

Brill, William H. *Military Intervention in Bolivia: The Overthrow of Paz Estenssoro and the MNR*. Washington, D.C.: Institute for the Comparative Study of Political Systems, 1967.

Buechler, Hans C., and Judith Maria Buechler. *The Bolivian Aymara*. New York: Holt, Rinehart and Winston, 1971.

Calderón, Fernando, and Jorge Dandler. *Bolivia: La fuerza histórica del campesinado*. La Paz: Centro de Estudios de la Realidad Económica y Social (CERES), 1984.

Camacho Omiste, Edgar. *Política exterior independiente*. La Paz: n.p., 1989.

Campesinado y desarrollo agrícola en Bolivia. Estudios e Informes de la CEPAL, No. 13 (E/CEPAL/G.1211, July 1982). Santiago de Chile: Comisión Económica para América Latina (CEPAL), 1982.

Canelas Orellana, Amado, and Juan Carlos Canelas Zannier. *Bolivia: coca cocaína*. La Paz: Editorial Los Amigos del Libro, 1983.

Carter, William E., and Mauricio Mamani P. *Coca en Bolivia*. La Paz: Editorial Juventud, 1986.

Crabtree, John, et al. *The Great Tin Crash: Bolivia and the World Tin Market*. London: Latin American Bureau, 1987.

Delgado Gonzales, Trifonio. *100 años de lucha obrera en Bolivia*, with notes by Guillermo Delgado P. La Paz: Ediciones ISLA, 1984.

Debray, Regis. *Ché's Guerrilla War*, translated by Rosemary Sheed. London: Penguin Books, 1975.

Doria Medina, Samuel. *La economía informal en Bolivia*. La Paz: Editorial Offset Boliviana (EDOBOL), 1986.

———. *Estabilización y crecimiento, reto del mañana: balance y perspectivas de la economía boliviana*. La Paz: Editorial Offset Boliviana (EDOBOL), 1988.

Dunkerley, James. *Rebellion in the Veins: Political Struggle in Bolivia, 1952–82*. London: Verso Editions, 1984.

Evaluación económica 1989. Informe Confidencial. La Paz: Müller & Asociados, January 1990.

Fifer, J. Valerie. *Bolivia: Land, Location, and Politics Since 1825*. Cambridge: Cambridge University Press, 1972.

Gill, Lesley. *Peasants, Entrepreneurs, and Social Change: Frontier Development in Lowland Bolivia*. Boulder, Colo.: Westview Press, 1987.

Gómez, Walter. *La minería en el desarrollo económico de Bolivia, 1900–1970*. La Paz: Editorial Los Amigos del Libro, 1978.

González, Luis J., and Gustavo A. Sánchez Salazar. *The Great Rebel: Ché Guevara in Bolivia*. New York: Grove Press, 1969.

Healy, Kevin. *Caciques y patrones: una experiencia de desarrollo rural en sud de Bolivia*. Cochabamba: Ediciones El Buitre, 1982.

Heath, Dwight B., Charles J. Erasmus, and Hans C. Buechler. *Land Reform and Social Revolution in Bolivia*. New York: Praeger, 1969.

Hermosa Virreira, Walter. *Breve historia de la minería en Bolivia*. La Paz: Editorial Los Amigos del Libro, 1979.

Hillman, Grady, with Guillermo Delgado P. *The Return of the Inca: Translations from the Quechua Messianic Tradition*. Austin, Texas: Place of Herons Press, 1986.

Kelly, Jonathan, and Herbert S. Klein. *Revolution and the Rebirth of Inequality: A Theory Applied to the National Revolution in Bolivia*. Berkeley: University of California Press, 1981.

Klein, Herbert S. *Bolivia: The Evolution of a Multi-Ethnic Society*. New York: Oxford University Press, 1982.

_____. *Parties and Political Change in Bolivia, 1880–1952*. London: Cambridge University Press, 1969.

Knudson, Jerry W. *The Press and the Bolivian National Revolution*. Lexington, Ky.: Journalism Monographs, 1973.

_____. *Bolivia's Popular Assembly of 1971 and the Overthrow of General Juan José Torres* (Council on International Studies). Buffalo: State University of New York, 1974.

Ladman, Jerry R., ed. *Modern-Day Bolivia: Legacy of the Revolution and Prospects for the Future* (Center for Latin American Studies). Tempe: Arizona State University, 1982.

Laserna, Roberto, ed. *Crisis, democrácia y conflicto social*. Cochabamba: Centro de Estudios de la Realidad Económica y Social (CERES), 1985.

Leonard, Olen E. *Bolivia: Land, People and Institutions*. Washington, D.C.: Scarecrow Press, 1952.

Lora, Guillermo. *A History of the Bolivian Labor Movement, 1848–1971*. Cambridge: Cambridge University Press, 1977.

McEwen, William J., et al. *Changing Rural Society: A Study of Communities in Bolivia*. New York: Oxford University Press, 1975.

Magill, John H. *Labor Unions and Political Socialization: A Case Study of Bolivian Workers*. New York: Praeger, 1974.

Malloy, James M. *Bolivia: The Uncompleted Revolution*. Pittsburgh, Pa.: University of Pittsburgh Press, 1970.

Malloy, James M., and Eduardo Gamarra. *Revolution and Reaction: Bolivia, 1964–1985*. New Brunswick, N.J.: Transaction Books, 1988.

Malloy, James M., and Richard S. Thorn, eds. *Beyond the Revolution: Bolivia Since 1952*. Pittsburgh, Pa.: University of Pittsburgh Press, 1971.

Marsh, Margaret Charlotte Alexander. *The Bankers in Bolivia: A Study in American Foreign Investment*. New York: Vanguard Press, 1928.

Mayorga, René, ed. *Democrácia a la deriva*. La Paz: Centro de Estudios de la Realidad Económica y Social (CERES), 1987.

Mitchell, Christopher. *The Legacy of Populism in Bolivia: From the MNR to Military Rule*. New York: Praeger, 1977.

Nash, June. *We Eat the Mines and the Mines Eat Us: Dependency and Exploitation in Bolivian Tin Mines*. New York: Columbia University Press, 1979.

Osborne, Harold. *Bolivia: A Land Divided*. New York: Oxford University Press, 1964.

Paredes, Rigoberto M. *Mitos, supersticiones y supervivencias populares de Bolivia*. La Paz: Ediciones ISLA, 1963.

Paz Estenssoro, Víctor. *La revolución boliviana*. La Paz: Dirección Nacional de Informaciones, 1964.

Prado Salmón, Gary. *Como capturé al Ché*. Barcelona: Ediciones B, 1987.

———— . *Poder de las fuerzas armadas, 1949–1982*. 2nd ed. La Paz: Editorial Los Amigos del Libro, 1987.

Quiroga Santa Cruz, Marcelo. *El saqueo de Bolivia*. Buenos Aires: Ediciones de CRISIS, 1973.

Rivera Cusicanqui, Silvia. *'Oprimidos pero no vencidos.' Lucha del campesinado Aymara y Quechua, 1900–1980*. La Paz: Instituto de Historia Social Boliviana (HISBOL), 1984.

Rolón Anaya, Mario. *Política y partidos en Bolivia*, 2nd ed. La Paz: Editorial Juventud, 1987.

Saavedra Weise, Agustín. *Bolivia en el contexto internacional*. Cochabamba: Editorial Los Amigos del Libro, 1985.

Selser, Gregorio. *La CIA en Bolivia*. Buenos Aires: Hernández, 1970.

———— . *Bolivia: el cuartelazo de los cocadolares*. Mexico City: Editorial Mex-Sur, 1982.

Stearman, Allyn MacLean. *Camba and Kolla: Migration and Development in Santa Cruz, Bolivia*. Gainesville: University Presses of Florida, 1985.

Torres, Juan José. *El General Torres habla a Bolivia*. Buenos Aires: Crisis, 1973.

Urioste F. de C., Miguel. *Resistencia campesina: efectos de la política económica neoliberal del Decreto Supremo 21060*. (Centro de Estudios para el Desarrollo Laboral y Agrario [CEDLA], No. 6). La Paz: CEDLA/EDOBOL, 1989.

Weil, Thomas E., et al. *Area Handbook for Bolivia* (Foreign Area Studies, American University). Washington, D.C.: Government Printing Office, 1974.

Wennergren, E. Boyd, and Morris D. Whitaker. *The Status of Bolivian Agriculture*. New York: Praeger, 1975.

Whitehead, Laurence. *The United States and Bolivia: A Case of Neo-Colonialism*. London: Haslemere Group, 1969.

Wilkie, James W. *The Bolivian Revolution and U.S. Aid Since 1952: Financial Background and Context of Political Decisions* (Latin American Center). Los Angeles: University of California at Los Angeles, 1969.

———— . *Bolivian Foreign Trade: Historical Problems and MNR Revolutionary Policy, 1952–1964* (Council on International Studies). Buffalo: State University of New York at Buffalo, 1971.

Zavaleta Mercado, René. *Bolivia: el desarrollo de la conciencia nacional*. Montevideo: Diálogo, 1967.

———— . *Lo nacional-popular en Bolivia*. Mexico City: Siglo Veintiuno Editores, 1986.

———— , ed. *Bolivia, hoy*, 2nd ed. Mexico City: Siglo Veintiuno Editores, 1987.

Zondag, Cornelius H. *The Bolivian Economy, 1952–65: The Revolution and Its Aftermath*. New York: Praeger, 1966.

Articles, Chapters, and Reports

Alexander, Robert J. "Bolivia's Democratic Experiment." *Current History* 84 (February 1985):73–76, 86–87.

Burke, Melvin. "Bolivia: The Politics of Cocaine." *Current History* 90 (February 1991):65–68, 90.

_____ . "Does 'Food for Peace' Assistance Damage the Bolivian Economy?" *Inter-American Economic Affairs* 25 (Summer 1971):3–20.

_____ . "Land Reform and Its Effect Upon Production and Productivity in the Lake Titicaca Region." *Economic Development and Cultural Change* 18 (April 1970):410–450.

_____ . "The Stabilization Programs of the International Monetary Fund: The Case of Bolivia." *Marxist Perspectives* 6 (Summer 1979):118–133.

Burke, Melvin, and James M. Malloy. "From National Populism to National Corporatism: The Case of Bolivia, 1952–1970." *Studies in Comparative International Development* 9 (Spring 1974):49–73.

Burke, Melvin, and Waltraud Queiser Morales. "Bolivia." In Jack W. Hopkins, ed., *Latin America and Caribbean Contemporary Record*, Vol. 3 (1983–1984), pp. 295–306. New York: Holmes & Meier, 1985.

Camacho Omiste, Edgar. "Bolivia en 1986: la política exterior del neoliberalismo." In Heraldo Muñoz, ed., *Las políticas exteriores de América Latina y el Caribe: continuidad en la crisis.* Buenos Aires: PROSPEL/Grupo Editor Latinoamericano, 1987.

"Coca: The Real Green Revolution." (Five-article series, by various authors, North American Congress on Latin America [NACLA]). *NACLA Report on the Americas* 22 (March 1989):12–40.

Dunkerley, James. "Bolivia at the Crossroads." *Third World Quarterly* 8 (January 1986):137–150.

Dunkerley, James, and Rolando Morales. "The Bolivian Crisis." *New Left Review* 155 (January/February 1986):86–106.

Eckstein, Susan. "Transformation of a Revolution from Below: Bolivia and International Capital." *Comparative Studies in Society and History* 25 (January 1983):105–135.

Eckstein, Susan, and Frances Hagopian. "The Limits of Industrialization in the Less Developed World: Bolivia." *Economic Development and Cultural Change* 32 (October 1983):64–95.

Gamarra, Eduardo A., and James M. Malloy. "Bolivia: Revolution and Reaction." In Howard J. Wiarda and Harvey F. Kline, eds., *Latin American Politics and Development*, 3rd ed., pp. 359–377. Boulder, Colo.: Westview Press, 1990.

Greene, David G. "Revolution and the Rationalization of Reform in Bolivia." *Inter-American Economic Affairs* 19 (Winter 1965):3–25.

Hanson, Simon G. "Fraud in Foreign Aid: The Bolivian Program." *Inter-American Economic Affairs* 11 (Autumn 1957):65–89.

Healy, Kevin. "The Boom Within the Crisis: Some Recent Effects of Foreign Cocaine Markets on Bolivian Rural Society and Economy." In Deborah Pacini and Christine Franquemont, eds., *Coca and Cocaine: Effects on People and Policy in Latin America, Cultural Survival Report, No. 23*, pp. 101–144. Cambridge, Mass.: Cultural Survival and Latin American Studies Program, Cornell University, 1986.

_____ . "Coca, the State, and the Peasantry in Bolivia, 1982–1988." *Journal of Interamerican Studies and World Affairs* 30 (Summer/Fall 1988):105–126.

Heath, Dwight B. "Hacendados with Bad Table Manners: Campesino Syndicates as Surrogate Landlords in Bolivia." *Inter-American Economic Affairs* 24 (Summer 1970):3–13.

————. "New Patrons for Old: Changing Patron-Client Relationships in the Bolivian Yungas." *Ethnology* 12 (January 1973):75–97.

Henkel, Ray. "The Bolivian Cocaine Industry." In *Drugs in Latin America, Studies in Third World Societies*, No. 37, September 1986, pp. 53–80. Williamsburg, Va.: Department of Anthropology, College of William and Mary, 1986.

Heyduk, Daniel. "The Hacienda System and Agrarian Reform in Highland Bolivia: A Re-evaluation." *Ethnology* 13 (January 1974):71–81.

Klein, Herbert S. "American Oil Companies in Latin America: The Bolivian Experience." *Inter-American Economic Affairs* 18 (Autumn 1964):47–72.

————. "The Creation of the Patiño Tin Empire." *Inter-American Economic Affairs* 19 (Autumn 1965):3–23.

————. "The Crisis of Legitimacy and the Origins of Social Revolution: The Bolivian Experience." *Journal of Inter-American Studies* 10 (January 1968):102–110.

————. "David Toro and the Establishment of 'Military Socialism' in Bolivia." *Hispanic American Historical Review* 45 (February 1965):25–52.

————. "Germán Busch and the Era of 'Military Socialism' in Bolivia." *Hispanic American Historical Review* 47 (May 1967):166–184.

————. "Social Constitutionalism in Latin America: The Bolivian Experience." *The Americas* 22 (January 1966):258–276.

Labrousse, Alain. "Dependence on Drugs: Unemployment, Migration and an Alternative Path to Development in Bolivia." *International Labour Review* 129:3 (1990):333–348.

Ladman, Jerry R., and Ronald L. Tennermeir, "The Political Economy of Agricultural Credit: The Case of Bolivia." *American Journal of Agricultural Economics* 63 (February 1981):66–72.

Lambert, Robert F. "Ché in Bolivia: The 'Revolution' That Failed." *Problems of Communism* 19 (July–August 1970):25–37.

Leons, Madeline Barbara. "Land Reform in the Bolivian Yungas." *América Indígena* 27:4 (1967):689–713.

Malloy, James M. "Bolivia's Economic Crisis." *Current History* 86 (January 1987):9–12, 37–38.

————. "Revolution and Development in Bolivia." In Cole Blasier, ed., *Constructive Change in Latin America*, pp. 177–232. Pittsburgh, Pa.: University of Pittsburgh Press, 1968.

Malloy, James M., and Eduardo A. Gamarra. "The Transition to Democracy in Bolivia." In James M. Malloy and Mitchell A. Seligson, eds., *Authoritarians and Democrats: Regime Transition in Latin America*, pp. 93–119. Pittsburgh, Pa.: University of Pittsburgh Press, 1987.

Mann, Arthur J., and Manuel Pastor, Jr. "Orthodox and Heterodox Stabilization Policies in Bolivia and Peru: 1985–1988." *Journal of Interamerican Studies and World Affairs* 31:4 (Winter 1989):163–192.

Mendelberg, Uri. "The Impact of the Bolivian Agrarian Reform on Class Formation." *Latin American Perspectives*, Issue 46, Vol. 12, No. 3 (Summer 1985):45–58.

Mitchell, Christopher. "The New Authoritarianism in Bolivia." *Current History* 80 (February 1981):75–78, 89.

Morales, Juan Antonio. "Inflation Stabilization in Bolivia." In Michael Bruno et al., eds., *Inflation Stabilization: The Experience of Israel, Argentina, Brazil, Bolivia, and Mexico*. Cambridge, Mass.: MIT Press, 1988.

Morales, Juan Antonio, and Jeffrey Sachs. "Bolivia's Economic Crisis." Monograph, National Bureau of Economic Research (NBER), Conference on Developing Country Debt, Washington, D.C., September 1987.

Morales, Waltraud Queiser. "Bolivia." In Abraham F. Lowenthal, ed., *Latin America and Caribbean Contemporary Record*, Vol. 5 (1985–1986), pp. B23–B47. New York: Holmes & Meier, 1988.

————. "Bolivia Moves Toward Democracy." *Current History* 78 (February 1980):76–79; 86–88.

————. "Bolivian Foreign Policy: The Struggle for Sovereignty." In Jennie K. Lincoln and Elizabeth G. Ferris, eds., *The Dynamics of Latin American Foreign Policies*, pp. 171–191. Boulder, Colo.: Westview Press, 1984.

————. "La Geopolítica de la Política Exterior de Bolivia" (Centro Para el Estudio de las Relaciones Internacionales, CERI). *Relaciones Internacionales, Revista Boliviana* (La Paz) Year 1, Vol. 2 (Second Trimester, 1986), pp. 69–94.

————. "The War on Drugs: A New U.S. National Security Doctrine?" *Third World Quarterly* 11:3 (July 1989):147–169.

————. "Philosophers, Ideology, and Social Change in Bolivia." *International Philosophical Quarterly* 24 (March 1984):21–38.

Morales Anaya, J. "Estabilización y nueva política económica en Bolivia." *Trimestre Económica* 54 (September 1987):179–211.

Mortimore, Michael D. "The State and Transnational Banks: Lessons from the Bolivian Crisis of External Public Indebtedness." *CEPAL Review* (August 1981):127–151.

Patch, Richard W. "United States Assistance in a Revolutionary Setting." In Robert D. Tomasek, ed., *Latin American Politics*, pp. 344–374. New York: Anchor Books, 1970.

————. "Peasantry and National Revolution: Bolivia." In Kalman H. Silvert, ed., *Expectant Peoples: Nationalism and Development*, pp. 95–126. New York: Vintage Books, 1967.

Pearse, Andrew. "Peasants and Revolution: The Case of Bolivia," Vols. 1 and 2. *Economy and Society* 1 (August 1972):225–280; 2 (November 1972):399–424.

Petras, James. "Bolivia Between Revolutions." *Monthly Review* 23 (June 1971):11–24.

Sachs, Jeffrey. "The Bolivian Hyperinflation and Stabilization." *American Economic Review* 77:2 (May 1987):279–283.

St. John, Ronald Bruce. "Hacia el Mar: Bolivia's Quest for a Pacific Port." *Inter-American Economic Affairs* 31 (Winter 1977):41–73.

Sanabria, Harry. "Coca, Migration and Social Differentiation in the Bolivian Lowlands." In *Drugs in Latin America, Studies in Third World Societies*, No. 37, September 1986, pp. 81–125. Williamsburg, Va.: Department of Anthropology, College of William and Mary, 1986.

Shumavon, Douglas H. "Bolivia: Salida al Mar." In Elizabeth G. Ferris and Jennie K. Lincoln, eds., *Latin American Foreign Policies: Global and Regional Dimensions*, pp. 179–190. Boulder, Colo.: Westview Press, 1981.

Weston, Charles H., Jr. "An Ideology of Modernization: The Case of the Bolivian MNR." *Journal of Inter-American Studies* 10 (January 1968):85–101.

Whitehead, Laurence. "Banzer's Bolivia." *Current History* 70 (February 1976):61–64, 80.

————. "Bolivia Swings Right." *Current History* 62 (February 1972):86–90, 117.

————. "Bolivia's Failed Democratization, 1977–1980." In Guillermo O'Donnell, Phillipe Schmitter, and Lawrence Whitehead, eds., *Transitions from Authoritarian Rule: Latin America*, pp. 49–71. Baltimore, Md.: Johns Hopkins University Press, 1986.

Yopo H., Mladen. "Bolivia 1987: una política exterior de sobrevivencia." In Heraldo Muñoz, ed., *Las políticas exteriores de América Latina y el Caribe: un balance de esperanzas*, pp. 147–168. Buenos Aires: PROSPEL/Grupo Editor Latinoamericano, 1988.

About the Book and Author

Located in the heart of the Andes, Bolivia is a microcosm of the region's chronic political instability and socioeconomic underdevelopment. It has undergone more military coups since independence than any other Latin American republic and is the second-poorest country in the hemisphere. This comprehensive survey introduces the general reader to Bolivia's turbulent political history, its beleaguered economy, and its vibrant Indian culture and customs. It traces the causes of Bolivia's predicament to the intractable problems that confront many developing countries—poorly managed natural resources and foreign political and economic intervention. The study emphasizes the contemporary crises of international debt and the ongoing Andean war on drugs and concludes with the 1952 Bolivian National Revolution and its enduring legacy of popular struggle for democracy and economic equality.

Waltraud Queiser Morales is associate professor of political science at the University of Central Florida in Orlando. A generalist in international affairs and a specialist in Latin America, Third World development, and comparative revolutionary change, she has published articles on Bolivian domestic and foreign policies, the Andean drug war, Nicaraguan foreign relations, and television coverage of Latin America. She is the author of *Social Revolution: Theory and Historical Application* (1974), the coauthor of *Human Rights: A User's Guide* (1989), and a major contributor to *Violence and Repression in Latin America* (1976). She has been the recipient of grants from the National Endowment for the Humanities and of a Fulbright teaching and research grant to Bolivia in 1990.

Index

Acción Cívica Boliviana, 75–76(n37)
Acción de Defensa del MNR. *See* Action in
  Defense of the MNR
Acción Democrática Nacionalista. *See*
  Nationalist Democratic Action
Achá, José María de, 43
Achacachi, 113
Action in Defense of the MNR, 85
Act of Bolivia's Economic Independence, 78
ADN. *See* Nationalist Democratic Action
Agency for International Development
  (AID), 175
Agrarian Reform Decree, 79
Agreda, Sebastián, 42, 43
Agribusiness, 117, 122, 165
Agricultural fertilizers. *See* Guano; Nitrates
Agriculture, 5, 112, 146, 160–161
  Altiplano, 8–9
  and cocaine trafficking, 66, 164–165
  lowland, 11, 14
  and NPE, 159
  pre-Columbian, 31, 33
  sub-Andian region, 10
AID. *See* Agency for International
  Development
Air transport, 11, 12
Alasitas celebration, 24–25
Alfonsín, Raúl, 192
Allende, Salvador, 177
Almagro, Diego de, 35
Altiplano, 7–9, 9(photo), 44, 142
Alto Perú, 37–40
Alvarez, Waldo, 58
Amazonian region, 4
Amnesty International, 128
Anaya, Ricardo, 28, 58, 63

Andean Development Corporation, 193
"Andean Initiative," 154–155, 198(n20)
Andean Pact, 97, 152–153, 194
  and seacoast issue, 178, 179
Andean region, 4, 6–9
Andes Mountains, 5, 7, 14
Anticommunism, 63, 124
  and human rights abuses, 129
Antifascist Democratic Front, 65, 67, 68, 69
Antimony, 5
Antofagasta (city), 5, 46
Apaza, Julian. *See* Tupac Katari
APDH. *See* Permanent Assembly of Human
  Rights
Aquí (weekly), 126
Aramayo, Carlos, 49, 50, 62, 143
Araoz de la Madrid, Gregorio, 38
Arawak Indians, 16
Arce, Aniceto, 48, 49
Arce Gómez, Luis, 97
  and cocaine, 125, 126–127, 128, 189
  and foreign relations, 184, 185
Argentina, 4
  confrontations with, 6, 174
  economic aid from, 154
  and García Meza government, 184
  independence rebellion of, 38
  and independent Bolivia, 39–40, 41–42
  relations with, 181, 192, 194
  trade with, 150–151
Arguedas, Alcides, 2, 26, 27
Arica, 5
Aristocracy, 35, 36, 47
Arze, José Antonio, 28, 58, 63, 65, 68, 75–
  76(n37)
Arze Quiroga, Eduardo, 180–181

215

Atacama Desert, 45
Audiencia of Charcas (Upper Peru), 35, 37, 39, 45
Austerity programs, 83, 84, 103, 104, 106, 157–160
  and cocaine traffic, 155
  and economic injustice, xiii, 99, 128, 130–131
  and economic models, 144
  and health and education, 132–133
  and social unrest, 100, 115, 117, 157
  and U.S. aid, 154–155
Authentic MNR (MNRA), 85, 86, 87. See also Authentic Revolutionary Party
Authentic Revolutionary Party (PRA), 85, 88, 96
Ayacucho Declaration, 177
Ayares Indians, 33
Aylwin, Patricio, 180
Aymara Indians, xii, 1, 14–15, 32–33
  and national identity, 203

Baldivieso, Enrique, 60, 62, 66
Ballivián, Adolfo, 44
Ballivián, Hugo, 65, 72
Ballivián, José, 42, 45
BAMIN. See Mining Bank of Bolivia
Banking, international, 93, 120, 156–160
Banzer Suárez, Hugo, xii, 12(photo), 87, 92–94, 123
  and Brazil, 192
  drug connection, 126, 164
  economic policy, 145, 147
  ideology, 124
  1979 and 1980 elections, 96, 97
  1985 election, 102
  1989 election, 99, 104–106
  and the peasantry, 114
  and seacoast issue, 177–178
  and U.S., 182, 184
Baptista, Mariano, 47, 48
Barbie, Klaus Altmann, 126, 186
Barrientos Ortuño, René, 86, 87–89, 90
  ideology, 124
  and the peasantry, 113
  and U.S., 182, 183
Battle for La Paz, 73–74
Battle of Ayacucho, 39
Battle of Ingavi, 42
Battle of Junín, 39
Battle of Tumusla, 39

Battle of Zepita, 39
Belgrano, Manuel, 38
Belzu, Manuel Isidoro, 42–43
Beni department, 16
Bennett Plan, 168
Bernal Pereira, Waldo, 125
Beta Gama Socialist Action group, 64
Bilbao Rioja, Bernardino, 66, 75–76(n37)
Black market, 136, 157
Blanco, Pedro, 41
Bloc for the Defense of the Revolution, 86
Bloque de Defensa de la Revolución. See Bloc for the Defense of the Revolution
Bloque Parlamentario Minero. See Miners' Parliamentary Bloc
Bloque Reestructurador, 85
Bolívar, Simón, 2, 4, 39–40, 203, 204
Bolivian Bishops' Conference (CEB), 130, 131
Bolivian Communist Party (PCB), 70
  factionalism in, 100, 102
  foreign policy, 196
  ideology, 28
  and labor, 82, 101, 119
  and 1956 election, 85
  and 1966 election, 88
  and Siles government, 100
Bolivian Confederation of Private Entrepreneurs (CEPB), 92, 101, 103, 122, 145–146
Bolivian Democratic Union, 65
Bolivian Development Corporation (CBF), 145
Bolivian Gulf Oil Company, 89, 183
Bolivian Iron and Steel Corporation (SIDERSA), 144
Bolivian Labor Central (COB)
  and NPE, 121
  and Paz government, 103, 104
  and the peasantry, 115
  and political power, 81–82, 119–120
  and postrevolutionary military government, 89, 93, 95, 96, 97
  repression of, 128. See also Repression, of labor
  and Siles government, 85, 100–101, 157–158
Bolivian Left of Gainsborg in Chile, 64
Bolivian Mine Workers' Federation (FSTMB), 64
  and COMIBOL takeover, 101

ideology, 28, 70
and MNR, 68, 81
and NPE, 120–121
and Paz government, 104
political power of, 110, 119
and postrevolutionary military
government, 89, 93, 94
repression of, 134. *See also* Repression, of
labor
Bolivian Mining Corporation (COMIBOL)
and austerity measures, 86, 88, 104, 120–
121
and cocaine trafficking, 162
demise of, 110, 120, 122, 149
formation, 78
production and employment, 144, 145,
146, 147
worker management issue, 101, 119
Bolivian Nationalist Action, 63
Bolivian Ranger Battalion, 123
Bolivian Revolutionary Front (FRB), 88
Bolivian Socialist Falange (FSB)
formation, 61, 62–63
and FPN coalition, 93–94
ideology, 28, 63
1956 election, 85
and postrevolutionary governments, 86,
89, 92
and World War II, 65
Bolivian State Petroleum Enterprise (YPFB),
58, 80, 144, 145, 146, 147
privatization of, 150
Border disputes, xi, 5
and geopolitics, 174
See also Chaco War; Seacoast
Brazil, 4
and Banzer government, 92
confrontations with, 6, 174
relations with, 192, 194
trade with, 150, 151
British-Chilean Nitrates and Railroad
Company of Antofagasta, 44, 46
Bulnes, Manuel, 42
Bureaucracy
and drug enforcement, 162
and middle class, 121
Busch, Germán, 57, 58, 59–61
economic policy, 143, 147
Busch Code. *See* Labor Code
Bush, George, 180
Bush administration, 155, 168, 169, 188, 190

Cabinets
1964–1982 military, 87, 90
MNR postrevolutionary, 81, 83
and Paz Estenssoro government, 103
and Paz Zamora government, 106
and Siles government, 99–100
stability of, 176
Calahumana, Juana Basilia, 41
Calchas Indians, 15
Callahuaya Indians, 15
Camacho, Eliodoro, 47, 48
Camba, 18
Campero, Narciso, 48
Campesinos. *See* Peasant associations
Canada, 151, 154
Capitalism, 43, 90
as exploitative, 143–144
state, 144, 145, 146
See also Economic development, models
Caracoles Tin Company, 181
Cartagena Drug Summit Agreement, 115
Carter, Jimmy, 184
Carter, Rosalynn, 96
Carter administration, 94, 96, 126
Castelli, Juan José, 38
Castro, Fidel, 183, 194
Catari, Tomás. *See* Tupac Katari
Catavi Massacre, 67
Catavi mining center, 9
Catholic Church
and culture, 20
and government, 47, 102, 106
and social justice, 110, 128–131,
129(photo), 203–204
Caudillos, 41, 42–44
CBF. *See* Bolivian Development Corporation
CEB. *See* Bolivian Bishops' Conference
Central Bank, 61
Central Intelligence Agency (CIA), 89, 189
Central Obrera Boliviana. *See* Bolivian
Labor Central
CEPB. *See* Bolivian Confederation of Private
Entrepreneurs
Cerro Magnífico, 6
Céspedes, Augusto, 62, 68
Chaco (subregion), 13–14, 53
Chaco War (1932–1935), xi, xii, 51, 53, 55–
57
and tin decline, 143
Chapel of the Virgin of Socavón, 21, 23
Chaquies Indians, 15

Charangas province, 15
Charango (musical instrument), 24
Charcas (city), 35. *See also* Sucre
Chávez Ortiz, Ñuflo, 82, 85
Chayantas Indians, 15
"Ché" Guevara, Ernesto, xi, 89, 123, 183
Cheysson, Claude, 186
Chile, 4
  Andean Pact, 152
  confrontations with, xi, 43, 44, 174. *See also* War of the Pacific
  expansion in, 45
  and Peru-Bolivian Confederation, 41–42
  relations with, 194
  and seacoast issue, 94, 177–178, 179, 180
  and U.S. influence, 192
Chilean Nazi party, 63
Chipaya Indians, 15
Chiquitano Indians, 16
Chiriguano Indians, 16
Cholo, 17–18
Christian Democratic Community, 88, 91
Christian Democratic Party (PDC), 100, 101
Chulumani (city), 10
Chuquisaca province, 6
CIA. *See* Central Intelligence Agency
Class
  conflict, 65, 101, 104, 110–111, 116–117, 120, 121, 155. *See also* Political power
  consciousness, 110, 118–119
  and postrevolutionary society, 110–125
  See also Elites; Labor; Middle class
Climate, 7, 8, 10, 11
Cliza peasant syndicates, 113
CNTCB. *See* National Confederation of Peasant Workers of Bolivia
COB. *See* Bolivian Labor Central
Cobija (city), 12
Coca, Ariel, 125
Cocaine, xi, xiii, 1
  and the economy, 3, 110, 115, 122, 161–165
  and government corruption, 2, 97, 104, 125–128. *See also* Drug enforcement, corruption in
  military connection, 100
  production, 10, 11, 162, 190(table)
  and regional power, 6
  societal effects of, 136, 137–138
  See also Drug enforcement
Cochabamba (city), 10, 21, 35, 38

Cochabamba (department), 10
  and coca production, 11, 162, 168
  ethnic groups, 15
  and politics, 63
Cochabamba Army Command School, 100
Cochabamba–Santa Cruz highway, 11, 79, 165
Código Busch. *See* Labor Code
Colombia
  Andean Pact, 152
  and cocaine, xi, 188
  population of, 4
  relations with, 193
  and U.S. aid, 168
Colonialism, 28
COMIBOL. *See* Bolivian Mining Corporation
Comintern, 63
Communication
  and geography, 5
  Incan, 35
Compulsory Civil Service Law, 94
Concordancia, 65, 66
CONDEPA, 105
Condorcanqui, José Gabriel. *See* Tupac Amaru
Con el ojo izquierdo mirando a Bolivia (Seoane), 28
Confederación de Campesinos. *See* Peasant Confederation
Confederación Nacional de Trabajadores Campesinos de Bolivia. *See* National Confederation of Peasant Workers of Bolivia
Confederación Perú-Boliviana. *See* Peruvian-Bolivian Confederation
Confederación Sindical de Trabajadores de Bolivia. *See* Confederation of Bolivian Workers
Confederación Sindical Unica de Trabajadores Campesinos de Bolivia. *See* Sole Unionist Confederation of Peasant Workers of Bolivia
Confederation of Bolivian Workers (CSTB), 60, 63, 68
Confederation of Workers' Republics of the Pacific, 63
Congress
  and presidential elections, 96, 97, 98, 102, 105
  and Siles government, 100

Connally, John B., 183
Conservatism
  and peasantry, 82
  in politics, 65, 70
Conservative Party, 47, 48
Constitution
  of 1851, 43
  of 1879, Liberal, 44
  of 1880, 48
  1938 constitutional convention, 59–60, 62
  Santa Cruz's democratic, 41
CORACA. See Peasants' Agricultural
  Corporation
Cordillera Occidental, 7
Cordillera Real, 7
Cordova, Jorge, 43
Corporación Minera de Bolivia. See Bolivian
  Mining Corporation
Corporatism, 59, 63
Corr, Edwin G., 100, 163, 168, 185, 186–187
Corruption
  and drug enforcement, 138, 163, 164
  and drug money, 2, 97, 104, 125–128
  intellectuals on, 27, 29
Cosmology. See Mythology
Cotton, 160, 166
Council of Amazonian Cooperation, 193
Coup(s)
  attempts, 68, 90, 93, 138
  during 1930s, 56, 58, 59
  during 1940s, 65, 67–68
  1951, 65
  1964, 77, 87
  during 1970s, 92, 95, 96
  during 1980s, 97, 114, 125
Creación de la pedagogía nacional (Tamayo),
  26
CSTB. See Confederation of Bolivian
  Workers
CSUTCB. See Sole Unionist Confederation
  of Peasant Workers of Bolivia
Cuba, 182, 185, 186, 194
Cuban Missile Crisis, 182
Cueca (dance), 23
Culture
  and indigenism, 19–20
  and regionalism, 15, 20
  and social status, 17–18
Currency devaluations, 101, 157, 159
Cuzco, 33, 34

Dalence, Alfonso, 126

Dances, 22–23, 24(photo)
Daza, Hilarión, 44, 46
DEA. See United States Drug Enforcement
  Agency
Debray, Regis, 91
Debt, 89, 99, 200–201
  agricultural, 160
  and Chaco War, 57
  crisis, 3, 117, 132, 143, 153, 156–160, 194,
  196
  and Santa Cruz, 41
  and state capitalist model, 147
  See also Foreign loans
DeConcini, Dennis, 127
Defense spending, 55, 123. See also Military
de la Serna, José, 38, 39
Democracy, 201
  and U.S. policy, 154–155
Democratic Alliance. See Concordancia
Democratic and Popular Unity Front
  (FUDP), 95
Democratic Party, 48
Democratic Popular Unity (UDP), 95
  and "La Gaiba" incident, 127
  1979 election, 96
  and Siles presidency, 99–102
Demography, 4, 8, 121, 136
Desaguadero River, 7
D'Escoto, Miguel, 193
Devaluations. See Currency devaluations
Diablada (devil dance), 23
Díez de Medina, Fernando, 27, 28
DIN. See National Office of Investigations
Dirección Revolucionaria Unitaria. See
  Unitary Revolutionary Direction
Disease, 36
Doria Medina, Arturo, 125
Doria Medina, Samuel, 191
DRU. See Unitary Revolutionary Direction
Drug enforcement
  and alternative development plans, 115–
  116
  corruption in, 138, 163, 164
  legislation, 115, 168–169
  and social unrest, 165
  and U.S. policy, 154–155, 166–169, 185,
  187–191
  See also Cocaine

Eastern Europe, 183, 186
Echeverría Tardío, Hugo, 125

Economic dependency, 110, 119, 141–143
  and cocaine trafficking, 161, 166
  and development models, 143–148, 160.
    See also Economic development
  and foreign interference, 68, 80, 173, 174–
    176
  and underdevelopment, 202
Economic development, 142
  and Banzer, 92–93
  and cocaine trafficking, 115–116, 165–169
  and military ideologies, 124–125
  and MNR postrevolutionary government,
    79–80, 86–87
  models, 59, 122, 143–148
  and 1980s economic crisis, 155
  See also Underdevelopment
Economic stabilization. *See* Austerity
    programs
Economy
  and cocaine, 138, 161–165
  colonial, 35
  crisis of 1980s, 155–160, 161
  and development models, 143–148. *See
    also* Economic development
  and economic dependency, 141–142. *See
    also* Economic dependency
  Incan, 142
  mining, 49–51, 142–143
  as political issue, 104–105
  postindependent, 44–45, 59, 60
  and postrevolutionary military
    government, 89
  See also Black market; Investment;
    Underdevelopment
Ecuador, 152, 193
Eder, George Jackson, 84
Eder Mission, 175
Education, 60, 79, 121, 131–132, 139(n20)
  austerity and privatization of, 132–134,
    136, 139–140(n21), 140(n23)
Eisenhower administration, 182
Ejército de Liberación Nacional. *See*
    National Liberation Army
Ejército Productora, 122
Elections
  fraud in, 48, 94, 95, 105
  1884, 48
  1936, 58
  1938, 60
  1940, 63, 65, 66
  1944, 68

1947, 70
1949 congressional, 70
1951, 71, 72, 75–76(n37)
1956, 85
1960, 86
1966, 88
1978, 94, 95
1979, 95–96
1980, 97
1985, 99, 102, 103(table)
1987 municipal, 104
1989, 104–106, 106(table), 109(n31)
  and voter behavior, xii, 71–72
  and voter turnout, 72, 97, 102, 105
  See also Electoral law
Electoral law
  franchise, 48, 65, 78
  May 1986 reform, 105
  Padilla reform of, 95–96
  postrevolutionary reforms, 78, 83
Elío, Tomás Manuel, 70, 75–76(n37)
Elites
  and postrevolutionary military
    government, 92
  prerevolutionary political power, 47, 48,
    49–51, 66–72, 143
  and reformers, 57, 59, 61
  rural, 116, 122
ELN. *See* National Liberation Army
El Salvador, 185, 186
El Trompillo Airport, 11
Emigration, xi, 6
Employment
  and COMIBOL, 149
  and NPE, 120–121, 159
  and public sector, 121, 145
  rural, 166
ENAF. *See* National Smelting Company
Encomienda, 36–37, 142
Environmental pollution, 137
Escalier, José María, 52
Espinal Camps, Luis, 126, 128, 130
Ethnic groups, 14–19, 30(n10)
Europe
  relations with, 179–180, 186
  trade with, 151
Exploitation. *See* Underdevelopment
Export-Import Bank, 66
Exports, 142, 148–152, 158
  dependence on raw, 143
  mineral, 50

nitrate, 44
public sector, 145
and state capitalist model, 146–147
and transportation, 5, 13, 49
Expropriation. *See* Nationalization

Factionalism
    and FPN coalition, 93–94
    in military, 123–125
    and MNR, 77, 83–84, 85–86
    and 1985 election, 102
    and Siles government, 100
Falange Socialista Boliviana. *See* Bolivian
    Socialist Falange
Falklands War, 178
Family planning, 136, 140(n25)
Fascism, 63, 67, 68, 71
Federación Sindical de Trabajadores
    Mineros de Bolivia. *See* Bolivian Mine
    Workers' Federation
"Federal Revolution," 48–49
Federation of University Students of Bolivia
    (FUB), 64
Fellmann Velarde, José, 86, 183, 195
Festivals, 20, 21–22, 23, 24–25
FIB. *See* Front of the Bolivian Left
Figueiredo, João, 192
First Treaty of Limitation. *See* Treaty of 1866
Flores Santos, Genaro, 101, 114–115
Folklore, 19, 20–26
Foreign aid
    and austerity programs, 86, 160
    and drug war, 116, 168, 169, 187, 188,
        189(table), 190, 190(table), 191,
        198(n20)
    as political weapon, 78, 80, 90, 93, 97,
        153–155, 175–176, 182, 183, 186. *See
        also* Foreign influences
    sources of, 153–155, 154(table), 186, 193,
        196
    See also Foreign loans; Military, foreign
        aid for
Foreign exchange, 143, 155, 157, 158, 160
Foreign influences, 110, 202
    and drug enforcement, 115–116, 168, 169,
        187, 188, 190, 191
    and economic aid, 78, 80, 90, 93, 97, 153–
        155, 175–176, 182, 183, 186
    South American, 174
    U.S., 68, 84, 181–191, 192, 193, 195, 197
    See also Economic dependency

Foreign investment
    and Andean Pact Decision, 24, 152–153
    and nationalists, 57, 60. *See also*
        Nationalism
    and NPE, 160
    and oil, 90, 150
    and postrevolutionary military
        governments, 88, 93
    and Republican era, 52
Foreign loans, 93, 147
    and Peñaranda government, 66
    and Republican era, 52, 53
    See also Debt; Foreign aid
Foreign policy
    and Banzer government, 94
    determinants, 173–176, 197
    inter-American relations, 191–194
    Salamanca and, 55
    seacoast issue, 177–181
    Third World, 176, 185–186, 195–196
    and U.S. relations, 181–191
FPN. *See* Popular Nationalist Front
FPU. *See* Front of a United People
Franco, 186
Franchise. *See* Electoral law, franchise
FRB. *See* Bolivian Revolutionary Front
Frente de Izquierda Boliviana. *See* Front of
    the Bolivian Left
Frente de la Revolución Boliviana. *See*
    Bolivian Revolutionary Front
Frente del Puebo Unido. *See* Front of a
    United People
Frente de Unidad Democrática y Popular.
    See Democratic and Popular Unity
    Front
Frente de Unidad Nacionalista. *See* Front of
    Nationalist Unity
Frente Popular Nacionalista. *See* Popular
    Nationalist Front
Frías, Tomás, 44
Front of a United People (FPU), 102
Front of Nationalist Unity, 86
Front of the Bolivian Left (FIB), 63
FSB. *See* Bolivian Socialist Falange
FSTMB. *See* Bolivian Mine Workers'
    Federation
FUB. *See* Federation of University Students
    of Bolivia
FUDP. *See* Democratic and Popular Unity
    Front
FULKA. *See* Katarist Liberation Front

Fundamental Agrarian Law, 116
Fund for Social Investment, 136
Funeral services. *See Velorio*

Gainsborg, José Aguirre, 64
Gainsborg Trotskyists, 64
Gamarra, Agustín, 39, 40–41, 42
García, Alan, 196
García Meza, Luis, 94, 96–97, 98(photo)
    and the church, 130
    and cocaine, 125, 128, 164, 190
    and repression, 114–115, 125, 128
    U.S. and, 184–185
GDP. *See* Gross domestic product
Geisel, Ernesto, 177
Gelbard, Robert, 187, 188, 191
General Law of Agrarian Development, 116
General Services Administration (GSA), 175
Genuine Republican Party, 52, 65
Genuinos. *See* Genuine Republican Party
Geography, xxii(map), 1, 4–5
    Bolivian regions, 6–14
    and isolationism, xi–xii
    and regionalism, 5–6
Geopolitics, 173–174
Germany, 186
GNP. *See* Gross national product
Gold, 5
Gosálvez, Gabriel, 72
Government
    and the *caudillos*, 40–44
    during Chaco War (1930–1936), 53, 55–57
    civilian (1982–1989), 99–107
    and labor, 119, 134
    military reformers (1936–1939), 58–61
    1964–1982 military, 87–99
    oligarchy versus reformers (1939–1952), 65–72
    and the peasantry, 113, 115
    postrevolutionary MNR, 77–86
    Republican (1880–1930), 47–53
    See also Government spending
Government spending
    on education, 133–134, 139–140(n21)
    and foreign aid, 153
    and health, 135
    See also Defense spending; Social welfare programs
Goyeneche, José Manuel de, 38
Gran Chaco territory, 55

Gran Colombia federation, 39
Great Depression, 51, 143
Grenada, 193, 196
Gross domestic product (GDP), 142, 145, 160
Gross national product (GNP), 142
"Group of 77," 179
Group of Exiles of Peru, 64
GSA. *See* General Services Administration
Guadelupe mines, 49
Guano, 43, 45
Guaraní Indians, 16
Guarayos Indians, 16
Gueiler Tejada, Lydia, 96–97
Guerra de Quince Años. *See* Heroic Era of the Fifteen Years War
Guevara Arze, Walter, 62, 84, 85–86, 87, 96
Gulf Oil, 80, 88, 89, 90, 184
Gumucio, Mariano Baptista, 90
Gutiérrez, Alberto Bailey, 90
Gutiérrez, Mario, 85, 92, 94
Gutiérrez Guerra, José, 49
Gutiérrez Vea Murguía, Guillermo, 75–76(n37)

Haig, Alexander, 184
Health, 131, 134–137, 157, 203
    privatization of, 132–133, 136
Henman, Anthony, 164
Heroic Era of the Fifteen Years War, 38
Hertzog, Enrique, 70, 71
Highlands
    culture, 23
    ethnic groups, 14–15, 18
    and regionalism, 5–6
History
    Chaco War, 55–57
    independence, 37–40
    National Revolution of 1952, 72–74
    1936–1939 military government, 57–61
    oligarchy era, 61–72
    postindependence era, 40–46
    pre-Columbian, 31–35
    Republican era, 47–53
    Spanish colonial rule, 35–37
Hochschild, Mauricio, 50, 62, 143
Housing, 117(photo), 133(photo), 135
    construction, 13, 13(photo)
Huanchaca Mining Company, 49
Huanuni mining center, 9
Human rights, 2

and the church, 128–131
and foreign relations, 94, 185, 194
and military repression, 128
See also Indian, rights
Hydrocarbon exports, 148, 150

Identity, Bolivian national, 2, 14, 19–20, 27, 29, 203–204. *See also* Ideology, nationalist
Ideology
  and Banzer, 92
  and contemporary politics, 107
  FSB, 63
  FSTMB, 70
  and labor unions, 82
  and military, 124–125
  MNR, 62
  nationalist, 19–20, 26–29
  PIR, 63
  POR, 64
  and Socialist Party, 62
Illampu mountain, 7
Illanes, Fernando, 196
Illimani mountain, 7
IMF. *See* International Monetary Fund
Immigration, 18–19. *See also* Migration
Imperialism
  economic, 59, 72. *See also* Economic dependency; Nationalism
  and labor exploitation, 119
  and military populist school, 125
Imports, 149, 151–152
INC. *See* National Institute of Colonization
Incas, 33–35
  economic structure, 142
  and Lake Titicaca, 7
  and Quechua Indians, 15
Income
  and coca production, 162
  distribution, 147, 203
  and economic crisis, 157, 159
  per capita, 141, 142, 166
  See also Poverty
Independence, 37–40
Independent Socialist Party, 62
Indian(s), 1
  and Chaco War, 57
  and coca plant, 165
  cultural traditions, 19, 20, 26. *See also* Folklore
  and education, 132

groupings, 14–16
  and national identity, xii, 27, 203
  pre-Columbian civilizations, 31–35
  rights, 60, 62, 69, 116
  and Spanish colonialism, 35–37
  See also Indigenism
Indian Congress, 69
Indianist (*Katarismo*) movements, 117, 165, 171(n30)
Indigenism, 19–20, 26–29
Infant mortality, 134–135, 203
Inflation, 84, 142, 155, 157, 158, 160, 200
Infrastructure
  and cocaine trafficking, 165, 166
  See also Transportation
Instability
  and Bolivian history, xi, 2, 31, 200, 204
  and change, 111
  and drug money, 127
  and foreign policy, 173, 174, 176
  and Republican government, 47–48
  and Siles government, 99–100
  and War of the Pacific, 44
  See also Coup(s); Unrest
Institutional Revolutionary Party (PRI; Mexico), 81
Intellectuals
  and indigenism, 1, 19–20
  and landscape, 14, 26
  and Marxist parties, 64
  and national ideology, 26–29
Inter-American Commission for Human Rights of the OAS, 128
Inter-American Development Bank, 86, 145, 159, 184
International Monetary Fund (IMF), 185, 196
  austerity programs, 80, 84, 99, 115, 128, 132, 157–160
  and development models, 145
International Tin Agreement (ITA), 170(n7)
International Tin Council (ITC), 148, 175, 170(n7)
Investment
  and public sector, 145
  and state capitalist model, 146
  See also Foreign investment
Ipiña Melgar, Enrique, 134
Isolationism, 5
Israel, 184
ITA. *See* International Tin Agreement

ITC. *See* International Tin Council

Japan, 151–152, 184
Jesuits, 16, 37
Jesús de Machaca festival, 21–22, 22(photo)
Jews, 61

Katarismo. See Indianist (*Katarismo*)
   movements
Katarist Liberation Front (FULKA), 171(n30)
Kennedy, Edward, 128
Khrushchev, Nikita, 182
Koening, Abraham, 45
Kolla, 18
Kolla Indians, 18, 32, 35
Kullawada (dance), 23

Labor
   and austerity programs, 157–158
   militancy, 67
   mita, 34, 36, 142
   and MNR postrevolutionary government,
      78
   and NPE, 159
   serf, 15, 79
   See also Labor unions
Labor Code, 60
Labor unions
   and government repression, 88–89, 94,
      134
   Labor Code, 60
   and Marxist parties, 63
   and MNR postrevolutionary government,
      81–82, 83, 85, 86–87
   and Paz government, 103, 104
   and political parties, 68–69
   and political power, 110, 111, 118–121
   and Siles government, 100–101
   See also Peasant associations; Strikes;
      specific organizations
La Calle (MNR newspaper), 62, 67
LAFTA. *See* Latin American Free Trade
   Association
"La Gaiba" incident, 127
Lago Minchín, 8
Laimes Indians, 15
Lake Ballivián, 8
Lake Poopó, 7–8, 15
Lake Titicaca, 1, 7, 8
   and Aymara Indians, 14–15, 32
Landownership, 116–117

and *encomienda*, 36–37
and Melgarejo policies, 43
See also Land reform
Land reform, 69, 116–117
   and CSUTCB, 115, 116
   and 1938 constitution, 60
   and PIR, 63
   postrevolutionary, 28–29, 78, 79, 111
   See also Reform
Language
   and ethnic groupings, 15, 16, 30(n10)
   and Incas, 35
Lanza, José Miguel, 40
La Paz (city), 73(photo)
   culture, 20–21, 24–25
   1809 rebellion in, 38
   foundation, 35
   geography, xii, 1, 7, 8(photo)
   and 1971 coup, 92
   and political power, 6
   transportation to, 10
La Paz department
   and coca production, 162–163
   ethnic groups, 15
La Plata Basin nations, 178, 192–193
Lara, Jesús, 27
Latin America
   and debt, 158
   relations with, 191–194
   trade with, 151–152
   See also specific countries
Latin American Bishops' Conference, 129
Latin American Free Trade Association
   (LAFTA), 152
Latin American parliament, 180
Law of Controlled Substances (1988), 115,
   187
Leadership
   and CSUTCB, 116
   military, and cocaine, 125–128
   and miners, 119
   MNR postrevolutionary government, 84
   postindependence era, 40–44
   Republican era presidents, 48
   See also Government
LEC. *See* Legion of Veterans
Lechín Oquendo, Juan
   COB and FSTMB, 68, 81, 93, 100
   in exile, 71, 87, 89, 97
   and MNR, 84, 85, 86
   and National Revolution of 1952, 73

political parties of, 91, 102
popularity of, 115, 119
and Siles-UDP coalition government, 101, 120
Leftist Revolutionary Movement (MIR)
-ADN alliance, 99, 105–106
factionalism in, 102
formation, 91
and political repression, 128
and Siles government, 100
Legión de Ex-Combatientes. *See* Legion of Veterans
Legion of Veterans (LEC), 60
Legislation
Decree Law 21060 (21660), 153
and drug enforcement, 115, 168–169, 187
labor, 60
postrevolutionary, 77, 78
and Santa Cruz, 41
See also Reform
"Leopardos" (UMOPAR), 100, 115, 138, 187
Ley de Substancias Controladas. *See* Law of Controlled Substances
Liberalism, 27
Liberal Party, 47, 48–49, 65, 70
1966 election, 88
split of, 52
Linares, José María, 43
Llallagua. *See* Catavi mining center
Llanos de Chiquitos, 11
Llanos de Moxos, 11
Lora, Guillermo, 64, 70
Lowlands
culture, 23
economic development of, 165–166
ethnic groups, 15–16, 17, 18
geography, 7, 11–14
and regionalism, 5–6

MacKay Commission, 90
Madre de Dios River, 12
Magruder Commission, 67
Mama Ocllo, 33
Manco Kapac, 33
Manrique, Jorge, 130
Mariátegui, José Carlos, 28, 64
Marof, Tristán, 64
Marofistas, 64
Marxism, 28–29
and political parties, 63–65
and Torres government, 91

See also Socialism
"Massacre of All Saints," 130
"Massacre of Loreto," 43
Massacre of Tolata, 93, 114
Matarani, 5
Matto Grosso, 43
Media, 127
Medici, Emilio, 192
Medinaceli, Carlos, 27
Mejillones, 43
Melgarejo, Mariano, 43–44, 142–143
Mendoza, Jaime, 27
Mennonites, 19
Mercado, José Ortiz, 90
Merino, Admiral, 179
Mestizos, 17–18
Middle class
and austerity programs, 85, 159
and Banzer, 93
and drug enforcement, 162
growth of, 121–122
and labor, 120
and MNR, 87
Migration
and cocaine enforcement, 165
to underpopulated areas, 79, 110, 117, 165–166
See also Emigration; Urbanization
Militarization
of drug war, 187–188, 191
Military, 124(table)
and Chaco War, 56–57
and cocaine, 100, 125–128, 137–138
coups by, 58, 65–66, 72, 77, 87, 92, 96, 97
factionalism in, 123–125
foreign aid for, 154, 168, 182
and labor, 120
and middle class, 122
and MNR postrevolutionary government, 80–81
and National Revolution, 73
and the peasantry, 87–88, 93, 113–114, 115
political intervention by, 65–66, 94, 96–99, 111, 124
postrevolutionary reorganization of, 122–123
and Siles-UDP government, 100
unrest, 67–68
and Villarroel-MNR government, 69
See also Government

Military-Campesino Pact of 1966, 87–88,
   93, 113, 114, 115
Mineral resources, 1
   economic dependence on, 49–51, 142–
      143, 149
   and lowlands, 13
   transporting, 5
   and War of the Pacific, 43, 44–45
   See also Mining; Tin
Miners
   and MNR postrevolutionary government,
      82
   and National Revolution, 73
   and peasants, 113
   and political power, 118–121
   See also Bolivian Labor Central; Bolivian
      Mine Workers' Federation; Mining
Miners' Parliamentary Bloc, 70
Mining, 149
   and colonial economy, 35, 36, 142–143
   decline of, 40
   highland, 9
   investment in, 146
   and labor unrest, 67, 70–71
   nationalization of, 78–79. See also
      Bolivian Mining Corporation
   See also Miners; Silver; Tin
Mining Bank of Bolivia (BAMIN), 61, 144
Mining Code, 42
MIR. See Leftist Revolutionary Movement
Miranda, Rogelio, 90, 124
MIR–New Majority, 105
MIR-NM. See MIR–New Majority
Mita, 34, 36, 142
MNR. See Nationalist Revolutionary
   Movement
MNRA. See Authentic MNR
MNR Andradista, 88
MNR Auténtico. See Authentic MNR
MNRH. See MNR-Histórico
MNR-Histórico (MNRH), 100, 102
MNRI. See MNR-Left
MNR-Izquierda. See MNR-Left
MNR-Left (MNRI), 85, 93, 100, 102
MNR Silista, 88
MNR Unificado, 88
Monetary Stabilization Commission, 84
Montenegro, Carlos, 62, 68
Montero (city), 112(photo)
Montes, Ismael, 49
Morales, Agustín, 43, 44

Morales Bermúdez, Francisco, 177
Morenada (slave dance), 23, 24(photo)
Mount Sajama, 7
Movimiento de Izquierda Revolucionaria.
   See Leftist Revolutionary Movement
Movimiento Nacionalista Revolucionario.
   See Nationalist Revolutionary
   Movement
Movimiento Popular Cristiano. See Popular
   Christian Movement
Movimiento Revolucionario Tupac Katari de
   Liberación. See Tupac Katari
   Revolutionary Liberation Movement
Moxos Indians, 16
MPC. See Popular Christian Movement
MRTA. See Tupac Amaru Revolutionary
   Movement
MRTKL. See Tupac Katari Revolutionary
   Liberation Movement
Murillo, Pedro Domingo, 37
Music, 24, 25(photo)
Mythology
   Aymara, 33
   and Bolivian nationalism, 27–28
   and cultural traditions, 24, 25–26
   Incan, 7
   Tiwanakan, 32

Napoleon, 38–39
National Association of Medium-Sized
   Mine Enterprises, 92
National Conciliation, 70
National Confederation of Peasant Workers
   of Bolivia (CNTCB), 82, 112–113, 114,
   115
National Electoral Tribunal, 95
National Institute of Colonization (INC),
   112(photo)
Nationalism, 26, 28
   and Chaco War, 57
   cultural, 20
   versus economic dependency, 80
   and military reformers, 57, 59, 61
   and MNR, 62
Nationalist Democratic Action (ADN)
   elections, 96, 102, 105
   -MIR alliance, 99, 105–106
   -MNR pact, 103–104
   and Siles government, 100
Nationalist Party, 52, 53, 62

Nationalist Revolutionary Movement
(MNR)
elections, 85, 96, 102, 105
formation of, 61–62
and FPN coalition, 93
ideology, 26, 28, 62
and labor, 118
and National Revolution, 72–74
organization, 81–82
and Paz government, 102–104
postrevolutionary government, 77–87,
113, 131
and postrevolutionary military
government, 88, 89, 92
and prerevolutionary conservative
government, 66–67, 70, 71
-RADEPA government coalition, 67–69
and Siles government, 100
support for, 71, 81–84
and World War II, 65
Nationalization
of banks, 61
and economic policy, 78–79, 144, 145
of mines, 29
of oil companies, 58–59, 89, 90, 183
and PIR, 63
National Liberation Army (ELN), 90, 91
National Liberation Front, 88
National Office of Investigations (DIN), 128
National Political Committee of MNR, 81–
82, 85
National Revolution of 1952, 72–74, 76(n38)
causes of, 55, 57, 77
consequences of, 110, 116–117, 131–132
ideology of, 20, 26, 28
National Smelting Company (ENAF), 144,
145
National Social Security Fund, 136
National Unity government, 105–107
Natural disasters, 153–154, 157, 161
Natural gas, 5, 150–151, 192
Natural resources, 1
foreign exploitation of, xi, 89, 141
and geopolitics, 174
See also Mineral resources
Natusch Busch, Alberto, 96, 114, 125
Navarro, Gustavo Adolfo. See Marof, Tristán
"Nazi Putsch," 66–67
Neoliberalism, 144, 156
New Economic Policy (NPE)
Decree Law 21060 (21160), 103, 153

and economic development models, 146,
158–160
education and health privatization, 132
and middle class, 122
social inequities and unrest, 104, 106, 115,
120–121, 128, 149, 159
and U.S. relations, 196
Nicaragua, 185, 186, 193
Nitrates, 43, 44–45
Nixon administration, 183
Nonaligned Movement, 178, 179, 182–183,
184, 195
NPE. See New Economic Policy
Nueva Política Económica. See New
Economic Policy
Ñuflo de Chávez, Captain, 16, 35

OAS. See Organization of American States
Occidental Boliviana, 150
Oil
and Chaco War, 55
and economy, 146, 160, 161
export prices for, 148
and foreign investment, 80, 90
and lowlands, 6, 11
reserves, 5, 149–150
See also Nationalization, of oil companies
Olañeta, Casimiro, 40
Olañeta, Pedro Antonio de, 39
Oligarchy. See Elites
Orbegoso, Luis José de, 41
Organization of American States (OAS),
176, 178, 179, 182, 192, 193, 194, 195
Oriente, 11–14, 18. See also Lowlands
Oruro (city)
festivals in, 21, 23
foundation of, 35
and National Revolution, 73
Oruro department, 6, 15
Ovando Candia, Alfredo, 87, 89–90, 123
and economic development, 147
foreign policy, 183
ideology, 125

Pachamama, 25–26
Pacheco, Gregorio, 48, 49
"Pact for Democracy," 103–104
Padilla Arrancibia, David, 95, 96
Palestine Liberation Organization, 186
Palm trees, 13
Panama, 193

Pando, José Manuel, 49, 52
Pando department, 11
Panoan Indians, 16
Paraguay, 4, 16, 174, 193
   and Chaco War, xi, xii, 53, 55–57
Paraguay River, 5
Paramilitary organizations, 126, 128
Partido Comunista de Bolivia. *See* Bolivian
   Communist Party
Partido de la Izquierda Revolucionaria. *See*
   Party of the Revolutionary Left
Partido Demócrata Cristiano. *See* Christian
   Democratic Party
Partido Demócrata Cristiano
   Revolucionario. *See* Revolutionary
   Christian Democratic Party
Partido Obrero Revolucionario. *See*
   Revolutionary Workers' Party
Partido Revolucionario Auténtico. *See*
   Authentic Revolutionary Party
Partido Revolucionario de la Izquierda
   Nacionalista. *See* Revolutionary Party
   of the Nationalist Left
Partido Social Demócrata. *See* Social
   Democratic Party
Partido Socialista. *See* Socialist Party
Partido Socialista Uno. *See* Socialist Party–
   One
Partido Unico, 88
Party of the Republican Socialist Union
   (PURS), 70–72, 88
Party of the Revolutionary Left (PIR)
   coalition with traditional parties, 65, 68,
      70
   and elections, 65, 88
   formation of, 61–62, 63–64
   ideology, 28, 63
   and labor, 68–69, 82
   and World War II, 65
Pastoralism, 9, 11, 14
Patiño, Simón, 50, 62, 143
Patiño Mines, 181
Patriotic Accord, 106
Paz Estenssoro, Víctor, xii
   and the church, 130
   early MNR years, 62, 68
   economic policy, 143, 144, 150, 152–153,
      155–156, 157, 158–160
   and elections, 70, 72, 95, 96, 97, 99, 102
   foreign policy, 176, 177, 179, 182–183,
      187–188, 194, 196, 197

   government of (1985–1989), 103–104
   and labor, 120
   and military government, 87, 91
   MNR postrevolutionary government
      (1952–1956), 74, 80, 84
   and peasantry, 113, 115
Paz Zamora, Jaime
   and the church, 131
   economic policy, 152–153, 155–156, 158,
      160
   foreign policy, 176, 177, 179–180, 185,
      188, 194, 196, 197
   government of, 105–107
   and military government, 91
   1989 election, 99, 164
   and peasantry, 115–116
   and Siles government, 100
   and teachers, 134
PCB. *See* Bolivian Communist Party
PDC. *See* Christian Democratic Party
PDCR. *See* Revolutionary Christian
   Democratic Party
Peasant associations, 69, 112–113, 114, 117–
   118
   and Banzer government, 93
   and Barrientos, 87–88
   and cocaine enforcement, 165
   and MNR postrevolutionary government,
      81, 82–83
   UCAPO, 91
   See also Sole Unionist Confederation of
      Peasant Workers of Bolivia
Peasant Coca Growers' Unions, 115
Peasant Confederation, 88
Peasantry, 111–118
   and cocaine, 137, 162–165, 168, 169
   division with miners, 113
   and education, 131
   and labor-student alliance, 110, 114, 115,
      118
   and military, 113–114
   and political power, 111, 112–118
   See also Peasant associations
Peasants' Agricultural Corporation
   (CORACA), 115
Peñaranda, Enrique, 65, 66, 182
People's Nationalist Union (UNP), 95
Pereda Asbún, Juan, 94, 95, 114, 126
Permanent Assembly of Human Rights
   (APDH), 125–126, 130
Peru, 4

Andean Pact, 152
and cocaine, xi, 188
confrontations with, 45–46, 174
independence of, 39
and independent Bolivia, 39–41, 42
and seacoast issue, 177–178
Shining Path, 118
and U.S. aid, 168
Peruvian-Bolivian Confederation, 41, 174
Petroleum. *See* Oil
Petroleum Code, 90, 93
Philosophy. *See* Ideology
PIDYS. *See* Substitution of Coca Cultivation
Pinochet, Augusto, 177, 179, 192
PIR. *See* Party of the Revolutionary Left
Pizarro, Francisco, 35
Pizarro, Gonzalo, 35
Plains of Grigotá, 11
Plan Trienal Para la Lucha Contra el
    Narcotráfico (1987), 115
Police, 73, 169
Political culture, 48
Political instability. *See* Instability
Political parties
and Banzer government, 93–94
and classes, 121
and elections, 88, 95, 102
formation of radical and reformist, 61–65,
    66
founding of, 27, 46, 47–48, 51
and military reformers, 58
and 1979 coup, 96
See also individual parties
Political power
elites, 47, 50–51, 65–66
labor, 118–121
and multiclass alliance, 111
peasantry, 79, 112–118
regional, 6
Political prisoners, 94
Political repression. *See* Repression
Political system, 2
dictatorship versus democracy, 41, 201
multiparty, 51–52
one-party, 88
of pre-Columbian groups, 32–33, 34–35
See also Government
Politics
and drug enforcement, 169
and ideology, 27–29
Popular Assembly, 91

Popular Christian Movement (MPC), 88
Popular Nationalist Front (FPN), 92, 93
Population. *See* Demography
Populism, 111. *See also* Reform
POR. *See* Revolutionary Workers' Party
Portales, Diego, 42
Potato, 8–9
Potosí (city), 35
Potosí department
ethnic groups, 15
independence uprising in, 38
mining deaths in, 36
and silver, 5, 6, 35, 49
Poverty, 1, 136
and austerity programs, 132–133
and national unity, 201–203
and social instability, 117
and Spanish rule, 35
and War of the Pacific, 44–45
See also Income
PRA. *See* Authentic Revolutionary Party
Pragmatism, 107
Pre-Columbian civilizations, 31–35
Pre-Incan peoples, 31–33
Presencia (Catholic daily), 125–126, 130
Presterío, 20, 20(photo), 21
PRI. *See* Institutional Revolutionary Party
Prices, export, 148, 149. *See also* Inflation
PRIN. *See* Revolutionary Party of the
    Nationalist Left
Privatization
and development models, 145–146
of health and education, 132–133, 136
of YPFB, 150
Prudencio, Roberto, 27
PS. *See* Socialist Party
PSD. *See* Social Democratic Party
PSOB. *See* Socialist Workers' Party of
    Bolivia
PS-1. *See* Socialist Party–One
Public sector, 145, 155
Pueblo enfermo (Arguedas), 26
Puente, Carlos, 63
Puerto General Busch (city), 5
Puerto Suárez (city), 5
PURS. *See* Party of the Republican Socialist
    Union

Quechua Indians, xii, 14, 15
Quintanilla, Carlos, 65, 66
Quiroga, Alberto, 184

Quiroga, Cuadros, 78
Quiroga, Ovidio, 72

Race, 14–19
    and national character, 26–27
Racism, 29
RADEPA. *See* Reason of the Fatherland
Railways, 5, 11, 12, 50
Razón de Patria. *See* Reason of the
    Fatherland
Reagan administration, 120, 126, 145, 169,
    184, 186–187
Real Socavón Mining Company, 49
Reason of the Fatherland (RADEPA)
    -MNR government coalition, 67–69
Reform
    and Belzu, 42–43
    electoral, 95–96, 105, 78, 83
    and Linares, 43
    MNR-RADEPA government and, 69
    and 1936–1939 military reformers, 57–61
    1953 education, 131
    postrevolutionary, 28–29, 77, 78–80, 83,
        116
    and Saavedra, 52
    and Santa Cruz, 41
    See also Land reform
Regionalism, 2, 173–174
    and geography, 5–6
    and race, 15, 18
Religion
    and coca plant, 165
    See also Mythology
Repression
    and Banzer, 92, 93
    and the church, 129, 130
    and García Meza, 97, 114–115, 128
    of labor, 67, 94, 103, 104, 118, 120, 147
    Melgarejo and, 43–44
    and National Unity government, 106
    and NPE, 159
    of popular classes, 111
    and postrevolutionary military
        government, 88, 89
Reprivatization, 144, 145
Republican Party, 51–52, 70
"Republican Revolution," 49
Republican Socialist Party, 58
Restorative Revolution, 87
Revolution
    and Bolivian history, 1–3, 200, 204

See also National Revolution of 1952;
    Unrest
Revolutionary Christian Democratic Party
    (PDCR), 91
Revolutionary Party of the Nationalist Left
    (PRIN),86, 88, 91
Revolutionary Socialist Cell, 62
Revolutionary Workers' Party (POR)
    and elections, 85, 88
    formation of, 61–62, 64
    ideology, 28, 64
    and labor, 70, 82
    and postrevolutionary government, 86
    and World War II, 65
Reyes, Simón, 102
Riberalta (city), 12
Rico Toro, Faustino, 98, 100, 125
Río Acre, 12
Río Beni, 11, 12
Río de la Plata region, 4
Río Mamoré, 12
Rivera, Primo de, 63
Rojas, José, 113
Rojos, 44
Rondeaux, José, 38
Rosas, Juan Manuel de, 41–42
Rosca, 51, 65, 72, 88. *See also* Elites
Royal Dutch Shell, 55

Saavedra, Bautista, 52, 58
Saavedristas. *See* Socialist Republican Party
Sainz, Luis, 130–131
Salamanca, Daniel, 52, 53, 55–57
Salar de Uyuni, 8
Salas, Toribio, 113
Salaverry, Felipe Santiago, 41
Salomón, Norberto, 100, 125
Salt, 8
San Andrés University, 87
Sánchez de Lozada, Gonzalo, 103, 105
San Juan celebration, 25
San Juan Massacre, 88–89
San Martín, José de, 39
Santa Cruz, Andrés de, 39, 41–42
Santa Cruz, Marcelo Quiroga, 90, 91, 97,
    114, 128
Santa Cruz de la Sierra (city), 11, 12(photo),
    122, 137
    foundation of, 16, 35
    housing in, 117(photo)
Santa Cruz department, 10

and Chaco War, 56
and cocaine, 166
ethnic groups, 16
migration to, 79
and oil, 90, 161
and political power, 6, 92
uprisings and unrest in, 6, 38, 92
Saravia, Rolando, 100
School of Higher Military Studies, 123
Seacoast
    and Bolivian development, 4–5
    as foreign policy issue, 3, 173, 176, 177–
        181, 193
    and War of Pacific, 46
Secessionism. See Separatism
Sector Pazestenssorista (MNR
    Pazestenssorista), 86, 88
Sejas Tordoya, Simón, 100
Seleme, Antonio, 73
Selich, Andrés, 93
Seoane, Manuel A., 28
Separatism, 6
Serrano, José Mariano, 40
SES. See Special Security Services
Shultz, George, 187
SIDERSA. See Bolivian Iron and Steel
    Corporation
Siete ensayos de interpretación de la realidad
    peruana (Mariátegui), 28
Siles, Hernando, 52–53
Siles Salinas, Jorge, 179
Siles Salinas, Luis, 88, 89
Siles Zuazo, Hernán, xii
    economic policy, 90–91, 144, 145, 147–
        148, 157–158
    and elections, 95, 96, 97
    in exile, 87
    foreign policy, 176, 177, 178–179, 185–
        187, 192–194, 195–196, 196–197
    and labor, 120
    and National Revolution of 1952, 71, 72–
        73
    and peasantry, 69, 113, 115
    and political factions, 62, 86, 93
    postrevolutionary government of (1956–
        1960), 84, 85
    as president (1982–1985), 94–95, 98, 99–
        102, 126, 138
Silver, xi, 5, 6, 35, 49–50, 143
    elite, 47, 48
Sirionó Indians, 16

Sixth International Tin Agreement, 121
Slavery, 16. See also Labor
Social Democratic Party (PSD), 88
Social groups. See Class
Social injustice
    and austerity programs, xiii, 99, 128, 130–
        131
    inequities, 29, 146, 202–204
    See also Human rights
Socialism, 58, 59, 71, 90–91, 120, 144, 147
Socialist Party (PS), 58, 62, 91
Socialist Party–One (PS-1), 97, 128
Socialist Republican Party, 52–53, 65
Socialist Workers' Party of Bolivia (PSOB),
    64
Social mobility, 17, 116, 121
Social security, 132
Social status
    and festival sponsorship, 21
    and race, 14, 16–18
Social welfare programs, 104, 116, 132–137,
    159
    and National Revolution, 131–132
Society
    and Chaco War, 57
    effects of drugs on, 137–138
    pre-Columbian, 33, 34–35
Sole Unionist Confederation of Peasant
    Workers of Bolivia (CSUTCB), 114, 115,
    116
Sotomayor, Colonel, 46
Sotomayor, Oscar Céspedes, 114
SOUTHCOM. See Southern Command's
    School of the Americas
Southern Command's (SOUTHCOM)
    School of the Americas, 123, 124(table)
Soviet Union
    economic aid from, 153, 186
    relations with, 182, 183, 186
Spanish colonial rule, xi, 5, 35–37, 39, 142
Special Security Services (SES), 126, 128
Standard Oil, 52, 55, 182
    nationalization of, 58–59, 66
State capitalism. See Capitalism, state
Strikes
    and austerity programs, 85, 157
    and Banzer government, 94
    and Busch government, 59, 60
    Catavi Massacre, 67
    1978 hunger, 130
    and 1979 coup, 96

and Paz government, 103, 104
political power of, 118
and Siles government, 101
teacher, 106, 134
and Vildoso government, 98
See also Labor unions
Student movements
and Paz government, 104
and politics, 53, 63, 64
and Torres government, 91
Suárez Gómez, Roberto, 126, 164, 190
Sub-Andean region, 7, 10
Substitution of Coca Cultivation (PIDYS),
1987, 116
Sucre, Antonio José de, 39, 40–41
Sucre (city), 6, 37, 48
Sucre department, 10, 15
Sugar, 166
Supreme Council for National Defense, 123
Sweden, 154
Switzerland, 154

Tacanan Indians, 16
Tacna, 5
Tamayo, Franz, 14, 26, 27, 29
Tannenbaum, Frank, 132
Tarabucos Indians, 15
Tarija (city), 35
Tarija department, 6, 10, 38, 56
ethnic groups, 15, 16
Teacher unions, 134
Technology, mining, 49
Tejada Sorzano, José Luis, 56, 58
Tellurism, 26
Teoponte guerrilla foco, 90
Terrazas, Julio, 131
Tesoro Bolivian Petroleum, 150
"Thesis of Pulacayo," 70, 78
Third World, 141
and debt crisis, 156
and foreign policy, 176, 177, 178–179,
185–186, 194, 195–196
Thornburgh, Richard, 187
Tin
and economic dependency, xi, 57
elite, 47, 49, 50–51, 59, 61, 62, 143
metal exports, 148
1985 market collapse, 121, 148, 161
production, 5, 146, 149
and regional power, 6
and U.S., 66, 72, 175, 181

Tirinas Indians, 15
Tito, Josip Broz, 182–183
Tiwanaku civilization, 1, 14, 31–32
Tiwanaku (village), 21
Toro, David, 57, 58, 59, 61, 147
Torrelio Villa, Celso, 97–98
and the peasantry, 115
and U.S. relations, 185
Torres, Juan José, 87, 90–92
economic policy, 147
foreign policy, 183–184
ideology, 125
Torres Ortiz, Humberto, 73
Trade balance, 146–147, 151
and debt crisis, 143
and NPE, 160
Trading partners, 151–153
Transportation
and economic system, 4–5, 10, 12–13, 49,
50, 51
Incan, 35
and lowlands, 11, 165, 166
postrevolutionary construction, 79
public, 145
and U.N. aid, 196
Treaty of 1866 (First Treaty of Limitation),
43, 45
Treaty of 1874, 46
Treaty of Ancón, 46
Treaty of Montevideo, 152
Triangular Plan, 88, 118, 182
Trinidad (city), 12
Tristán, Pío, 41
Tumiri, Julio, 130
Tupac Amaru, 37, 41
Tupac Amaru Revolutionary Group, 64
Tupac Amaru Revolutionary Movement
(MRTA; Peru), 118, 191
Tupac Katari, 37, 171(n30)
Tupac Katari Revolutionary Liberation
Movement (MRTKL), 114–115

UCAPO. *See* Unión de Campesinos Pobres
Ucumaris Indians, 15
Ucureña (city), 79, 113
UDP. *See* Democratic Popular Unity
UMOPAR. *See* "Leopardos"
UNCTAD. *See* United Nations Conference
on Trade and Development
Underdevelopment, 2, 200, 201–202
and cocaine trafficking, 166

and tin economy, 143
UNICEF. *See* United Nations, Children's
    Fund
Unidad Democrática y Popular. *See*
    Democratic Popular Unity
Unified Socialist Party, 65
Unión de Campesinos Pobres (UCAPO), 91
Unión Nacionalista del Pueblo. *See* People's
    Nationalist Union
Unitary Revolutionary Direction (DRU), 102
United Nations, 193, 195–196
    Children's Fund (UNICEF), 133, 136
    and human rights abuses, 128
    and seacoast issue, 178, 179, 180
United Nations Conference on Trade and
    Development (UNCTAD), 195–196
United Provinces of South America, 39
United States
    aid from, 78, 80, 86, 90, 93, 116, 123,
        153–155, 154(table), 160, 168, 169, 182,
        183, 186, 187, 188, 189(table),
        190(table), 191, 198(n20)
    and Banzer government, 92
    business interests, 79, 80, 93
    drug policy, xiii, 126–127, 128, 161, 166–
        169, 187–191
    and economic stabilization, 84
    and García Meza government, 97
    and Peñaranda government, 66–67
    political interference from, 68, 77, 84, 115,
        192, 195, 197
    and postrevolutionary military
        government, 89
    relations with, 72, 98, 175–176, 181–191,
        196
    trade with, 151
    and Villarroel government, 68
United States Army Special Warfare School,
    123
United States Catholic Conference, 128
United States Drug Enforcement Agency
    (DEA), 116, 126, 138
United States Information Agency (USIA),
    91
United States Peace Corps, 91
United States Senate
    Foreign Relations Committee, 187
    Subcommittee for Inter-American Affairs,
        128
United States Steel, 88
Unity, 111, 173–174

and foreign policy, 176, 197
and national identity, 202–204
Universities, 134, 140(n23)
University of San Francisco Xavier of
    Chuquisaca, 37
UNP. *See* People's Nationalist Union
Unrest, 43
    and austerity programs, 100, 117, 157
    and Banzer government, 93, 94
    and cocaine enforcement, 165, 169,
        171(n30), 188
    Indian uprisings, 37, 52
    labor, 60, 70–71, 120, 201. *See also* Strikes
    military, 67–68, 100
    and military reformers, 58
    1949 civil war, 71
    and Paz government, 104
    peasant, 43, 112, 115
    and Peñaranda government, 66
    and postrevolutionary military
        government, 88–89, 98
    and postrevolutionary MNR government,
        86–87
    secessionist revolts, 6
    student, 53, 91, 104
    and Villarroel government, 69
    See also Instability
Unzaga de la Vega, Oscar, 63, 85
Uprisings. *See* Unrest
Urbanization, 57, 121, 142
Urquidi, Arturo, 28
Urriolagoitia, Mamerto, 71, 72
Uruguay, 193
Uru Indians, 15
USIA. *See* United States Information
    Agency

Valverde Barbery, Carlos, 94, 126
Vatican Councils, 129
Veizaga, Miguel, 113
Velasco, José Miguel de, 41, 42
Velorio, 20–21
Venezuela, 152
Veterans, 58, 60
Viceroyalty of Buenos Aires, 37
Vicuña, 9
Vildoso Calderón, Guido, 97–98, 126, 185
Villarroel, Gualberto, 67–69, 192
    and economic development, 143, 147
    and U.S., 181
Virgin of Copacabana shrine, 21

Virgin of Urquina shrine, 21
Voter turnout, 72, 97, 102, 105
Voting behavior, xii, 71–72

Wallace, Henry, 66
Warisata school, 60, 131–132
War of the Pacific (1879–1884), 43, 44–46
Waterways, 7–8, 11
  and transportation, 5, 12
Wayño (dance), 23
Welles, Sumner, 66
West Germany, 86, 154
Whites, 16–17, 18–19
WHO. *See* World Health Organization

World Bank, 132, 136, 140(n25), 196
World Council of Churches, 128
World Health Organization (WHO), 136
World War II, 66, 75(n27), 181–182
  and political parties, 65

Yacimientos Petrolíferos Fiscales Bolivianos.
  See Bolivian State Petroleum Enterprise
YPFB. *See* Bolivian State Petroleum
  Enterprise
Yungas, 10
Yuras Lipes Indians, 15

Zampona (musical instrument), 24, 25(photo)
Zarate Willka Armed Liberation Front, 118